Virtues

Virtues

For Another Possible World

LEONARDO BOFF

Translated by
Alexandre Guilherme

CASCADE *Books* · Eugene, Oregon

VIRTUES
For Another Possible World.

Cascade Books
An Imprint of Wipf and Stock Publishers
199 W. 8th Ave., Suite 3
Eugene, OR 97401
www.wipfandstock.com

ISBN 13: 978-1-60899-075-7

Cataloging-in-Publication:

Boff, Leonardo.
[Virtudes para um outro mundo possivel (Hospitalidade—direito e dever de todos ;
Convivencia, respeito e tolerancia ; Comer e beber juntos e viver em paz). English.]
Virtues : for another possible world / Leonardo Boff ; translated by Alexandre
Guilherme.

ISBN 13: 978-1-60899-075-7

x + 272 p. ; 23 cm.—Includes bibliographical references (110–115, 189–192, 267–271).

1. Virtues. 2. Virtue. 3. Ethics. 4. Globalization—Moral and ethical aspects.
5. Hospitality—Religious aspects—Christianity. I. Guilherme, Alexandre. II. Title.

BJ1012 .B58 2011

Contents

Preface

Which virtues are minimally necessary to guarantee a human face to the process of globalization?

I start from the premise that we face a crisis situation but not a tragedy. Every crisis refines, precipitates, and liberates constructive energies. Crisis implies transition and change. We are currently making the transition from an understanding of history that is connected to cultures, religions, nation-states, social classes, and reference figures to an understanding of history that is collective and encompasses the entire human species. In order to understand this transition properly we must place it within the evolutionary process, the process of biogenesis, of anthropogenesis, and of planet-genesis.

Every change involves risks and opportunities. There is the real opportunity to build a global human society that is single in substance and different in manifestations, and that offers a promising future for all. But there is also the risk that each nation will only take account of itself and will try to impose itself on other peoples, and in so doing lose the understanding that we all form a great family, the human family, within the community of life, of which we are part and parcel. The danger posed by the weapons of mass destruction (WMDs) already built, which can seriously wound the biosphere and make it impossible for the global human project, has not been overcome.

Independent of risks and opportunities, every transition represents a dimension of continuity and of innovation. It continues something that happened before and as such it is linked to all values and countervalues that are in place. But it also breaks away from these and inaugurates something that is new. Continuity and innovation always coexist, and the change is always dramatic. What will prevail: continuity or innovation? If continuity predominates, then the crisis will be aggravated, and destructive elements will emerge. If innovation triumphs, then hope will emerge and a new pathway will be opened.

In fact, I believe we already find ourselves within this innovative aspect of change, we are already experiencing things globally. It is imperative for us now to become aware of this fact so that the process of change can release itself from the continuity of the past and in doing so inaugurate something that is effectively new. The process of change must leap forward in such a way that it becomes irreversible.

We must get used to the idea that we are passengers in a spaceship, blue-and-white, our Common Home, the Earth, which possesses limited resources, which is overpopulated, and which faces threatening risks. These risks will only be avoided if we guide our practices through the virtues that will be presented in this book, such as hospitality, co-living, tolerance, respect for differences, communality and a culture of peace. Along with these virtues we must adjoin the virtues that are appropriate to the ecological age, such as care, co-responsibility, cooperation, and reverence. Only thus are the conditions for the emergence of something new created.

Moreover, we are increasingly aware that sciences, technology, economy, finance and trade, however important these are, are not sufficient to confer a human face to the process of globalization. The process itself demands a spiritual, ethical, and aesthetic dimension, which ascribes direction and meaning to the other dimensions of the process. The dimensions of the process are not juxtaposed but intertwined and interdependent. The ecological, economic, political, social, ethical and spiritual challenges we currently face are interretroconnected, and therefore, only a holistic perspective and inclusive solutions will do justice to this complex global reality.

I understand that this web of connections can only be established if the following directions are followed: the individual well-being is connected to the collective well-being, economy is compliant to politics, politics is guided by ethics, and ethics is inspired by spirituality. That is to say, it is inspired by a new perspective of the universe, of the place that the human being occupies in the universe, and of the mystery of being.

For centuries we have overvalued the economic and political fields to the detriment of the ethical and spiritual spheres. This asymmetry constitutes one of the reasons for the current crisis of civilization, and of the loss of meaning and of idealistic horizons in the history of humankind.

My theoretical and practical efforts focus on recovering ethics and spirituality as a basis over which a global project of civilization that is sustainable and that presents a proper future for the biosphere, for the community of life and for humanity as a whole can be built.

I shall focus on four core virtues which, I believe, are necessary for a more humane coexistence and for a process of globalization that is beneficial and loaded with hope for all: these four virtues are hospitality, co-living, tolerance, and communality.

The first book deals with the issue of hospitality within the dramatic context of the global flux and influx of populations (usually in search of better living conditions or purely and simply in search of survival) that challenge the geographical limits of nation-states.

The second book will tackle issues connected to co-living and tolerance, and it will discuss various modern theories that seek to understand the current transitional situation of the world, which is dominated by fear, which is threatened by fundamentalism, and which is affected by terrorism.

The third book will engage the distressing question of communality and issues such as famine, commercial control of seeds, and the genetic manipulation of life. The ultimate outcome of these cardinal virtues is the generation of a long-desired culture of active nonviolence and of peace.

Virtues constitute the realm of excellence and of values, and as such, virtues clearly possess a utopian appeal. It belongs to the nature of utopia to transport us to increasingly higher and broader horizons. And as has already been said, their function is to unsettle and to bring about change. Virtues are similar to the stars: we can never touch them, but they guide navigators and enchant our nights. They can always suggest to us practices that are increasingly more creative and that allow utopia not to remain only a utopia. We can always grow and better ourselves.

The challenge consists in finding under the inspiration of these virtues historical mediations and the best social and judicial conditions to allow these virtues to actualize themselves in the best possible manner, and thus in avoiding their suppression within the framework of given situations.

For this reason, I shall make a great effort to incorporate in my ethical-spiritual discourse concrete mediations, attitudes, and stances so that the dream is allowed to become a process of continuous change.

These cardinal virtues for a process of globalization that is minimally ethical are not merely a desire and a project. They are being reflected upon and practiced by groups that seek an alternative to the present global order, by international movements connected to ecology, to the preservation of nature, to the defense and promotion of social and environmental human rights, by movements inspired by the principles of the Earth Charter, and by global initiatives such as the World Social Forum and by the Alliance for a Responsible, Plural, and United World.

Within these movements and initiatives, despite their limitations and contradictions, simmers an *ethos* of care, of welcoming the other, of tolerance, of sharing, and of productive and consuming ways that are based on solidarity. Values are historically incorporated and organized, and convey to us the hope that, with certainty, another kind of world and another kind of globalization is historically possible. Paraphrasing the poet Fernando Pessoa,[1] I could say: I want to imagine the world as it has never been.

We should encourage *hospitality* from one to another, for the Judaeo-Christian Scriptures say that we are sojourners on earth, and that we do not dwell permanently here. We must strive to *co-live* one with another because we dwell in the same Common Home, and we do not have another place to live in. We must incorporate *tolerance* from one to another in those issues we find difficult to understand and abide. It is important to *respect* differences. It is necessary to live in *communality*, that is: to sit together at the table and to celebrate with joy the fact of being together as a family, as brothers and sisters, savouring the generosity of Mother Earth. What is the point of having *hospitality*, *co-living*, *respect*, and *tolerance* if there is no *communality*, if we are dying of hunger and thirst, and if we do not have a common table at which we can satiate our needs with solidarity?

If these virtues become a habit and part of our culture, then the conditions for the so-desired and liberating globalization, for the kind of globalization that reunites the tribes, that brings back prodigal sons and daughters, and that brings closer those who are distant; that better preserves Mother Earth, and that open us up to the original Fountainhead that is the source of all gifts, of the infinite goodness of life and happiness, will emerge.

Petrópolis, Easter 2005

1. Translator's note: Fernando Pessoa (1888–1935) is considered to be one of the greatest poets of the Portuguese language.

book 1

Hospitality—
The Right and Duty of All

one

The Global Phase of the Earth and of Humanity

We are entering a new phase in the evolutionary process of the Earth and of humanity, the global phase. People who are scattered in the various continents and who are enclosed in their respective nation-states are increasingly aware of their place in our Common Home, the planet Earth.

Increasingly, people are more aware that we only have this planet to inhabit, a planet which is small and limited in resources. Thus, it is important to treat it with care so that it can accommodate all humans and the whole chain of life. We want our planet to have a very long future.

We have also become acquainted with something that deeply touches us: the astronaut's perspective from space. From space it is not possible to distinguish the Earth from humanity, the Earth from the biosphere. They form a great, unique, and complex reality. We have the same origins and the same destiny, and for this reason insofar as the future is concerned, we are a single subject.

And this slowly provokes a progressive new state of consciousness. From being ethnically and class conscious, we become species conscious, we become conscious that we are part of the *homo sapiens and demens* species (i.e., we are rational, *sapiens*, but we can also be irrational, *demens*). We discover ourselves to be members of the great human family and of the community of life; we discover ourselves as brothers and sisters, and as cousins of the other representatives of the immense biodiversity (plants and animals) that characterizes the biosphere—that thin layer that envelops the Earth and that constitutes the life-system. Certainly, it is more than a thin membrane of life; it is the most visible

3

part of the planet Earth itself, which should be understood as a living supraorganism, the Great Mother, Pachamama,[1] and Gaia.

In the face of this new moment in our common history everybody is affected. People have started to ask themselves: what is the function of each human person, of cultures, of nations, and of religions? And inquire: Will our traditions, our regional cultures, our convictions, our arts and religions matter? In short, will that which constitutes our identity matter? How are we to transform ourselves so that we are in synchrony with this new phase that is emerging? What must we be?

The accelerated process of globalization presents a dramatic crossroads for humanity. It can produce the opportunity for all peoples of all cultures and traditions to meet. It can be a pleasurable experience of discovering differences, and this represents a possibility to form new partnerships and to co-live.

However, it can also present a strange experience that gives rise to mistrust, anxiety, and even fear in the face of differences. Moreover, close contact can reignite old hatreds, tensions, sorrows, and prejudices that have accumulated over centuries between regions and peoples.

Now more than ever hospitality, mutual welcome, and kind receptivity are imperative; for those virtues require a detachment of conceptions and preconceptions. Only in this way can we perceive difference as something that is different and not as something that is unequal and inferior. Thus it is necessary to be willing to co-live in the same Common Home, for we have no another alternative. We must also be tolerant, because without tolerance the logic of the friend/enemy, of wars, and of exclusion endures. Last, we need communality, which is the ultimate implication of globalization, so that we can all sit at the table together to eat and celebrate the generosity of nature and the fact that we are together. Thus, the virtues for a successful globalization are four: hospitality, co-living, tolerance, and communality. And these are the object of my investigations in these books.

The process involving these four virtues inevitably encompasses comings and goings, getting it right and making mistakes. But this process will consolidate and expand the points of convergence, and in doing

1. Translator's Note: *Pacha Mama* or *Mana Pacha* is a fertility goddess in Inca mythology. *Pacha Mama* is usually translated "Mother Earth," but a more correct translation would be "Mother Universe"—in the Aymara and Quechua languages *mama* means "mother," and *pacha* means "universe."

so it will create a common foundation, which will provide the conditions for a new kind of collective consciousness and for a new global citizenship. When this happens, we will see the rise of a new form of identification that is collective; it is the human-species-identity. All previous identities, national or regional, which have produced so many conflicts and tensions, will not cease to exist; but individually these will not be the defining factor in the future. The future will be molded by all of us and by the common elements that are being identified and taken up by us.

We will emerge as citizens of the Earth, who are different, but who also share a common humanity. The ancient and basic concept *humanitas* will become pivotal and the common reference value. Only then, will we live as communal sojourners on Earth, our common fatherland and motherland.

In order to understand this complex process with all its presupposed developments, we must become aware and pass judgement on two basic attitudes that are present in the process of globalization: one attitude that is guided by the past and another attitude that is directed toward the future. These attitudes provide us with two different paradigms, for each of them try to shape in their own way the process of globalization, and this provides us with two distinct futures.

Looking Behind: The Paradigm of the Enemy and of Confrontation

When faced with something new, a great number of societies and people look to what has happened before, look to the past, in search of guidance. In redefining their identity, they appeal to traditions, to language, to religion, to custom, to the glories of their culture, to national heroes, to the values that characterize their culture, to traditional feasts, to literary and other artistic masterpieces, to long-lasting institutions, to the singularity and the beauty of their ecology. Moreover, they look to those peoples and cultures with whom they have an affinity and with whom they share a destiny, but they also refer to those peoples with whom they maintain tense and even hostile relations.

Identities that are reaffirmed by taking the past as the reference point are usually constructed by emphasizing the difference with other identities. This form of identity clearly defines one's enemies and friends. One modern theorist of political philosophy, Carl Schmitt (1888–1985), analyzed this issue in his well-known *The Concept of the Political* where he states: "For as long as a people exists in the political sphere, this people must, even if only in the most extreme case . . . determine by itself the distinction between friend and enemy."[2] Who is the enemy? The enemy "is . . . the other, the stranger; and it is sufficient for his nature that he is, in a specially intense way, existentially something different and alien, so that in the extreme case conflicts with him are possible. . . . Each participant is in a position to judge whether the adversary intends to negate his opponent's way of life and therefore must be repulsed or fought in order to preserve one's own form of existence. Emotionally the enemy is easily treated as being evil and ugly."[3]

Another well-known modern theorist on political philosophy and on globalization, Samuel P. Huntington, states something similar in his *The Clash of Civilizations* when he says: "For peoples seeking identity and reinventing ethnicity, enemies are essential. . . . We know who we are only when we know who we are not and often only when we know whom we are against."[4]

This perspective, as one may gather, is full of risks, for it is guided by the paradigm of the enemy and by a predisposition to conflict and even to war. Certainly, the post–cold war era is being characterized by wars in various parts of the world, wars that have origins in those groups that seek to defend their identity, whether because they judge their identities are threatened by traditional enemies, or whether because they feel their identities are threatened by the homogenization caused by the dominant process of globalization, which is so characterized by the Westernization of the world (and some call this the "Western intoxication" of the world), and which is so characterized by the standardization of the economy and of political thinking. Alongside the process of globalization we can also see, unfortunately, the process of balkanization and of fragmentation of humanity.

It is important to seriously consider the question, how can we consider others to be enemies, enemies to be faced, if we must co-inhabit a small place, the planet Earth? This paradigm of friend/enemy, even if it is realistic, must be set aside if we want to share a sole and unique space (for we do not have another), our Common Home, the Earth. This kind

2. Schmitt, *The Concept of the Political*, 49.

3. Ibid., 27.

4. Huntington, *The Clash of Civilizations*, 20–21.

of paradigm stands for the endurance of the past and does not present us with a future. The reaffirmation of ethnic identities through definitions and outlines vis-à-vis others, through disregarding the search for points in common, represents a battle that has been lost from the outset, for it ignores the minimal and unique identity that will necessarily emerge as the outcome of the process of globalization of the human species. Moreover, by conducting a war with the current technological resources, we have could put in danger the biological future of our species.

It is this reductionist perspective that has inspired world politics after the terrorist attacks on that sad day, September 11th of 2001 in the USA. The discourse is very clear: it is a war between "the world of order and the world of disorder," a world of disorder characterized by "rogue states"; it is a war between the "evil axis" and the "good axis." President George W. Bush in his political-religious fundamentalism sought to pursue wars with no limits, an "infinite war" against terrorism and against those who provide strategic support for terrorism. The dominant superpower confronts all countries with the following alternative: you are either with the USA (and thus pro-civilization) or with the terrorists (and thus pro-barbarism). There is no other alternative. Curiously, Islamic fundamentalists follow the same reasoning, and only invert the terms: there is a need to fight against the Empire of Evil, against Western arrogance, against atheism, and against the materialism of Western culture, which is dominated and represented by the USA; and it is imperative to opt for the kingdom of good represented by Islamic religion and culture. Islamic religion and culture place everything under the reign of the unique and true God, Allah, and for this reason it invalidates the separation of religion and politics, the separation between the sacred and the secular—and it encourages fraternity between peoples.

It becomes clear that we are faced with two fundamentalisms, which are belligerent and threatening to a humane process of globalization.

Due to this scenario of conflict, global analysts, such as Thomas L. Friedman, who is a columnist for the *New York Times*, and Ephraim Halevi, who is the former head of the Israeli Intelligence Service (Mossad) and current president of the Israeli National Security Council, sustain the thesis that on 9/11 of 2001 the Third World War started—a war that is being fought between the world of order and the world of disorder. The question here is this: what kind of war is this? Will all weapons available in the arsenals of destruction eventually be used, or will a conscious self-restraining take place? If the West launched a mas-sive military offensive, the results would be so monstrous in terms of the genocide of civilians that it would be contradictory to the values of Western and democratic civilization, in the name of which the war is being fought. As one may gather, the paradigm of the enemy and of confrontation still persists.

To continue to build the human family through the inspiration of this old paradigm would take us to dramatic scenarios and it could pres-ent us with the serious risk of the destruction of humankind's global project. This old paradigm perpetuates the destructive dialectic of friend/enemy, which characterizes a dramatic past for the majority of peoples.

This old paradigm, if viewed from within the new global phase, seems to be very simplistic, linear, and reductionist. It does not possess realities capable of providing a new horizon of hope for tomorrow. For this reason, Eric Hobsbawm's warning at the end of his book *The Age of Extremes*, when he concludes his balance of the twentieth century, makes sense: "Our world risks both explosion and implosion. It must change . . . the alternative to a changed society, is darkness."[5] The great historian Arnold Toynbee (1889–1975) held a similar opinion at the end of his life and after having had written twelve tomes on the great civilizations. In his autobiography, titled *Experiences*, he says sombrely: "I . . . have lived on to see the ending of human history become a mundane possibility that would be translated into fact by an act, not of God, but of Man."[6]

This paradigm is only capable of creating a unipolar world that is built on the imperialist mentality of a sole hegemonic superpower that imposes itself on all and by all means. The superpower does not hesitate in using its might in conventional wars, in preventive wars; and eventually it may use its arsenal of weapons of mass destruction. It puts under its control markets and finance, and it entraps countries within a unique global strategy that includes the generation of information by a few global conglomerates associated with political-economic-military power. And this political-economic-military power legitimizes a culture based on material goods, favors an impoverished perception of reality, aims at the standardization of the images that are produced, supports

5. Hobsbawm, *The Age of Extremes*, 585.
6. Toynbee, *Experiences*, 371.

the imposition of designed customs and the manufacturing of induced tastes.

This is a dead end. We must find new pathways.

Looking Ahead: The Paradigm of the Sojourner and of Alliance

Another possible attitude in the face of the process of globalization is to turn toward the future and to the opportunities that it offers. It is important to bear in mind when we do this that we are experiencing a new and singular phenomenon. New wine requires new skins.

Those who formulated a new understanding of the world, such as Albert Einstein, Max Planck, Werner Heisenberg, Mm. Marie Curie, Ilya Prigogine, Dana Zohar, Edgar Monn, Sigmund Freud, Carl Gustav Jung, Pierre Teilhard de Chardin, Mahandas Gandhi, Martin Luther King Jr., Nelson Mandela, and Dom Helder Câmara, among others, have clearly expressed during their time that the tools available to rationality did not account for the new facts that were emerging. We either require new scientific theories or new social categories to comprehend those new facts emerging about reality. With imagination and reasoning they created instruments more in tune with knowledge and social relations. They enriched our experiences with theories that nourish us to this day.

The philosopher of sciences Thomas Kuhn and the quantum physicist Fritjhof Capra theorized about this creative process when they commented on the issue of paradigm change. Fundamental transformations of consciousness and of society trigger a change of paradigm. This is our current situation. We are changing our paradigm of civilization. I mean that (and here I am also explaining what a paradigm is) another kind of perception of reality is emerging, with new values, with new dreams, with a new form of organizing knowledge, with new types of social relations, with a new way of dialoguing with nature, with a new way of experiencing the Ultimate Reality, and with a new manner of understanding ourselves and of defining our place within the chain of being.

The new, emerging paradigm occurs in progressive stages: we move from the parts to the whole, from the simple to the complex, from the local to the national, from national to global, from global to cosmic, from cosmic to mystery, and from mystery to God.

This new paradigm no longer understands the Earth as discretely made up of the physical, of the mental, of the spirit, and of life. The Earth is simultaneously all these dimensions forming a complex totality and a system that is open to new incorporations. All beings are intertwined in webs of inter-retro-connections within this totality that is complex, cosmic, terrestrial, biological, anthropological, and spiritual. Neither the Earth nor the human is a finished entity. Both continue to dawn, to expand, and to evolve in continuous processes of generation.

A perspective that looks toward the future is vital for the dawn and consolidation of this new paradigm. It is important to set aside the kind of enclosed metaphysics that identify an understanding of reality with reality itself. Reality transcends the representations we construct about it, because it is bursting with opportunities and promises that can potentially be realized. Therefore there are an infinite number of prospects within the current critical stage. And our challenge is to allow these prospects to burst through.

It is at this point that visionaries, idealists, prophets, and those who formulate new utopias appear. Their visions are indeed idealistic, but not wrong. They represent what ought to be and what certainly is needed. But it is important to understand their discourse properly: they are guiding images, maps, charts to direct our searches, to help us to make right decisions, and to give rise to a new state of conscience.

These essential visions make us aware of the singularity of our historical moment. Our perception of our settings has changed: we are all interdependent; we cannot live and survive on our own and without the community of life and the remaining energies of the universe; the common destiny has been globalized. We either take care of humanity and of the planet Earth as a whole, or we will not have a future. Every thing is definitely connected to everything.

Up to now we could consume natural resources without worrying about their exhaustion. We could use drinking water without being aware of its extreme scarcity; we could have children without being anxious about overpopulation; we could go to war without fearing a total catastrophe for the biosphere and for the future of the human species. Today we cannot continue to live so naively and unconcerned. We must change our habits so that we are not responsible for serious crises and terrible disasters. Change is a condition for our survival and for the preservation of the biosphere.

Hence we are faced with a risk of a total disaster, or we are faced with a unique opportunity where we are called, personally and collectively, to be responsible for the common future of Humankind and the Earth; we are called to reinvent a new paradigm of civilization. We must be creative. Creativity is written in our genetic code and culture; we were created creators and copilots of the evolutionary process. Therefore we will only express our creativity if we look forward. We must learn from the past, but we must not repeat the past.

The paradigm of the enemy and of confrontation must be balanced out by the paradigm of the equal, of the guest, and of the communal. From confrontation we must pass to conciliation, and from conciliation we must pass to co-living, and from co-living we must pass to communion and from communion to communality. People who were scattered in the various continents and enclosed in their nation-states are increasingly aware of their place in our Common Home, the planet Earth. And thus some questions arise: How are we to take care of ourselves? How are we to build a common future? How are we to poetically and prosaically inhabit the world? What is the common basis that will permit us to understand each other and that will allow us to converge globally?

To answer these questions it is imperative to practice the virtues of hospitality, co-living, tolerance, and communality, which I have already mentioned above. It is the practice of these virtues that will provide us with the basis for a future with hope for all.

The Burning Flame of Prophets and Visionaries

There have already been prophets and visionaries who in their respective times have picked up the first signs of this kind of globalization that offers a future with hope for all. One of these is without doubt Dom Helder Câmara, who was the greatest prophet of the developing world. He was full of compassion and concern for the impoverished masses of the world. He argued for an ethical, global mobilization founded on at least a minimum of justice and on the natural generosity of human beings to give rise to a world where wealth was not generated at the cost of the poor, where unlimited solidarity and communality flourished, and where social justice is in place and universal fraternity embraced. To start with, this dream was meant to be built out of the nightmare of poverty, out of the sons and daughters who live in chaos, and then it would involve everybody's constructing a possible heaven on earth for us. In this pantheon of prophets and visionaries are also Mahatma Gandhi,

Martin Luther King Jr., Paulo Freire, Desmond Tutu, Mother Teresa of Calcutta, and Robert Müller, among others.

Another prophet and visionary was, without doubt, the palaeontologist and Christian mystic Pierre Teilhard de Chardin (1881–1955). By observing the ascending evolutionary process and the tendency of intercommunication between peoples as well as the increasing awareness of these, he identified, already in the 1930s, the seeds of a new era, which he called the *noosphere*. According to Teilhard de Chardin, we are moving towards a new phase in the history of the Earth and of Humankind, a new phase that offers the possibility of convergence of minds and hearts (*noos* means "heart" in Greek), and therefore of a more loving relationship between all human beings within our Common Home, and this is something that has never before been seen in the history of humanity.

In our modern times, Robert Müller, who is an established United Nations employee and the founder of the University for Peace in Costa Rica (of which he is the chancellor), dreamt of *the birth of a global civilization* (which is the title of his main book)[7] founded in a spiritual and ecocosmic perspective, in fraternity between all peoples, in living together in the Common Home, the Earth, as a family. In the mode of Paulo Freire, he developed a pedagogy used by a chain of schools all over the world, a pedagogy according to which, from a very early age, students, with educators, look at the universe, the Earth, and the human being in a globalized and ecological way, examining these as an expression of the immense evolutionary process that has taken place for more than 15 billion years.

Recently, after years of intense work involving dozens of peoples, the Earth Charter was elaborated (and taken up by UNESCO in 2000), and this is one of the most important documents within the new paradigm based on inclusion and on the articulation between every thing with every thing, and which aims to encourage an essential care for the planet and for a new sustainable way of being.

It is against this background that I wish to deal with the issues of hospitality, co-living, tolerance, and communality. We either feel, as the psalmist says, sojourners in this world, we either show hospitality to each other and learn to co-live as partners in a common cause, we either eat at the same table, or we can behave like enemies and move toward devastating conflicts such as have never been seen before.

7. Müller, *The Birth of a Global Civilization*.

There will be a multicivilizational Earth, which will be colored by all kinds of cultural values with various means of production, with typical social structures, with various musical styles, with the most varied cuisine, with different symbols, and with extraordinary religions and spiritual pathways. All these will be embraced as legitimate expressions of the human being, as rightful expressions within the great confederation of tribes and peoples of the Earth.

For this reason, we must be creative, we must look forward, we must take account of all the signs pointing us to a happy ending in our dangerous journey, and we must encourage an atmosphere of warmth and of fraternity that may allow us to live with at least a minimum of happiness in this small planet in the interior of a planetary system of small dimensions, hidden in a corner of a medium-size galaxy, but which is also under the auspices of human goodwill and divine goodness.

The enlightening words of the president of the Czech Republic, Václav Havel, the writer and human-rights activist, when he received the Philadelphia Liberty Medal on 4th July 1994 in Philadelphia confirms our dream: "The central political task of the final years of this century, then, is the creation of a new model of coexistence among the various cultures, peoples, races, and religious spheres within a single interconnected civilization."[8] This will not happen without virtues, such as hospitality, co-living, tolerance and communality.

These virtues will build, slowly, a common basis for a single civilization, the civilization of the human species. Unaccountable internal differences will continue to exist, but all these differences will be placed over a consensus that has been assumed by all, the consensus always to treat each other with humanity, to co-live peacefully as brothers and sisters, to take care of the Earth and to preserve the integrity and beauty of nature, to guarantee the bare minimum for all, and to create the conditions for all human beings to humanly and spiritually develop themselves.

Only then will the flame become a radiating and warm burning flare.

---

8. Translator's note: Václav Havel's speech, "The Need for Transcendence in the Postmodern World," is available online: http://www.worldtrans.org/whole/havelspeech .html/.

two

Returning from the Great Scattering

The new historical phase is centred on the indissoluble union of the Earth and Humanity. In order to understand this unity, it is necessary to rediscover the Earth, to identify our common roots, our cosmic, terrestrial, biological, anthropological, historical, social and spiritual roots. These are roots long forgotten in the discourse and practice of current, pretentious global leaders, who are only concerned with power, which is exercised as domination over others and nature. These leaders are hostages to a kind of reductionist and impoverished view of the human being, of culture, of means of production, and of dialogue with nature.

Our real situation is the following: we are inserted into a universal process that has already been on course for billions and billions of years. The current process of globalization is founded in the previous dynamics that involves all: the universe, the Earth, life, and humanity. We are not and we have never been juxtaposed to each other. We have always been intertwined with each other, forming an organic, complex, dialectic, and complementary whole. Let me briefly go over the stages of this universal process.

Everything has its origins in the energy that comes from the ends of the universe, which is called the quantum vacuum by quantum physicists and modern cosmologists. This is a vacuum that is not empty; it is the source of everything that exists, for it is impregnated by the original, mysterious, and creative energy. For this reason some people prefer to call it a fecund vacuum, or empty plenitude, or simply as the original fountain where everything originates. This energy contained in the quantum vacuum was extremely concentrated, and it was billions of times smaller than the head of a pin. There we find infinite peace and quietness.

Suddenly, and we do not know why, this miniscule point inflated to the size of an apple and exploded with unimaginable power. Elemental energies and particles were thrown on all directions. This is the *big bang* that occurred about 15 billion years ago.

The process of expansion started with a subtle balance of factors. If gravity (the force of attraction) was too strong, it would prevent expansion, and successive explosions would take place. If gravity was too weak, everything would be diluted, and solid bodies, which are the basis of the universe, would not be formed. Immediately after the great explosion, immense clouds of gas full of elemental particles, especially hydrogen and helium (which are the most simple and abundant elements in the universe), where formed.

Then, the gas started to condense. forming the great red stars. These stars function as immense atomic reactors because they synthesized for billions of years in their interior the 92 heavy chemical elements that compose the universe and human reality: at first, silicon, nitrogen, potassium, magnesium, iron, phosphorus, uranium; and later, carbon and others.

Atomic reactions inside these red stars were so violent that they caused these stars to explode. Thank God that this occurred, for without their self-sacrifice we would not be here, alive, and able to talk about it. These explosions caused matter to spread all over the universe. This matter, this cosmic by-product, was responsible for the birth of nebulas, conglomerates of galaxies, galaxies (such as our Milky Way), stars (such as our sun), planets (such as our Earth) and the life in our own bodies. But how did the Earth, our Common Home, come into being?

A Star Is Dead, the Earth Is Born

The Earth was not born as it is today. It possesses a prehistory of millions of years before it became Earth, the third planet of the solar system. Below is a brief account of the events leading to this as envisaged by cosmologists.

First, the grandmother of the Earth was a star that turned supernova and exploded five billion years ago. A supernova is a star that suddenly has its brightness greatly increased, and this is provoked by internal explosions that throw internal matter into space, which in turn gives origin to nebulas and stellar debris. Scientists call this star *Tiamat*, the name of a Middle Eastern deity, the parts of which formed the heavens and the earth according to the myth. With the death of the grandmother *Tiamat*, in a grand finale of brightness and beauty, an immense nebula was formed. Elements that were inside this star were thrown into space and constitute the basis of our world and of life.

These elements were not present when the first gases and particles condensed within the Higgs Field (i.e. the first crystallizations of energy in the form of material particles such as top quarks). It was *Tiamat* who forged these elements inside herself (e.g., phosphorus, which made photosynthesis possible). It was *Tiamat* who threw into space oxygen and sulphur, which are the basis of life. With her death carbon and nitrogen were liberated, which are fundamental for the various combinations that structure life, genetic information, memory, and rationality. Without her sacrificing her existence in an incommensurable explosion, nothing would have existed with regard to our history of intelligence, creativity, love, and reverence toward reality.

Tiamat is also the origin of *planet cores*, which are fragments that became part of the composition of planets. These fragments occurred in various sizes, from ten meters to two thousand kilometers in radius. These planet embryos coexisted within the nebula, colliding and amalgamating with each other due to the force of gravity on them, and due to their own particular revolutions. Over a period of a million years, the nebula became more dense until it reached the point in which a radiating star, the Sun, appeared at its center.

Another chapter starts with the appearance of the Sun. The mother, and if you wish the father, of the Earth enter the scene: a star, the Sun. The Sun, with its gravitational pull, arranged around itself the orbits of the *planet cores*. The ardent solar rays scalded us and caused the volatile components to evaporate. This cleaning-up operation counted on the help of solar winds, and it gave rise to the larger planets, such as Jupiter, which is so voluminous because it accumulated the gases produced during the evaporation of those volatile components around itself. During a period of a hundred million years the other planets were formed. These planets are the result of a process of progressive aggregation (which is technically called accreation) of *planet cores*. The first of these planets to appear was Mercury, then Mars and Venus. Afterwards, other large *planet cores* merged together during a period of one hundred million years; then finally, the Earth, our Earth, our Cosmic Home, was born.

The Earth is a very singular planet within the solar system. It possesses optimum characteristics, which allowed it to be what it is today. It is an ideal distance from the Sun, which allows the Earth to seize and preserve various volatile chemical elements, and which stops water from completely evaporating from the Earth's surface. If the Earth was closer to the Sun, such as Venus is, then the solar winds would have scorched the Earth. If the Earth was much farther away from the Sun, such as Jupiter and Saturn are, then its composition would fundamentally be based on gases, such as hydrogen and helium, and the solidification of physical-chemical elements would not occur, and this is something that is necessary for the formation of an atmosphere, of oceans and rivers, and lastly of life. But to reach the current stage, the Earth underwent dramatic convulsions. For eight hundred million years it remained a molten body because of the immense heat generated by the Sun, and also because of the heat caused by the impact of asteroids and meteorites. When the terrestrial crust cooled down, thanks to its ideal distance to the Sun the conditions for the appearance of a magnificent garden and cradle of an immense diversity of life were in place.

Life is part of the cosmic evolutionary process, and it is written in the physical and chemical laws. If there was no equilibrium in the gravitational force, as I mentioned above, and if the physical and chemical laws were slightly different, the kind of life we are familiar with would not have emerged. Computer simulations suggest that life springs spontaneously when a group of amino acids, proteins, and alkaline phosphates reach a certain degree of interaction and complexity.

Once it has appeared, life continues to create the most adequate conditions for its own development, and this is something that is consonant with James Lovelock's Gaia hypothesis, and which allows us to say that the biosphere is the creation of life itself. Life expanded and increased in complexity in our galaxy, in our solar system, and on our planet Earth; then finally, life broke through as conscious human life, as a bearer of love and of care, and in synchrony with and aware of God.

The Earth was formed 4.44 billion years ago, when it assumed its current mass and dimensions of radius of 6.400 km and circumference of 40.000 km. It is composed of a series of concentric layers. Externally, we find the atmosphere, which is rarefied and filled with gases. On the surface we find the hydrosphere composed of oceans, seas, and continental rivers, and we also find the risen lands of continental plates. Below these, there is the terrestrial mantel, which constitutes about 70 percent of the Earth's volume; and at 2,900 km under our feet we find the Earth's nucleus, which is composed of liquid iron and solid nickel.

During its long history, the Earth was geologically very active. From time to time volcanoes exploded and huge meteors hit the Earth leaving immense craters but also bringing in considerable quantities of water and metals, and according to some the meteors also brought in those most basic molecules (i.e., amino acids, proteins, and alkaline phosphates), the building blocks of life.

Parts are United and Torn Apart: The Continents

Geologists and palaeontologists inform us that during the Archean period, which spans the period from formation of the Earth 4.44 billion years ago to 2.7 billion years ago, the continents did not exist. The waters covered the whole of the Earth, which was dotted with immense volcanic islands.

Around 3.8 billion years ago vast extensions of lands emerged, but these were dispersed all over the place and shifting. These lands started to join together, always with great friction, tidal waves, and devastations, in a process that lasted one billion years and which led to the formation of the continents. Floating on a layer of basalt, these continents moved about and joined together until they formed one vast continent, *Pangaea*. For 50 million years this supercontinent moved around the globe, and then a million years later it became fragmented and the continents we know today appeared.

Underneath the continents, we find tectonic plates, which are always active, which are always colliding with or superimposing on each other (producing mountain ranges), or moving away from each other (the so-called continental drift). Each time these plates collide, they produce unimaginable cataclysms, such as the one that occurred 245 million years ago, which caused the rupture of *Pangaea*. It was so devastating that 75 to 95 percent of the species of that time disappeared.

The Earth experienced fifteen great mass extinctions. Two of these are notable by the fact that they completely reorganized ecosystems on land and sea.

The first of these is the one I have just mentioned above. The second occurred 65 million years ago and was caused by climate and sea-level changes, and by the impact of an asteroid measuring 9.6 km on Central America. It provoked infernal fires and gigantic tidal waves; it produced considerable quantities of poisonous gases and a long-lasting darkening of the sun. Plants and animals that depended on sunlight died. The dinosaurs, which for 130 million years dominated the Earth, disappeared completely as well as 50 percent of all other species. It took the Earth 10 million years to recover and re-create its enormous biodiversity.

Geologists and biologists maintain that a third great decimation is on course. It started 2.5 million years ago when vast glaciers started to cover part of the planet, changing climate and sea levels. Coincidently, at the same time emerged *homo habilis*, who invented instruments (e.g., from a stone or a piece of wood) to more efficiently intervene in nature. Later, *homo sapiens sapiens* will show itself to be so destructive that it could be compared to a threatening meteor. In our modern times, due to irresponsible and careless consumerism, the practice of systematic depredation of ecosystems was introduced, and as a consequence of this the process of mass extinction of species has accelerated to a level that outpaces nature itself.

Thus, we are at the mercy of uncontrollable forces that can destroy our species just as many other species were destroyed in the past. Life, however, was never exterminated. There was a new genesis after each mass extinction. Because intelligence occurs first in the universe and then in us, we can presuppose that it will continue to exist in other beings who, let us hope, will behave better than we have done. As Peter Ward, the geologist based at the University of Washington, observed in his book *The End of Evolution*: "Who can say that some currently insignificant species might not be the rootstock of some far-flung intelligence ultimately of greater achievement, wisdom, and insight than our own? Who would have predicted that the first protomammals migrating into the frigid Karroo 275 million years ago would give rise to the mammals, or that the small arboreal mammals trembling in fear of the mighty dinosaurs 75 million years ago would one day give rise to us?"[1] This is one of the reasons for the preservation of all species; that is, we should preserve them not as much for their economic, medicinal, and scientific

1. Ward, *The End of Evolution*, 270.

value to us but for the evolutionary potential that is contained in them. The future of intelligence and conscience could be inherent in them.

Hence, here is our Earth, already mature and with its current characteristics; with its oceans, rivers, volcanoes; with its atmosphere, flora and fauna, and immense biodiversity. Its distinctive elements (e.g., rocks, mountains, waters, plants, animals, human beings, and microorganisms) are not, as I have previously said, juxtaposed on each other. Every thing is intertwined and interdependent with everything, forming a complex and living system. This is the Gaia system, the Earth as a live supra-organism, endowed with a very subtle equilibrium of elements, of oxygen in the air, of nitrogen in soil, of salt in the oceans, in order that it can only be a living being. Within the complex and ascending process of life it is the most magnificent phenomenon we are acquainted with—it is our planet.

The Most Beautiful Child: Life

Until recently, life was conceived of as something outside the cosmosgenesis; it was conceived of as something miraculous, originating directly from God. But in the 1950s the discovery of the genetic code (i.e., DNA) that is present in cells completely changed our understanding of the origins of life. Life is not outside the cosmological process. On the contrary, life is its best expression. Scientific research has revealed that life is composed of the same physical-chemical elements that are shared by all other beings and which are organized in extremely complex relations. All living organisms possess the same basic alphabet: twenty amino acids and four nucleic acids (i.e., adenine, guanine, thymine and cytosine). We are all brothers and sisters and cousins. We are differentiated by the different combinations of the syllables of this alphabet of life.

In the 1970s, with research into thermodynamics and physics of chaos (and it is worth mentioning here the name of the seminal scientist on this issue, the Russian-Belgian, Ilya Prigogine, who died in 2003), it became clear that life appears when matter has reached a high level of complexity and within a context of turbulence and chaotic situations. Chaos is never merely chaotic. From the very beginning chaos shows itself to be generative. It generates higher and more complex orders. Life is an expression of this organizational chaos. When matter finds itself unbalanced, it overcomes chaos through life, matter finds a new dynamic, auto-organizing and autoregenerative equilibrium—life represents the reorganization of matter. When a certain degree of complexity is reached, life emerges as a cosmic imperative and this is valid anywhere in the universe where this degree of complexity is reached. Life is the most beautiful child of the known universe, the most enchanting child that evolution has produced, a child that is at the same time vigorous and tender, fragile and, up to now, indestructible.

Around 3.8 million years ago, probably in the depths of a primeval ocean or in a primordial swamp on this miniscule planet Earth, in a small solar system, in a corner of our galaxy (i.e. our planet is located in the minor Orion spiral arm and is 29 thousand light-years from the center of the galaxy), the first live cell appeared, a primordial bacteria named *Aries*. It is the original mother of all live beings, the true Eve, for all living beings (including human beings) are derived from it.

With the appearance of this uniqueness an intense dialogue between life, the Sun, the Earth, and all its elements, and the entire universe begins. The Earth collaborates with life and life collaborates with the Earth. As James Lovelock demonstrated with his theory of Gaia the atmosphere is by and large the creation of life itself, life that created the adequate conditions for the generation and expansion of its own habitat. Slowly the Earth ceases to be Earth and becomes Gaia, which Lovelock defines in his book *Gaia* as: "a complex entity involving the Earth's biosphere, atmosphere, oceans, and soil; the totality constituting a feedback or cybernetic system which seeks an optimal physical and chemical environment for life on this planet."[2]

Through the works of the German physicist Heinrich Schumann we learned that the Earth is wrapped in a complex electromagnetic circuit. It is the result of interaction between the Sun, the Earth (its soil, magma, waters, and ecosystems) and the inferior part of the Earth's ionosphere (i.e. the uppermost layer of the atmosphere) at about 55 km above sea level. It produces relatively constant resonance, which is called Schumann resonance, at a frequency of 7.8 hertz. It is equivalent to the vibration of brain waves, which are particular to mammals and human beings. It stands for the heartbeat of the Earth, the pacemaker that balances out all relations connected to life. This balance is fundamental for meteorology for it regulates the seasons, the verve of volcanoes, the flow of oceans and the movement of tectonic plates. There are scientists who

2. Lovelock, *Gaia*, 11.

affirm, and these are not few, that the cardiac and emotional balances of living beings, and in particular of human beings, rests on the Schumann resonance. This is another indication that the Earth is in fact a live supraorganism, Gaia. However, something happened during the 1980s and the frequency of the Schumann resonance changed. It changed from 7.8 hertz to 11 hertz, and sometimes even 13 hertz. The Earth's heart started to beat faster. Possibly, the change in the magnetic resonance constitutes one of the causes of natural disasters, of climate change, and even of the multiplication of social conflicts worldwide.

In more than 3 billion years of work, the Earth produced an immense biodiversity of viruses, bacteria, protists, fungi, plants, and animals. Due to the numerous crises it experienced, which resulted in mass extinctions, the vast majority of the species produced by the Earth have disappeared. Perhaps only 1 percent of these species remain. But this 1 percent represents a lot. It is reckoned that there exist five thousand kinds of bacteria, one hundred thousand species of fungi, three hundred thousand species of trees, eight hundred fifty thousand species of insects. Nobody knows exactly. Biologists assert that there are as much as 30 million species.

Around the time when human beings first appeared after the disappearance of dinosaurs, there was a rapid multiplication of species as was never seen before on Earth. Really, the Earth resembled a paradise and a true cradle of life. Suddenly, and we do not know why, the planet, which was totally green due to the chlorophyll, became multicolored. A spring of multicolored flowers broke through.

It was at this exact moment that there appeared on this world a being that was more complex, fragile and relational than the others, and because of these characteristics also more resilient—this being is the human being, man and woman. Nobody expressed this miracle of the universe better than did the ancient wisdom of the Mayas. The Mayas are one of the original peoples of Mexico and they maintained, "The time of dawn has come, let the work be finished, and let those who are to nourish and sustain us appear, the noble sons, the civilized vassals; let man appear, humanity, on the face of the Earth."[3]

3. Translator's note: *Popol Vuh*, part 3, chapter 1. Popul Vuh or Popol Wuj (Council Book or Book of Community) is a book containing mythological narratives and the genealogy of the rules of the post–Classic Quiché Maya civilization. I have referred to the translation by Goetz and Griswold Morley, *The Book of the People*.

Drought: The Birthplace of the Human Being

Around 75 million years ago, when Europe, North America and Greenland formed a single continent, another chapter of life was written when the first simians, who are our ancestral relatives, appeared. These little animals, which are the size of a modern rat, fed on both flowers and insects, and not only on insects as had their ancestral forebearers. As they had to climb up and down trees, they developed their superior limbs. A particular finger was present in their paw, the thumb, which assumed an opposing position to the other fingers and this allowed these little animals to grab things, such as a fruit or a stone.

Around 35 million years ago the first primates appeared as the outcome of the evolution of those simians. These primates are a common ancestor to both human beings and higher simians. They were still quite small, about the size of a cat, and lived in isolation in Africa. They adapted themselves to climate changes, which ranged from great droughts to torrential rains caused by the expansion of forests.

These primates grew and evolved. The great African apes, chimpanzees, and gorillas, appeared. Around 7 million years ago an important split in the evolutionary process occurs: on the one side chimpanzees and gorillas (who have 99 percent of the genes we have) and on the other side the Australopithecus, which are primates in a process of hominization. This split was caused by a geological accident—the Great Rift Valley.[4] The formation of this African valley created a gigantic fault about six thousand kilometers in length. On one side of the fault we find tropical forests, which are well irrigated, and where higher primates lived comfortably. On the other side of the fault we find drought and savannahs where the Australopithecus could be found.

This change in the environment brought about two kinds of evolution. Those who were in the forests continued to be primates (gorillas and chimpanzees) as they did not require much adaptation as they lived in a *biological siesta* with their environment. The others, who were condemned to live in drought, had to develop their survival skills. They required intelligence and strategy—this is the basis of their biological sustainability—and therefore they evolved a more developed cranial

4. Translator's Note: The Great Rift Valley is a geological and geographical feature that runs from northern Syria in Southwest Asia to Mozambique in East Africa. It is approximately 6,000 km in length.

box. They walked upright to see further and were forced to eat every-thing they could catch—they are omnivorous.

As can be deduced from Lucy's bones (a young female discovered in 1974 in the Ethiopian Afar depression), the Australopithecus already presented humanoid characteristics around 3 to 4 million years ago.

As they evolved, an accelerated process of cephalization took place. From around 2.2 million years ago we see the successive emergence of the *homo habilis*, then the *homo erectus*, and then the *homo sapiens*, who are full-blown humans. They were social beings, they showed themselves to be cooperative beings, and they could speak. When they hunted they did not eat the catch alone but shared it with their fellows. During a period spanning 1 million years the brain box of the genus *homo* duplicated in volume. And during the following 1 million years, which stands for a period when the *homo sapiens* reigned, the brain did not grow any further. There was no need for any further increase as the brain was now capable of turning to its exterior, and in doing so it gener-ated knowledge through its capacity to learn; it created instruments and artefacts, it transformed the world and gave rise to culture, which is a particular characteristic of the *homo sapiens*. The *homo sapiens* is not dependent on any particular physical organ. It had to interact and in-tervene with nature to guarantee its survival. It extends its own abilities through technology, and in doing so it creates a cultural system. Culture is the outcome of the human being's activity over nature and over itself; sometimes, the human being adjusts itself to nature, at other times, the human being adjusts nature to its will, and always does either of these through an intense dialogue that is not always well balanced.

The Scattering of Human Beings and the Rise of Civilizations

As soon as human beings appeared in the evolutionary process, they started to spread out. From Africa they spread to Eurasia, to the Far East, to the Americas, and then finally reaching Oceania and Polynesia. At the end of the superior Palaeolithic period, around forty thousand years ago, human beings had already spread all over the planet and numbered around 1 million people.

During the Neolithic period, between 10,000 and 5,000 BCE, the Agricultural Revolution takes place, one of the greatest revolutions in the history of humankind. Human beings domesticated animals, selected seeds, developed irrigation, and created the first settlements. During this period the human population jumped to something around 5 to 10 million people.

From around 3500 BCE we see the rise of the great classical civilizations in Mesopotamia, of the great civilizations along the Nile in Egypt, and along the Hindus valley in India. We see the rise of cultures in China, we see the rise of the Olmec and Toltec cultures in Central America, and of Greek and Roman cultures in Europe, to mention a few. Around 1500 CE, when this period came to an end, the human population reached a figure between 500 and 600 million people.

From the fifteenth century CE we see the appearance of modern nations, with proper borders separating one nation from others, as well as frequent wars. The Industrial Revolution takes place and completely changes the relation human beings have with nature, for after the revolution the human being subjugates nature to its own interests without taking into account the autonomy of other beings and the interrelations between every thing with everything. This period reached its apex with a culture based on information, with the interference of technology on social relations, with the atomic and cybernetic revolution, and with the exploration of space aiming at the study of our solar system and cosmos.

During this period the human being gives rise to the concept of self-destruction. The human being shows itself to be not only *homo sapiens*, it shows itself to be also *homo demens*. It conquered around 83 percent of the surface of the planet and threatens all balances and species; it presents itself to be, in some cases, as the *Satan of life*. It gave itself the means to tremendously undermine the biosphere and to destroy itself.

At the same time, the human being placed in opposition to this folly the principles of care, of co-responsibility and of compassion, and through these it assumes its destiny, a destiny which is connected with the destiny of the Earth, and which is set within a perspective of self-limitation, of controlling mechanisms of destruction, of searching the golden mean, and of supporting efforts for the preservation and for the regeneration of the integrity of nature. From a potential *Satan of Earth*, the human being is transforming itself into a kind of *guardian angel* of nature and gardener of the terrestrial Garden of Eden.

In concluding this section it is important to bear in mind the following data. The process of evolution is dynamic, organic, contradictory (encompassing order and chaos), it is a complementary whole, and the human being is part and parcel of this process. It took 15 billion years for the human being to emerge. Through the human being, through the human being's brain, through the human being's eyes, through the human being's thought, through the human being's vibes, and through the human being's spirituality and reverence, the universe sees itself, the universe admires its amazing beauty, the universe contemplates its own reality and venerates the mystery it hides and reveals. The human being, as a part of the whole, enables the whole to come forward through its reflexive consciousness and through its foundational love. The human being comes from the Earth, fecund humus, and for this reason it is called *homo/human*. But the human being's horizon transcends the Earth for it is connected to the stars, stars which are the place where it came from and where it will always return.

The Return from Exile: The Globalization Process

Human beings, despite their being rooted in culture and nation-states, have never stopped migrating from one place to another on the planet. And human beings have carried their infections and diseases, their seeds, their animals and habits, and their understandings of the world in these migrations. There has always been in place a process of interbreeding between human beings: there is no race, and even less a pure race. Genes from all quarters have been mixed, but not fused. We are all interbred human beings. This is a constant stimulus in the continuous process of globalization.

The Iron Age of the Process of Globalization

The year 1492 of our Common Era is the starting point of an immense process of expansion of the West. In 1492 CE Christopher Columbus brings to the knowledge of Europeans the existence of other inhabited lands with completely different cultures. In 1521 Ferdinand Magellan demonstrates that the Earth is in fact round and that every place can be reached from any place. Then, for the first time in history, the superpowers of the sixteenth century, Spain and Portugal, give expression to the project-world. They expand to Africa, to the Americas, and to Asia. They started to Westernize the world.

Then in the nineteenth century Western colonialism submitted the known world to its cultural, religious and, particularly, commercial interests by force. All these interests were imposed on weaker peoples with extreme violence and terror. Rifles and canons are louder than reason and religion. Western Europeans revealed themselves to be the hyenas of humanity. And we, in the extreme West,[5] were born globalized, and by experience we know the meaning of globalization which is experienced and suffered as global-colonization.

This process reached its apex in the second half of the twentieth century with the great expansion of the United States of America. Technoscience, which brought us so many comforts in life, is used as a weapon of domination and as a tool to get rich. Multilateral and global corporations control national markets. A standardized Western culture weakens regional cultures. The sole mode of production becomes capitalism. And as capitalism is founded on competition, it destroys communality and cooperation. The sole way of thinking is neoliberal, and it is imposed on all quarters of the Earth. Most worrying, however, is the fact that the Earth has become a market; everything on Earth is commercialized (e.g. metals, plants, seeds, water, genes), everything is sold, and everything is a source of profit. There is no respect for the Earth's autonomy and subjectivity as Gaia. Our earthly roots and origins have become unfamiliar; it is being forgotten that we, men and women, have come from Earth, from the humus, from the fertile soil. As sons and daughters of Adam (which means son of the Earth in Hebrew), we are rooted in the fertile Earth (which is called *'adamah* in Hebrew).

This is the Iron Age of globalization, which I also call Tyrannosauric Age. I call it this because it is so vicious a period that it could be compared to the Tyrannosaurus, the most vicious of dinosaurs. In fact, the logic of mercantile competition, which has no trace of cooperation, tinges the current process of globalization with great cruelty as it excludes about half of humanity. It sucks the blood out of the economy of weaker and developing countries and mercilessly leaves millions and millions of people in hunger and malnutrition. It demands ecological costs so high that it poses a risk to the biosphere, for it pollutes the air, it poisons the soil, it contaminates the water, and taints the food. It does not put a stop to its tyrannosauric hunger even when it is faced with the real possibility of the demise of the global human project. It prefers to die

5. Translator's note: Boff makes an allusion here to Latin America.

than to reduce its material gains. Albert Jacquard, the French geneticist, rightly said: "The aim of society is exchange. A society whose engine is competition is a society that proposes suicide to me. If I put myself in competition with the other then I cannot exchange with the other, I must eliminate him, I must destroy him."[6]

This excluding model of globalization risks splitting the human family: on the one hand, a small group of opulent nations engulfed in material consumerism, experiencing frightful spiritual and humanitarian poverty, and putting all advantages of technoscience to their own benefit; and on the other hand, the multitude of victimized peoples who are left to their own devices, who are like the coal that propels the production machinery, who are condemned to die before their time, who are victims of chronic hunger, of the diseases that affect the poor, and of the general degradation of the Earth. There are a thousand reasons for us to oppose this kind of globalization. This kind of globalization cannot continue, for it compromises the future of the human species.

The Human Age of the Process of Globalization

The Iron Age of the process of globalization, despite the aforementioned contradictions, brings with it an important contribution to the process of globalization when viewed from a wider perspective. It creates the material and infrastructural conditions for other kinds of globalization. It projected the great avenues of global communication, it created a web of commercial and financial trading, and it favored the exchange between all peoples, continents and nations. Without these pre-conditions it would be impossible to dream about different kinds of globalization, which have always been in the background of economic globalization, but which could never attain their deserved importance.

Now that material globalization is well established, human globalization must gain control and rectify and share benefits within a wider and more inclusive perspective. This human globalization occurs simultaneously on various fronts, such as anthropological, political, ethical, and spiritual.

---

6. Albert Jacquard, *Da angústia à esperança*, 34. Translator's note: passage translated directly from the Portuguese. The reference for the French original is: Albert Jacquard, *De l'angoisse à l'espoir*. This text is not available in English.

Increasingly, people are becoming more aware of the unity of the human species, *sapiens* and *demens*. Even if cultural differences are great, a basic genetic unity is still in place; we all have the same anatomic constitution, the same psychological mechanisms, the same spiritual impulses, the same archetypal desires. No matter how different the modes of expression, we are all bearers of emotions, of intelligence, of freedom, of creativity, of care, of compassion, of love, of a playful and humoristic capacity, of musicality, of artistic expression and of spiritual experiences. And at the same time, we also see the manifestation of our capacity to be mean, to exclude the other, to be violent towards nature, to destroy, to seek revenge, and to kill. We are a complex unity of these opposing capacities.

Increasingly we see the conviction spreading, which emerged in the West but which is not exclusively Western for it is a human conviction, that each person is sacred (*res sacra homo*) and a subject of dignity. Each human being is an end in itself and cannot be treated as a means to an end. Each human being is an infinite project, it is the visible face of the Mystery in the world, and it is a son and daughter of God. Fundamental human rights, personal and social, were codified in the name of human dignity. The rights of peoples, of minorities, of women, of homosexuals, of children, of the elderly, and of the sick have been codified in detail. Last, the *dignitas Terrae* was elaborated, which is to be understood as the rights of the Earth as a living supraorganism, the rights of ecosystems, of animals, of everything that exists and that is alive.

Democracy as a universal value to be lived in all human instances, in families, in schools, in communities, in social movements, in governments, it slowly inserts itself into global political perspectives. That is to say, every human being has the right: 1) to participate in its own social realm; and 2) to help create and maintain with its presence and work its own social realm. Power must be controlled so that it does not become tyrannical. The pathway for long-lasting solutions is tireless dialogue, constant tolerance, the permanent striving for differences to meet, and saying no to violence. Peace is simultaneously a method (i.e., to always use peaceful means or to employ the least destructible means) and an aim, for it is the outcome of each person's care for everyone, for the Common Home, and for social justice. And institutions, as different as these are from society to society, must be at least minimally just, egalitarian, and transparent.

The minimum consensus for a global ethic is derived from *humanitas* (humanity), which is something each and every human being bears. More than a concept, *humanitas* is a deep feeling that we are brothers and sisters, that we have the same origins, that we possess the same physical-chemical-biological-social-cultural-spiritual nature, and that we share the same destiny. We must treat all in a humane way by following the golden rule: "do unto others what you would have them do unto you"; or put negatively: "do not do unto others what you would not have them do unto you."

Reverence for life, extreme respect for innocents, protection of the physical and psychological integrity of people and of everything that has been created, recognition of the right of the other to exist in its own singularity—all these constitute basic pillars upon which human sociability is built, all these are values that give meaning to our short stay on this planet.

Western and Eastern spiritual experiences, from ancient and modern peoples, meet and exchange perspectives. Through these experiences the human being reconnects itself to the original Fountainhead of all Being, the human being perceives a mysterious thread that runs through every thing in the universe, and in doing so, reunifies all inter-retroconnected things to a dynamic whole that is open to changes and to development. These spiritual experiences, which have been concretized in different religions and through different pathways, form human interiority and tear open vast horizons that go beyond the universe and toward the Infinite. It is only within this dimension of extrapolation and by going beyond all limits of space/time and of desire that the human being feels itself to be really human. This lesson was already taught by the ancient Greek masters, who said that it is only in the divine realm that the human being is plainly human.

The Human Age of globalization has not yet gained control. But its elements can already be seen, and are already simmering historically and in people's consciousnesses. It will break through, gloriously one day. It will inaugurate a new history, the history of the human family, who has travelled for so long in search of its common origins and of its Common Home.

The Ecological Age of the Process of Globalization

Modern cosmologists and anthropologists, such as Brian Swimme and Thomas Berry, have called our current age the Ecozoic Age. This is the era that follows from the Cenozoic Era, which is the era that started 65 million years ago, after the catastrophe that decimated the dinosaurs, when mammals experienced such a development as was never before seen. As a complex and advanced mammal, we human beings emerged during the Cenozoic period.

Slowly, this new era is emerging, a new era that is characterized by a new pact based on respect, veneration, and mutual collaboration between the Earth and humanity. This is the era of integral ecology, and thus the use of the term *ecozoic*. Human beings are increasingly more aware that they are just a moment in a process spanning billions and billions of years. Human beings are increasingly more conscious that they are part of, and co-responsible for, a web of vital relations. Human beings can either support life, ecosystems, and the future of Gaia, or they can continue to threaten these, frustrate the future, and decimate the biosphere.

After so many interventions with the rhythms of nature, we realize that we must preserve what is left and heal the wounds that we have inflicted.

This should be a concern of all and should become the basis for a new era in the process of globalization. The utopian dream of this phase is to seek the humanization of the human being, who is challenged to live in its own singularity as a communitarian being, as a cooperative being, as a compassionate being, as an ethical being that takes responsibility for its acts, and that makes sure all its deeds are good for all. This utopia must become a reality, and it must deal with those contradictions that are inevitable to historical processes or that are produced by conflict of interests. But it will stand for a new horizon of hope that will support the human journey toward the future.

From this new perspective a new ethic will emerge. Everywhere we see the rise of seminal forces that seek and that are already trying a new standard of human and ecological conduct. This new standard of conduct will grow, even if there are many difficulties, until it becomes the norm. It will represent that which Pierre Teilhard de Chardin called a *noosphere*. *Noosphere* stands for that sphere where minds and hearts enter into a fine synchrony characterized by love, by care, by a mutual respect, and by a spiritual collective intentionality. All these elements would be geared toward peace, toward guaranteeing the integrity of creation, and toward assuring the sustainability of resources (which are abundant to an extent) for the whole community of life. Free from the constraints of our consumerist and predatory society, we can co-live humanly as brothers and sisters who are able to articulate the local with the global, the part with the whole; we can combine work with poetry, efficiency with kindness; we can reconnect subjectivities and learn to play and worship as sons and daughters at home.

This awareness of belonging together, Earth-Humanity, is powerfully reinforced by the new perspective from astronauts' experiences in space. From their spaceships or from the Moon they have transmitted to us their powerful experiences. Gene Cernan, the astronaut, noted in his testimony: "I was the last man to step on the Moon in December 1972. From the lunar surface I looked with reverential fear to the Earth set in a deep blue background. What I saw was too beautiful for understanding; it was too logical and full of purpose to be the outcome of a cosmic accident. Deep inside, I felt an obligation to praise God. God must exist for God must have created that which I had the privilege to contemplate."[7]

Sigmund Jähn, another astronaut, when he returned to Earth, expressed his change of consciousness in the following manner: "Political borders are something of the past. National borders are also something of the past. We are a sole people and each of us is responsible for the upkeep of the fragile balance of the Earth. We are its guardians and we must be concerned with our common future."[8]

The perception of the Earth from outside the Earth gives rise to a new form of sacredness. It gives rise to a feeling of veneration and of respect. Perhaps there is a hidden meaning to travelling into space, which is nicely expressed by J. P. Allen: "There has been much discussion about the pros and cons of travelling to the Moon; I have not heard anyone argue that we should go to the Moon so that we could see the Earth from there. After all, this was without a doubt the true reason for us to have travelled to the Moon."[9]

---

7. Translator's note: passage translated directly from the Portuguese.

8. Translator's note: passage translated directly from the Portuguese.

9. Translator's note: passage translated directly from the Portuguese.

From the Moon there is no distinction between the Earth and Humanity, between whites and blacks, between the less educated and the sages. We all form a sole entity: the human family. And Humanity is not merely over the Earth, it is rather the Earth itself, which, as I have said previously, feels, reflects upon itself, loves, cares and venerates.

In order to transform this newfound consciousness into a permanent state, without having to think about it, we must live within the parameters of the Ecozoic Age. We must still evolve considerably if this kind of consciousness is to become a collective norm. But the first steps have already been taken. Slowly and increasingly it will flood all consciousnesses, and it will be everywhere. Only then will we achieve a new state of evolution.

The Earth Charter is intertwined with ecozoic views. In its introduction it says:

> Humanity is part of a vast evolving universe. Earth, our home, is alive with a unique community of life . . . The spirit of human solidarity and kinship with all life is strengthened when we live with reverence for the mystery of being, gratitude for the gift of life, and humility regarding the human place in nature . . . Our environmental, economic, political, social, and spiritual challenges are interconnected, and together we can forge inclusive solutions . . . The choice is ours: form a global partnership to care for the Earth and one another or risk the destruction of ourselves and the diversity of life. Fundamental changes are needed in our values, institutions and ways of living.[10]

These changes, despite the many challenges posed by the Iron Age of globalization, are already taking place in humanity: in youngsters, in students, in workers, in technicians, in researchers, in religious people; in short, in so many men and women who do not accept being hostages of a paradigm that is dehumanizing and that destroys horizons of goodness. As an alternative to this paradigm they commit themselves to small revolutions, small changes in themselves that irradiate over the whole of society.

In order for this human and ecozoic globalization to emerge and become the norm we require some basic virtues, which are linked to hospitality, to co-living, to tolerance, and to communality with the other,

10. Translator's note: the Earth Charter is available online on www.earthcharter inaction.org.

the different, the stranger. This is the object of my reflections in this book.

The time in exile is over. All tribes of the Earth now meet in the *taba*, in the great communal hut, in the communal *ilê*, in the communal home, in the bosom of the great and generous Mother Earth.[11]

11. Translator's note: Boff uses the words *taba* and *ilê* in this passage, and I have chosen to keep them in the English translation. *Taba* is a word from the Tupi-Guarani language, the language of most native Indians in Brazil, and it stands for the *native Indian hamlet*, or for the *great communal hut* in the middle of their settlement. *Ilê* is a word from Nago-Yoruba, an African language original of Western Africa, and which was spoken by many African slaves in Brazil, and it stands for "house," "terrain," "settlement," or "place." Both *taba* and *ilê* are words well known to Brazilians.

three

The Myth of Hospitality

In the previous chapters I have established the cosmological, biological, anthropological, and historical basis for the current process of globalization. I have considered some problems, which are true dramas and tragedies that can be the outcome of certain developments. But I have also pointed out opportunities that should not be lost, so that we do not hinder the development of a more advanced state of humanity and of the planet Earth.

The presence of some virtues that function as propelling energies is imperative for a very successful process of globalization. These virtues are not sufficient, but they are necessary. They require mediations of a technological and sociopolitical nature. They are like an airplane built with the most advanced technology. If its turbines are not in a perfect state, it will not fly. These virtues function as propelling forces for a new paradigm of globalization. Otherwise, the course of the process of globalization will remain the same and this can bring about a tragic end to the global human project. Thus, it is important to research these virtues and implement them in our daily lives at a personal and collective level, as principles for the generations of the future.

Let me start with the first of these virtues, that is, fundamental hospitality. I shall first approach this virtue in the light of one of the most beautiful myths of the Greek tradition, the myth of Baucis and Philemon.

This myth has been passed onto us by the Roman poet Ovid (43 BCE—37 CE). His *Metamorphoses* is divided into fifteen books, and it deals with the subject of the transformation of people into animals, plants, rocks, and as we shall see, with shrines and temples. One of the stories within the *Metamorphoses* is the myth of Baucis and Philemon.

I will provide the Latin original text below for the benefit of those who still appreciate classical Latin, and which is the very origin of all Latin languages. Here is the Latin text:

Tiliae contermina quercus
Collibus est Phrygiis, modico circumdata muro...
Haud procul hic stagnum est, telus habitabilis olim,
Nunc celebres mergis fulicisque palustribus undae.
Juppiter huc, specie mortali, cumque parente
Venit Atlandiades positis caducifer alis,
Mille domos adiere, locum requiemque petentes,
Parva quidem, stipulis et canna tecta palustri,
Sed pia Baucis anus parilique aetate Philemon
Illa sunt annis juncti juvenalibus, illa
Consenuere casa paupertatemque fatendo
Efecere levem nec iniqua mente ferendo.
Nec refert dominos illis famulosne requiras:
Tota domus duo sunt, idem parentque jubentque.
Ergo ubi caelicolae parvos tetigere penates
Summissoque humiles intrarunt vertice postes,
Membra senex posito jussit relevare sedili,
Quo super injecit textum rude sedula Baucis
Inque foco tepidum cenerem dimovit et egnes
Suscitat hesternos foliisque et cortice sicco
Nutrit et ad flammas anima producit anili,
Multifidasque faces ramaliaque arida tecto
Dedulit et minuit parvoque admovit aeno.
Quodque suus conjux riguo collegerat horto
Truncat holus foliis; furca levat ille bicorni
Sordida terga suis nigro pedentia tigno
Servatoque diu resecata de tergone partem
Exiguam sectamque domat ferventibus undis.
Interea medias fallunt semonibus horas
Concutiumque torum de molli fluminis ulva
Impositum lecto sponda pedibusque salignis;
Vestibus hunc velant, quas non nisi tempore festo
Sternere consuerant, sed et haec valisque vetusque
Vestis erata, lecto non indignanda saligno.

Accubuere dei. Mensam succincta tremesque
Ponit anus, mensae sed erat pes tertius impar:
Testa parem fecit. Quae postquam subdita clivum
Sustulit, aequatam mentae tersere virentes.
Ponitur hic bicolor sincerae baca Minervae
Conditaque in liquida corna autumnalia faece
Intibaque et radix et lactis massa coacti
Ovaque non acri leviter versata favilla,
Omnia fictilibus. Post haec caelatus eodem
Sistitur argento crater fabricataque fago
Pocula, qua cava sunt, flaventibus illita ceris.
Parva mora est epulasque foci misere calentes,
Nec longae rursus referuntur vina senectae
Dantque locum mensis paulum seducta secundis.
Hic nux, hic mixta est rugosis carica palmis
Prunaque et in patulis redolentia mala canistris
Et de purpureis collectae vitibus uvae.
Candidus in medio favus est; super omnia vultus
Acessere boni nec iners pauperque voluntas.
Interea totiens haustum cratera repleri
Sponte sua per seque vident succrescere vina.
Attoniti novitate pavent manibusque supinis
Concipunt Baucisque precis timidusque Philemon
Et neviam dapilus nullisque paratibus orant.
Unicus anser erat, minimae custodia villa,
Quem dis hospitibus domini mactare parabant.
Ille celer penna tardos aetate fatigat
Eluditque diu, tandemque est visus ad ipsos
Confugisse deos. Superi vetuere necari:
"Di que sumus meritasque luet vicinia poenas
Impia, dixerunt; vobis immunibus hujus
Esse mali dabitur; modo vestra reliquite tecta
Ac nostros comitate gradus et in ardua montis
Est simul." Parent ambo baculisque levati
Nituntur longo vestigia ponere clivo.
Tantum aberant summo quantum semel ire sagita
Missa potest: flexere oculos et mersa palude

Cetera prospiciunt, tantum sua tecta manere:
Dumque ea mirantur, dum deflent fata suorum,
Illa vetus dominis etiam casa parva duobus
Vertitur in templum: furcas subiere columunae,
Stramina flavescunt aurataque tecta videntur
Caelataeque fores adopertaque marmore tellus.
Talia tum placido Saturnius edidit ore:
"Dicite, juste senex et femina conjuge justo
Digna, quid optetis." Cum Baucide pauca locutus,
Judicium superis aperit commune Philemon:
"Esse sacerdotes delubraque vestra tueri
Poscimus, et, quoniam concordes egimus annos,
Auferat hora duo eadem, nec conjugis umquam
Busta meae videam, neu sim tumulandus ad illa."
Vota fides sequitur: templi tutella fuere
Donec vita data est. Annis aevoque soluti
Ante gradus sacros cum starent forte locique
Narrarent casus, frondere Philemona Baucis,
Baucida conspexit senior frondere Philemon,
Jamque super geminos crescente cacumine vultus,
Mutua, dum licuit, reddebant dicta Valeque
O conjux dixere simul, simul abadita texit
Ora frutex.
Ostendit adhuc Thyneius illic
Incola de gemino vicinos corpore truncos[1]

The translation reads:

Among the Phrygian hills
An oak tree and a lime grow side by side,
Girt by a little wall . . .
Not far from these two trees there is a marsh,
Once habitable land, but water now,
The busy home of divers, duck and coot.
Here once came Jupiter, in mortal guise,
And with his father herald Mercury,

---

1. Ovid, *Metamorphoses*, book 8, 620–720, in Gouast, *La poésie latine des origines au Moyen Age*, 319–24.

His wings now laid aside. A thousand homes
They came to seeking rest; a thousand homes
Were barred against them; yet one welcomed them
Tiny indeed, and thatched with reeds and straw;
But in that cottage Baucis, old and good,
And old Philemon (he as old as she)
Had joined their lives in youth, grown old together
And eased their poverty by bearing it
Contentedly and thinking it no shame.
It was vain to seek master and servant there;
They two were all the household, to obey
And to command. So when the heavenly ones
Reached their small home and, stopping, entered in
At the low door, the old man placed a bench
And bade them sit and rest their weary limbs,
And Baucis spread on it a simple rug
In busy haste, and from the hearth removed
The ash still warm, and fanned yesterday's embers
And fed them leaves and bark, and coaxed a flame
With her old breath; then from the rafters took
Split billets and dry twigs and broke them small,
And on them placed a little copper pan;
Then trimmed a cabbage which her spouse had brought
In from the stream-fed garden. He reached down
With a forked stick from the black beam a chine
Of smoke-cured pork, and from the long-kept meat
Cut a small piece and put it in to boil.
Meanwhile their talk beguiles the passing hour
And time glides unperceived. A beechwood bowl
Hung by its curving handle from a peg;
They fill it with warm water and their guests
Bathe in the welcome balm their weary feet.
They place a mattress of soft river-sedge
Upon a couch (its frame and feet were willow)
And spread on it their drapes, only brought out
On holy days, yet old and cheap they were,
Fit for a willow couch. The Gods reclined.

Then the old woman, aproned, shakily,
Arranged the table, but one leg was short;
A crock adjusted it, and when the slope
Was levelled up she wiped it with green mint.
Then olives, black and green, she brings, the fruit
Of true Minerva, autumn cherry plums.
Bottled in wine lees, endive, radishes,
And creamy cheese and eggs turned carefully
In the cooling ash; all served in earthenware.
Next a wine-bow, from the same 'silver' chased,
Is set and beechwood cups, coated inside
With yellow wax. No long delay; the hearth
Sends forth the steaming feast and wine again
Is brought of no great age, then moved aside
Giving a space to bring the second course.
Here are their nuts and figs, here wrinkled dates,
And plums and fragrant apples in broad trugs,
And sweet grapes gathered from pure vines,
And in the midst a fine pale honeycomb;
And—over all—a zeal, not poor nor slow,
And faces that with smiling goodness glow.
Meanwhile they saw, when the wine-bowl was drained,
Each time it filled itself, and wine welled up
All of its own accord within the bowl.
In fear and wonders Baucis and Philemon,
With hands upturned, joined in a timid prayer
And pardon sought for the crude graceless meal
There was one goose, the trusty guardian
Of their minute domain and they, the hosts,
Would sacrifice him for the gods, their guests
But he, swift-winged, wore out their slow old bones
And long escaped them, till at last he seemed
To flee for sanctuary to the Gods themselves
The Deities forbade: "We two are Gods,"
They said; "This wicked neighbourhood shall pay
Just punishment; but to you there shall be given
Exemption from this evil. Leave your home,

Accompany our steps and climb with us
The mountain slopes." The two old folk obey
And slowly struggle up the long ascend,
Propped on their sticks. A bowshot from the top
They turned their eyes and see the land below
All flooded marshes now except their house;
And while they wonder and in tears bewail
Their lost possessions, that old cottage home,
Small ever for two owners, is transformed
Into a temple; columns stand beneath
The rafters, and the thatch, turned yellow gleams
A roof of gold; and fine doors richly carved
They see, and the bare earth with marble paved
Then Saturn's son in gentle tones addressed them:
"Tell us, you good old man, and you, good dame,
His worthy consort, what you most desire."
Philemon briefly spoke with Baucis, then
Declared their joint decision to the Gods:
"We ask to be your priests and guard your shrine;
And, since in concord we have spent years,
Grant that the selfsame hour may take us both,
That I my consort's tomb may never see
Nor may it fall to her to bury me."
Their prayer was granted. Guardians of the shrine
They were while life was left, until one day,
Undone by years and age, standing before
The sacred steps and talking of old times,
Philemon saw old Baucis sprouting leaves
And green with leaves she saw Philemon too
And as the foliage o'er their faces formed
They said, while still they might, in mutual words
"Good bye, dear love" together, and together
The hiding bark covered their lips. Today
The peasants in those parts point out with pride
Two trees from one twin trunk grown side by side.[2]

---

2. Translator's note: I have referred to Melville, trans., *Metamorphoses*, 190–93.

Whoever passes through the region of Phrygia, which is currently located in Turkey, still hears the fantastic story which has been passed on from generation to generation. Whoever travels through this region can still see the two centennial trees, side by side, with their tops and branches intertwined. These trees remind us of Baucis and Philemon, that welcoming couple, and the metamorphosis they underwent because of their hospitality.

And the elderly repeat the story today: whoever welcomes a pilgrim, a foreigner, a poor person, welcomes God. Whoever welcomes God turns himself or herself into a temple of God. Whoever sees a stranger as part of his or her community inherits joyful immortality.

four

Explaining the Myth of Hospitality

Now that the narrative of the myth has been given I must explain it so that the lessons to be learned from it may guide a new kind of globalization. But before doing so it is imperative for me to go deeper into the nature of myths. Thus, some questions must be answered: What is a myth? What kind of language does it use? What does it want to teach? I understand that myths help us, even in our modern times, to understand important dimensions of personal and collective human existence.

Primordial Experiences and Myths

In Greek the term *myth* means "narrative" or "plot." A narrative is usually alive and filled with emotions. It has a plot that reveals the meaning of that which is being narrated. It is not something merely conceptual, although it does make use of concepts. It is something affectionate, and it follows the logic of emotions.

Why do we make use of narratives? Because human beings, during their lifespans, undergo fundamental experiences that determine the structure and meaning of life. These experiences are so significant that they cannot be properly expressed by simple words or by abstract concepts. And thus, stories are narrated, for they preserve the registry of those seminal experiences. When they are told or read again and again—and thus the relation between myth and literature—an increasing number of facets and meanings are discovered, which allow us to continuously relate to those narratives. In short, myths are crystallizations of those primordial experiences, and for this reason they are both outside time and related to every era, including our own era.

Mircea Eliade, one of the great experts on myths, said in his book *Aspects du mythe* that a myth has three functions, namely, to narrate, to explain, and to reveal.[1]

The myth *narrates*.

A myth is neither a treatise nor a rational discussion concerning fundamental experiential questions. It does not make use of conceptual logic; it rather makes use of the imaginary logic. It refers more to the heart than to the head. Myth narrates that which deeply affects us, and it stands for meaningful things in life. For this reason, all myths touch upon, grab, and speak to the innermost parts of listeners and readers.

The myth *explains*.

A myth explains that which is significant, and it also stands for an answer to those important questions we always ask ourselves, such as: What is the origin of the heavens with its myriad of stars? What is our relation to the earth, which is where we come from and where we return to? How are we to relate with those that we know and do not know? How to decipher the maddening relation between two lovers? Why does the suffering and anxiety of those we love affect our own happiness? Why do we suffer inconsolably with the death of a loved one? What is the meaning of one's personal I within the collection of all beings? Where do we ultimately go?

These questions are always on the human agenda. How are we to speak about these encompassing and deep realities? Rational theories and equations, which are certainly important, do not quite explain the dimensions implied in those existential questions. And as such, we are urged to tell life stories that provoke emotions that are capable of giving rise to illuminating explanations and of pushing history forward.

The myth *reveals*.

The mythical narrative uncovers deep dimensions of the human being and of the universe. Through the mythical narrative, we do not only have an objective and scientific understanding of things; we also have a subjective and symbolic understanding of the resonances of things in us. For instance, the sun is not just part of the empirical heavens; it also inhabits our soul, and it radiates light and warmth. James Hollis, a commentator on the function of myth in modern times, rightly noted in his book *Tracking the Gods*: "Myth takes us deep into ourselves and into the psychic reservoirs of humanity. Whatever our cultural and reli-

---

1. Mircea, *Aspects du mythe*; English trans., *Myth and Reality*.

gious background or personal psychology, a greater intimacy with myth provides a vital linkage with meaning, the absence of which is so often behind the private and collective neuroses of our time. Expressed in its most succinct form, the study of myth is the search for that which connects us most deeply with our own nature and our place in the cosmos."[2]

The mysterious depth of our psyche evokes divine categories that are most sacred and present in any culture. Only these divine categories are adequate to demonstrate, for they share the same essence with, foundational experiences. For this reason, masculine and feminine deities are continuously introduced into history's arena.

However, we must have a precise understanding of the function of these mythological deities. Otherwise, we may not understand their secret message.

The traditional interpretation is substantialist. It understands deities as entities that exist in their own right, and that are not dependent on our minds for their existence. This is connected to polytheism, since it, in fact, understands that there is a plurality of gods.

The modern interpretation is anthropological and transpersonal. Mythological deities are forms of expression, linguistic resources, which give body to energies acting in us and particularly in the innermost parts of human reality. For this reason, deities are realities present in the human psyche, and they also constitute universal and anthropological aspects. Deities are the incarnation of and stand for powerful energies that are both within us and outside us in the universe. Within us, these deities configure psychological aspects of great importance, aspects that are responsible to give meaning to our existence. To make use of C. G. Jung's terminology, deities are equivalent to important archetypes, that is to say, to dynamic standards of behavior that are rooted in the collective and transcultural unconscious of humanity and that help in the structuring of fundamental experiences.

As these archetypes and psychological aspects are numerous, we represent them through multiple divine figures, which give the impression of subscribing to polytheism. However, there is no real intention of multiplying the Divine, but only of emphasizing its numerous appearances in human, in natural, and in cosmic history.

2. Hollis, *Tracking the Gods*, 7–8.

This was well explained by Jennifer and Roger Woolger, who are experts in feminine myths, in their book *The Goddess Within*. I quote Jennifer and Roger Woolger:

> By *goddess* we mean a psychological description of a complex female character type that we intuitively recognize both in ourselves and in the women around us, as well as in the images and icons that are everywhere in our culture. For example, the smartly dressed, intelligent young career woman we see everywhere in our cities is the living embodiment of a goddess type we call the *Athena woman*, named after the Greek goddess who was patroness of the ancient city of Athens. Magazines, movies, and novels all reproduce her as a stereotype because she is so prevalent today.
>
> Yet a goddess type such as Athena is much more than just a media stereotype or cliché. Athena also represents a complex and highly evolved style of consciousness that characterizes everything about the way this type of woman thinks, feels, and acts.[3]

In the myth of hospitality, which is being analyzed, Jupiter and Mercury stand for the transcendent energy that is hidden in the figures of poor wandering people. But there is a moment when pretences are dropped, and this energy manifests itself in plenitude. The Divine bursts through and in doing so invites Philemon and Baucis to worship, to respect, and to serve in these deities' temple for the rest of their lives. The myth reveals deep dimensions of the human being.

Myths and the Development of Human Existence

As it has been demonstrated, myths possess universal and anthropological aspects. The American anthropologist Joseph Campbell, a notable researcher into transcultural myths, demonstrated how myths concretely function within the development of personal and collective human existence. Campbell identified four main functions to myths in his book *Myths to Live By*. I quote Campbell:

> The first is what I have called the mystical function: to waken and maintain in the individual a sense of awe and of gratitude in relation to the mystery dimension of the universe, not so that he lives in fear of it, but so that he recognizes that he participates

---

3. Woolger and Woolger, *The Goddess Within*, 7.

in it, since the mystery of being is the mystery of his own deep being as well . . .

The second function of a living mythology is to offer an image of the universe that will be in accord with the knowledge of the time, the sciences and the fields of actions of the folk to whom the mythology is addressed . . .

The third function of a living mythology is to validate, support, and imprint the norms of a given, specific moral order, that, namely, of the society in which the individual is to live. And the fourth is to guide him, stage by stage, in health, strength, and harmony of spirit, through the whole foreseeable course of a useful life.[4]

The best way to fulfil and develop these high purposes related to the meaning of life, of society, and of the universe is to resource to myths and to their unlimited imaginary and artistic potential. Civilizations have been founded more on myths than on documented historical facts. Even historical facts and people only continue to irradiate their influence when they become heroic acts and heroes, and in doing so, they become collective myths. It is thus the case, for instance, with the founding fathers of the United States of America such as Washington,[5] Jefferson, and others, as well as with those involved in the *Inconfidência Mineira* such as Tiradentes, Tomás Antônio Gonzaga, and their fellows in the movement, who dreamt of the independence of Brazil.[6]

The most important virtues for human sociability were expressed in myths, such as the virtues of hospitality, co-living, and communality, which are lived archetypically by Philemon and Baucis.

---

4. Campbell, *Myths to Live By*, 214–15.

5. Translator's note: In the Portuguese, Boff names Lincoln.

6. Translator's note: The Inconfidência Mineira (Minas Conspiracy) of 1789 was the first Brazilian independence movement. The movement was crushed by the Portuguese authorities in the same year. Various members of the movement were arrested and sentenced to death. All of them were pardoned by the Crown, but Joaquim José da Silva Xavier, known as Tiradentes, was hanged in Rio de Janeiro on the 21st of April 1792; his body was then quartered and displayed in various cities all over the country. When the republic was proclaimed in Brazil in 1889, the 21st of April became a national holiday, which is observed with pride by Brazilians to this date.

Myth and the Virtues of Hospitality,
Co-Living, and Communality

Let us apply the knowledge gathered thus far to the myth of Philemon and Baucis so that we can understand it better.

The myth *tells* a beautiful and touching story, despite Ovid's concise and affected language. The reader, however, can still appreciate it. The narrative develops until it reaches a *grand finale* that is wonderful, magical and happy: the revelation of the divine.

Then, the myth *explains* the story about hospitality, co-living and communality. And it does so by following a precise sequence whose moments we wish to uncover. The sequence is the following:

First, the myth explains *where* hospitality, co-living, and communality are being exercised, that is, in the most adverse situations. It is for this reason that the narrative is situated in Phrygia, a Roman province at the edges of the Empire that is notorious for the rough and brash attitudes of its population. This region is nowadays situated in Asia Minor between the Aegean Sea and the Black Sea, and it is currently located in Turkey. It is against this somber and inhumane background that the humane deed of welcoming those in need occurs.

Second, the myth explains *who* provides hospitality, that is, an elderly and humble couple living in a shack. They are hardworking, humble people and they do not live in dire poverty, for they have enough to live on. They live in great harmony, without patriarchal domination which causes inequality within relationships, and which gives rise to very tense relations. Ovid beautifully comments: "Tota domus duo sunt idem parentque jubentque," or "They two were all the household, to obey and to command." Humble people welcoming humble people.

Third, the myth explains to *whom* hospitality is being provided: to unknown, wandering, humble, tired, and famished people. Hospitality is always defined by the other. As I shall demonstrate later in more detail, there are many kinds of the other. However, the myth at hand provides us with a few instances of the other: (1) the other who is unknown, and who knocks at the door; (2) the other who is a foreigner, who comes from another country, speaks another language, has different habits and culture; (3) the other who belongs to a different social class and lives in poverty; (4) the other who has been snubbed by society, who is in need, tired, and starving; (5) the other who is the radical Other, who is

God hidden behind the figure of two wandering people. Hospitality is unconditional, and it applies to all kinds of the other.

Fourth, the myth explains the *attitude* of those wandering people who had to stand patiently the lack of solidarity and compassion, and even of verbal and gestural abuse, that greeted them at every threshold. What was most painful to them was that they were not even looked at. To be looked at represents recognition of the presence of the other, and from the perspective of those who are in poverty it represents a silent call for an encounter.

Nobody can experience a supplicant look without having its own humanity affected. To avoid looking is to intend to turn those who cry and exist into something nonexistent. It means to allow the other to succumb to its own needs. The two wandering people humbly stood their nonrecognition as human beings who are in need, and who have been excluded. They were placed at the same level as pestilent dogs. This attitude always causes an internal, quiet suffering, which becomes more painful the less compassion it encounters.

Fifth, the myth explains the *attitude* of those who offer hospitality: Philemon and Baucis. By their very nature, hospitality and co-living presume generosity, an open heart, and sensibility to the predicaments of the other. They imply overcoming certain attitudes, which are loaded with reserve and fear, that are present in people who are extremely cautious and suspicious; attitudes such as: "Who are these people?" "Are they thieves, swindlers, or people that cannot be trusted?" Whoever asks these questions can hardly show hospitality or welcome. They will always find an excuse or a reason for not welcoming those who are in need. Hospitality presupposes overcoming prejudices and an almost naive trust; these are indispensable if hospitality and co-living are to be true and without constraints. As I shall demonstrate later, hospitality must be unconditional and without reservations. In fact, this is what Philemon and Baucis showed. They did not ask questions, they did not prod for information. They simply and joyfully welcome strangers and are not concerned with strangers' appearances. They are aware of the needs of wandering people. They are willing to welcome and to offer all that they have.

A high member of staff of the government of Peru, who had previously worked as a social worker with indigenous communities in the Peruvian Amazon region, whilst visiting a community of the Achuar nation was received with a song about hospitality, which was personally conveyed to myself in 2004.[7] Here are the lyrics of this song: "Dove, who has left the nest and who comes from so far away, do not be sad. Our community is a great tree that opens up its branches and that welcomes you to its core. Dove, stay with us."[8]

She was so touched by the song that she stayed longer than needed, and whenever possible she always returns to this Achuar community. And this song is always sung on her arrival.

Sixth, the myth explains *how* hospitality, co-living, and communality concretely unfold. Ovid's narrative is outstanding and very refined. In the narrative of the myth it becomes clear that hospitality is connected to minimum human needs: to be welcomed with no reluctance; to be given shelter, food and drink; and to be able to rest. Without the bare minimum nobody lives or survives. And the material bare minimum is connected to the spiritual bare minimum, which is unfathomable, which has to do with that which make us human, which is that capacity of unconditional welcome of the other, of being charitable, cooperative, and communal. It was this attitude in the primordial times of the process of humanization that allowed us to rise from the animal kingdom to the human realm. The animal kingdom is ruled by competition and subordination, and the human realm is ruled by mutual care, cooperation, equality, and love.

The attitude of welcoming sheds light on the basic structure of the human being. We exist because we were welcomed without hesitation by the Mother Earth, of whom we are sons and daughters; by the chain of life that made us one of its links; by nature, who was so good to us; by our parents, whom we have not chosen; and especially by our mothers, who welcomed us in their arms with unconditional generosity; by our relatives and friends, who welcomed us to our families; by society, who accepted us as members. We exist because, in one way or another, we were welcomed. The worse possible feeling is the feeling of being rejected and excluded, and this is something that the two wandering people in the myth experience. This feeling of rejection and exclusion induces a psychological experience of death. The welcoming attitude by

7. Translator's note: The Achuar are an indigenous people from the Peruvian Amazon region. They amount to approximately 12,500 people living in 77 communities.

8. Translator's note: The lyrics of this Achuar song were translated directly from the Portuguese.

Philemon and Baucis represents a guarantee of life for those two wandering people.

Dimensions of Hospitality

And when Philemon and Baucis do so they realize hospitality. Hospitality involves various dimensions, which are clearly demonstrated within the narrative of the myth:

- *Sensibility* when confronted by the needs and predicaments of wandering people, which is something expressed by the phrase "come in, you must be tired and hungry." Without sensibility there is no reaching out for the other, there is no encounter to aid the other. Sensibility does not come from the structure of the *logos*; that is to say, from the human capacity to reason, and to logic for this capacity is something that comes later. Rather, sensibility is derived from something that is more primary and original; it is derived from the capacity to feel and to perceive the other and the other's own needs. This is *pathos* which is something that grounds *logos*. *Pathos* or affectivity is the ground-of-experiencing of the human being; and in our modern times *pathos* is also called emotional intelligence.

- *Compassion* is the capacity to forget oneself and in doing so encountering others with the willingness to welcome and to care. Philemon comes to the door quickly and addresses, smiling, those two wandering people. Compassion, the foremost virtue of Buddhism, does not stand for the lesser feeling of pitying others; it is rather the capacity to overcome oneself and, at the same time, to get hold of the other in the other's own concrete situation and to be willing to stay side by side with the other, to be happy with the other, to suffer with the other, and never to leave the other to endure their pain alone. In short, to have compassion is synonymous with sharing the *Passion* of the other.

- *Welcoming* is the fruit of sensibility and of compassion. Philemon welcomingly says: "Come into our home." This goodness impregnates their shack, and creates an aura of benevolence that is quickly noticed by the two wandering people. Philemon's welcome unfolds as a sequence of great gestures.

- *Inviting to sit*: When we are tired the first thing we search for is a place to sit or something to give us support. Baucis was quick to offer a bench to those two wandering people, and in doing so, offered an opportunity to co-live humanely.

- *Offering fresh water*: Water is life. Fresh water kills the thirst, brings back a sense of well-being and brings into mind the bubbling of a fountain; a fountain which is an archetype for the home.

- *Lighting a fire*: The fire is not only the means through which we prepare our meals. It stands for something that is very intimate, for it represents light and warmth, which are proper to a dwelling that becomes a home. For this reason, fire constitutes one of humanity's most ancient archetypes. A fire burning and a lamp shimmering is a sign that there is life in a place and the possibility of being welcomed. And therefore, it is understandable why Philemon, after having accommodated the strangers in his home, started feeding the cinders and reviving the fire.

- *Washing the feet*: Nothing is more comforting after a long walk than to refresh one's tired feet in fresh water or, if this happens in the evening, in warm water. To wash someone's feet is a supreme demonstration of welcome and of assistance, and this is something that slaves used to do. Jesus, before leaving this world and going to the Father, wanted to wash his disciples' feet—the disciples who were astounded by Jesus's action. This represents the supreme expression: "loved them to the end" (John 13:1, ESV). And Jesus explained to them his archetypal action: "If I then, your Lord and Teacher, have washed your feet, you also ought to wash one another's feet" (John 13:14, ESV). And in the myth Baucis washes the two strangers' feet, and this reminds me of my childhood when we, the children, had to wash our parents' feet in turn. And we used to do this with much reverence as if it was a sacred act. Whenever someone important was visiting us, we used to wash his or her feet also. This was a sign of a wholesome hospitality and an open invitation to co-living.

- *Providing something to eat*: Hospitality and co-living are ultimately concretized in communality. Philemon and Baucis prepare a meal with the best they had: with bread, vegetables, eggs, olive oil, wine, and a piece of smoke-cured pork for the soup. And then, for dessert, dried dates and figs. The preparation was not done mechanically. It was more like a ritual, for we (unconsciously) know that a meal is more than a meal. A meal is sharing those energies that give life to the universe and to all of us, and it is a communion between people. It is not just about getting nutrition; it is more than this; it is the ultimate act of relationships and of co-living.

- *Offering wine* represents another primordial gesture connected to communality. In the myth they drink wine that is aged and usually taken as a remedy. Wine is another powerful symbol of life, of feast, of joy and of being together.

- *Feasting with abundance*: The poor do not want their table to look poor for their guests. The table must be extremely plentiful and the dessert must be something special that is not normally served. The dessert gives that special touch to the meal. Philemon and Baucis offer dried dates and figs, which are reserved for special occasions such as the one they experience in the myth.

- *Offering all*: this is the ultimate test of unconditional hospitality. Hospitality must be unconditional if it is to be plainly human. Philemon and Baucis had already used their last bit of smoke-cured pork, and then were willing to sacrifice the only goose they had, the goose that, following an ancient practice, served as the guardian of the house. This is the same disposition displayed by Abraham, who orders the sacrificing of his only calf, and that it should be served to his guests. Everything is unconditionally put to the benefit of guests, and nothing is retained for later. This represents the maximum decentralization of the self and the maximum concern for the other. This is unrestricted and impartial hospitality. The two wandering people strongly opposed their willingness to sacrifice the goose but are full of admiration, for the elderly couple had passed the ultimate test of hospitality. They were filled with emotion.

- *Being communal*: When strangers are invited to share the same table, communality arises. This is the highest expression of co-living. It stands for overcoming all distances, suspicions, and enmity. Only those who are or who have become friends can be communal. Communality is an expression of communion, of co-living, of sharing, not only meals but also lives and hearts. In the myth, despite having already had their meal, Philemon and Baucis join their guests at the table and eat with them so that their guests do not feel awkward. This behaviour reminds me of a wonderful tradition in the Franciscan Order, which was something inherited from Saint Francis of Assisi. According to this tradition, one must never leave a guest to eat on his or her own. Even if the hosting brother or the superior brother of the convent himself had already eaten, he must sit at the table with guests so that the guest feels completely at ease and at home and without any feeling of awkwardness.

- *Offering one's own bed*: Just as expressive as washing the other's feet, as giving the other plenty to eat and drink, is offering one's own bed to other's to rest. And in the myth there was only one bed in the shack, which was offered to those two wandering people. To offer one's own bed means to completely release one's own intimacy. It implies bringing down all barriers between oneself and the other as a sign of goodwill and trust in the other. It is at this point that hospitality and co-living achieve their apex.

Last, the myth *reveals* that when hospitality and co-living are exercised in plenitude that they unveil that which they concealed: the logic of the universe and of life. To welcome strangers, foreigners, poor people, and people in need, and to co-live, even if for a brief moment, with them is to realize the basic structure of the universe. This basic structure is made of a web of inter-retro-relations and of chains of inclusive solidarity. Because every being was welcoming to all other beings, we were all able to reach this point. The universe continues to expand and to create orders that are increasingly more complex and more beautiful—bearers of meaning because every entity behaves as host, coexists, co-lives, and cooperates with the universe's efforts.

It is here that we find God's action, the originating Fountain of all Being and of all that is to come. In the myth, behind poor wandering people who were tired and famished, was hidden God, who then revealed himself in his full glory. God showed his powers, which are not threatening but upright. God transformed reality. The shack became a shining temple. The good hosts were transformed into clerics serving at the temple.

Everything that was touched by the deity became eternal. In order for Philemon and Baucis to pass into history as archetypes of hospitality, co-living, and communality they were transfigured into vigorous trees whose branches and tops are interlinked in an eternal caress and in everlasting love.

Because it is the case, and because it speaks the truth, this myth speaks to us in our modern days and inspires ideals and fundamental values in us so that we can build our Common Home where every one, including nature, can be; where every one can feel they are a guest of everyone; where every one can consider themselves to be brothers and sisters within an immense family, the unique human family.

five

Hospitality in Modern Societies

The myth of fundamental hospitality and the explanations that were given furnish us with the ideal of hospitality. This ideal is plain and enchanting, which is something proper to the nature of the ideal. This ideal represents hospitality in a pure, unconditional state and in a state without reservation.

But the ideal is not a reality yet, despite having a potential to become a reality. Reality is full of contradictions that, sometimes, seem to make the ideal unviable. But this does not mean that we should abandon the ideal. Without the ideal how are we to evaluate and improve concrete forms of hospitality that are found around us? Without the ideal how are we to instigate new forms of hospitality?

The ideal is never fully realized. This is not its function anyway. Its function is to both feed the will to always improve, and to guide in the direction of more creative practices that can replace conventional and outdated ones. The Brazilian poet Mário Quintana[1] wisely wrote:

> If things are unreachable . . . oh my goodness!
> This is no reason for not wanting them
> How sad paths would be without
> the magical presence of the stars![2]

The stars represent ideals and humanity's highest utopias.

We face limitations of all kinds, and in particular the fact that we live in complex and impersonal industrial societies, which are so dif-

1. Translator's note: Mário Quintana (1906–1994) is a famous Brazilian writer and poet.

2. Translator's note: Boff quotes here Quintana's short poem "Das Utopias," or "About Utopias."

ferent from past societies in which people knew each other and formed communities based on co-living.

As Jacques Derrida emphasized in his study on hospitality, *Of Hospitality*, our homes nowadays possess a number of "doors and windows" through which foreigners and strangers reach us, such as television, interactive programs, the telephone, mobile phones, fax machines, e-mail, and the Internet. How are we to live hospitality with these virtual beings, with these companions of human adventure?

We do not know yet, for this reality has only emerged recently, and we do not have enough experience and practice with it. What is sure at this point is that unconditional hospitality must inspire hospitality that is conditional and organized by society and governmental policies. The state has created norms and established rights that aim at not putting too much pressure on society, at not destabilizing the labor market, economy, and social services. It is difficult to imagine what would happen to the European Union if its borders were completely open and allowed in thousands, perhaps millions, of people from the rest of Europe and North Africa.

Conditional and Unconditional Hospitality

There ought always to be a dynamic articulation between conditional and unconditional hospitality so that one is not sacrificed in the name of the other. The ideal of hospitality must help with the formulation of good laws and to inspire generous public policies that welcome foreigners, immigrants, refugees, and those who are different. Otherwise, the ideal of hospitality becomes a utopia without concrete content.

Therefore, unconditional hospitality needs conditional hospitality so that it becomes effective. And conditional hospitality needs unconditional hospitality so that it does not become bureaucratic, and does not lose its openness, which is something essential when welcoming someone. Independently of the way through which we articulate one kind of hospitality with the other, we must always address the question: what can I do as a person, what can society do, what can the state do to welcome the foreigner and the different? Hospitality is a humanitarian and civilized response to this question, which is very pertinent to our modern times, for millions are awaiting a gesture of minimum humanity. It was not without justification that Immanuel Kant (1724–1804) placed hospitality as the central virtue of globalization, which is to be understood as a confederation of free republics.

The myth of Philemon and Baucis maintains the articulation of both forms of hospitality, the unconditional, which welcomes without reserve those two poor wandering people; and the conditional, which provides for all their needs—which provides shelter, food, and rest. Because of this successful articulation, the myth of Philemon and Baucis has a continuous relevance that applies to any historical age.

How are we to successfully maintain this articulation in humanity if 70 percent of human beings live in urban areas and in complex and extremely rational and functional industrial societies?

Moreover, the dominating culture places excessive value on the individual and on "celebrities," people of great social visibility or people who have succeeded in any of the various fields of human activity. The modern means of production, which is now globalized, is capitalist. That is to say, it places more value on the capital of the few than on the work of the many; it places more value on private enterprises than on social enterprises. Private groups who have a hold on economic power, which is associated with political, intellectual, military, and media power, accumulate wealth and advantages to the point that only a few hundred global groups practically control around 80 percent of all the wealth of the planet.

Urban and industrial society is also an impersonal society. The individual in its singularity and particularities disappears in the mass. Relations lose a direct approach and the biographical histories of common people become irrelevant.

In the society of the masses practically everything becomes standardized; it standardizes everything from the kind of food (fast food) to fashion to entertainment to the mobile phone, fax, and e-mail, to the way of speaking forged by means of communication such as television and music festivals, to consuming habits and collective values of reference (e.g., only those who practice a sport are healthy; only those who practice a particular form of diet will live longer; only those who subscribe to a particular spiritual pathway are happy; only those who consume such and such a product are members of a particular social group, and the like).

However, it is also important to recognize that this kind of society of anonymous people offers some opportunities to the individual that did not exist before, such as to think as an individual, to freely establish its social connections and relationships, and to characterize its differences by making use of, for instance, an e-mail address, a blog, and chat rooms. The mass of information available through the most diverse means of communication opens new horizons, expands consciousness, and allows for self-fulfilment. The phenomena of expansion of education, open universities, retraining courses, and enfranchising of individual human rights create the means for and ways through which the individual perceives itself to be an autonomous individual. The autonomization of individuals and the universalization of knowledge and education were and continue to be modern ideals that allow for the rise of contemporary societies.[3]

In such circumstances, how are we to live hospitality, as I have characterized it previously? How are we to articulate conditional and unconditional hospitality? It is needless to say that hospitality, by its own nature, presupposes reciprocity. Hospitality is a *duty* that must be practiced by all, and a *right* that all must enjoy.

Usually we live hospitality with those who are *similar* to us, with those who are close to us, with those whom we work with, with those who are part of our local community, with those who frequent the same social spheres, with those who are supporters of the same sports team or political party, with those who share the same faith. In this case, hospitality happens during visits, in family gatherings, in prayer meetings and in moments of need. This kind of hospitality does not present a problem, for it derives from minimum human sensibility and from a common feeling of solidarity.

More difficult is to live hospitality with those who are *different* from us and distant from us. The industrial society of the masses is deeply pluralist; it is composed by all sorts of people, ethnic backgrounds, religions, cultural traditions, and professions. And simultaneously it is also a society of high social mobility.

There are currently millions of economic, religious, political, and war refugees, that is to say, there are millions of people who have been expelled from their original homes. There are currently 50 million war refugees, of which 20 million are within their own countries and 30 million have been displaced to other countries. To these war refugees we must add 175 million people who emigrate for the most diverse reasons

3. Cf. Melucci, *Vivencia y convivência*, 43–61.

in search of another place to live. They are faced with a dramatic situation based on lack of support and on a generalized lack of a welcoming atmosphere, and this situation does not alleviate their dehumanizing situation.

Marx, Lenin, Einstein, Freud, Brecht, Thomas Mann, Walter Benjamin, Antonio Machado, Paul Tillich, almost all those who belonged to the Frankfurt School, Spanish intellectuals who founded the Casa de España and later the El Colégio de México (both of which are a source of intellectual and political renewal in modern Mexico)—all of them were refugees. Pablo Neruda, Paulo Freire, Josué de Castro, Celso Furtado, Betinho, Leonel Brizola, Fernando Henrique Cardoso (former president of Brazil), and many of the best intellectuals and politicians were also refugees. The pilgrims of the USA were refugees as were the founders of the United States of America.

My four Italian-Venetian grandparents (from the Fontana, Poletto, Rech, and Boff families) were economic refugees, for they were part of residual poor people who were left behind by the process of industrialization in the north of Italy. In order for them not be a factor of social destabilization and to abort Marx's prediction about the proletariat revolution, all those who were left behind were sent elsewhere: were sent to the USA, to Brazil, and to Argentina. All of them experienced hospitality positively when they were welcomed, when they were given lands to live and work, and when they were given the opportunity to live in a strange land without feeling themselves to be strangers.

Hospitality within the Boarders of a Nation-State

Faced with millions of refugees and with the mobilization of populations that come from poor countries that force their entrance into rich and highly developed nations, difficult questions arise. The problem is not only personal but also social and political. Entire societies and various nations are challenged to demonstrate minimum humanitarian feelings and to welcome hordes of people, the drifting sons and daughters of the Earth.

The magnitude of this global problem transcends the power of the nation-state and demands a solution that has been thought about and implemented from a global perspective. But this perspective is not in place yet, even if it is urgently needed. There are forces that have an interest in the nonimplementation of this global perspective, for they do not want to renounce their power over certain important sectors of the economy, now globalized, or they do not want to relinquish their political control over certain regions, a control which brings economic and geopolitical benefits to them.

Later in this book I shall point out the basic attitudes and social policies that are important to foster so that this global challenge can be met.

With the intention of seeking alternative and more benevolent forms of hospitality to deal with those who find themselves refugees or immigrants within a global context, it is appropriate to go further into this issue and, most important, to undergo self-criticism. The result of the dominant Western culture, which is now globalized, is clearly negative. We can no longer perpetuate the lack of hospitality and the dehumanizing behaviors of the past.

six

Lack of Hospitality in History

Generally speaking, we have confirmed that historically the West, from the ancient Greeks to our modern times, has always had a particular difficulty dealing with the topic of the other. This is so because Western culture is strongly centred in its own identity, almost to the point of not leaving any space for that which is different from itself.

This tendency is reflected even in the preamble of the Constitution of the European Union, which states: "Conscious that Europe is a continent that has brought forth civilization; that its inhabitants, arriving in successive waves from earliest times, have gradually developed the values underlying humanism: equality of persons, freedom, respect for reason."[1] This perspective is certainly true, but it is not dialectical. It does not mention the frequent violation of these values or the various tragic happenings created by European culture, such as totalitarian regimes, devastating wars, colonialism and imperialism that decimated entire nations, which is something in direct contrast with the values it proclaims. The current dramatic global situation is mostly due to the kind of globalization we experience for it proposes, in concrete terms, a kind of late Westernization of the world.

This tragic situation has only occurred because the other has never been recognized, and differences have never been properly respected. Let me demonstrate in some detail how the West dealt with the question of the other, and how it has defined the many others. This will increase our will to no longer foster this kind of paradigm.

1. Translator's note: Boff quotes here the first sentence from the preamble of the first draft of the text for the Treaty establishing the European Constitution (http://european -convention.eu.int/docs/Treaty/cv00850.en03.pdf/). This sentence is not part of the final draft of the Treaty.

The Many Others

First, the first other, the most immediate other, is the other in gender: *women*. In Western culture, as in various other cultures, a patriarchal and macho culture had a centrality that subjugated core values to a masculine form. Due to this domination, women were submitted, marginalized and turned into an entity that is socially invisible. An ideological justification for this inferiorization was created. This justification is based on Aristotle, who coined an expression loaded with prejudice, an expression which resonated in the thought of Saint Thomas Aquinas, and which also had some influence on Freud and on Lacan's views. Aristotle affirmed that the woman "is as it were an infertile male,"[2] an inferior and unfinished being.

Cultural bastions who keep this tradition alive, and who foster this inferiorization of women are still found in certain traditionalist sectors of churches. In these churches women do not enjoy complete ecclesial citizenship. Many interdictions are imposed on women, such as the impossibility of their ascending into priesthood, their nonparticipation in the decision-making process regarding the future of the church, and their not being allowed to exercise their freedom with reference to reproduction, to mention a few.

This inferiorization of women causes a division in humanity. It ascribes a considerable power to man. Man, because he does not recognize the alterity (i.e. otherness) and equality of women any longer, has lost the interlocutor that nature and God have given him so that they both, men and women, could grow together through cooperation. Man has also lost that which could put a limit to his powers so to avoid their becoming excess and domination. Without a woman, man focuses his physical force into the logic of competition, a logic in which only one gains and the others lose. This logic makes it impossible for cooperation, in which everybody gains. It allows for the rise of power structures based on hierarchy and exclusion. Effectively, the kind of centralized state we experience, the waging of wars, and the establishment of chauvinist social customs and discretionary laws are the outcome of patriarchalism and machismo.

2. Translator's note: Boff refers here to Aristotle, *Generation of Animals*, book 1, 728a.

But thanks to the historical endeavour of women, a systematic demolition of the false rationale of patriarchal societies has taken place. Women have elaborated a more holistic understanding of men and women, and of their historical mission; that is, to promote partnerships based on the respect of the different through a relationship that is more inclusive and less conflicting between genders, and to encourage relations that benefit of political and religious peace between peoples.

Second, the other is that which has a different sexual option to the established social norm. These are the *homosexuals*, men and women. They continue to face prejudice and to be victims of violence. The common interpretation, which is favored by religions, is that they represent a deviation from nature. The right to establishing stable unions is denied to them in the vast majority of countries.

Independent of the various readings about homosexuality that are pretentiously scientific or, to be frank, pseudoscientific or religious, it is appropriate to welcome homosexuals just as they are; it is appropriate to recognize their capacity to enter a loving relationship and their right to organize their existential realm, their *lifeworld* (*Lebenswelt*). This is the way a society should demonstrate its hospitality toward them. Nobody has a right to increase the suffering of those who already suffer because of social prejudice.

Third, the other may be someone who is affected by a *condition* such as HIV, Down Syndrome, Alzheimer's, and others; or, more concealed, afflicted by some sort of psychological disorder. Society tries to put them out of sight by placing them in institutions, and thus these people, even if their behavior is challenging, lack in human contact. To enter into their universe, to seek to see the world through their eyes, to be patient and to pay the necessary attention when listening to the long talk of a neurotic or even of a psychotic person, to know when to cheer them up and to unveil different life dimensions to them, when to be tactful and to be careful in the speech—all these are challenging ways, but still necessary ways, to live hospitality with all these people.

Fourth, the other may be someone from a different generation, the young or the *elderly*. The dominating global culture has an extreme focus on the figure of the young, on the vigor of the young, on its physical beauty, on its capacity to perform sexually, on its potential to consume, and on its capacity to mold the future, whilst the elderly is pushed aside as a used labor force with limited potential to consume, and not rarely, as a dead weight of history. Their experience and life histories, many of which are exemplary, are of little interest to the dominating culture of the young. To welcome them; to value their lives, their challenges and victories; to establish centers to rescue their memories; to create universities for the elderly;[3] and other such activities constitute a way of welcoming them within society.

Fifth, the other may be someone who is considered *illiterate*. All societies are school-based and incorporate written codes of communication. Whoever finds itself outside this setup is prejudiced against, is considered uneducated and backwards. A society's level of civilization is asserted through the extent to which it is able to insert its members into the world of letters. But this process of inclusion is not yet finished, and it is important to bear in mind that this "cultural other" is a bearer of another kind of culture based on an oral tradition, on knowledge of "experiential deeds" (Luis de Camões)[4] and on concrete living in all its expressions. Among these illiterate people we also place today those who have been excluded from digital culture, or who have not been initiated into the new computing alphabet.

Sixth, the other may be someone from a different *social class*, particularly from the so-called popular strata of society. These are millions and millions of people who live on low wages, who do not have a permanent job, who are unemployed, who are at the margins of society, despite having access to the media, to consumerism, and to entertainment, and being objects of demagogical political manipulation. They are seen as bearing imperfections, such as coarseness, lack of education, violence, and generalized ignorance.

This prejudiced attitude overlooks authentic values that are proper to the more popular strata of the population, such as its culture; its traditions, which are connected to life affairs and to the management of nature; its religiosity; and specially its art and its creativity, which is displayed in its survival skills and in its ascribing meaning to life in a world

3. Translator's note: Boff's idea to "create universities for the elderly" may strike many English-speaking people as rather odd. However, to Brazilians this is a matter of fact, as many states of the federation and the federal government itself have founded universities that focus solely on tertiary education for the elderly.

4. Translator's note: Luis de Camões (1524–1580) is considered the greatest poet of the Portuguese language. Boff alludes here to the following line of the *Os Lusíadas* or *The Lusiads*: "C'um saber experiência feitos" (IV.94).

that downgrades this strata and that penalize with grave social injustices those who belong to it.

If we pay close attention, a great part of the dominating culture in music, in fine arts, in literature, and even in scientific research, were inspired by themes from popular culture. We turn popular culture into a financial source; we accumulate academic titles and achieve fame from conducting research into or from being inspired by popular culture. However, we rarely ever give something back in the way of recognizing, ascribing value, and showing gratitude.

Seventh, the other may be someone who has been socially *excluded*. The current process of globalization based on an economic-financial strand produces, through its internal logic of competition and noncollaboration, a perverse social exclusion. Practically two-thirds of humanity lives under excluding conditions, enduring chronic hunger or death from all kinds of disease, earning extremely low wages, working in precarious conditions—victims of the market's voracity and of accelerated industrial production.

It could be said that humanity finds itself divided into, on the one hand, 20 percent that control 80 percent of the wealth and of natural resources consuming abundantly and considering themselves included within the global system; and on the other hand, 80 percent of the global population who have to do with the remaining 20 percent of the wealth and natural resources, who are excluded from the benefits of modern society based on information and knowledge.

Such a situation represents a generalized barbarism, and it is something never seen in this proportion before in the known history of humanity. This suffering part of humanity cries to the heavens and asks for justice and dignity, something that they do not experience on earth.

By looking at the geographical map of dire poverty and of richness, we discover a perverse relation in place between the North, which is rich but poor in natural resources, and the South, which is poor and drained but rich in natural resources. Those who come from the Great South are seen as the others by those in the developed world; those who come from the Great South are seen as underdeveloped and backwards, for they have not incorporated technical and scientific modernity and have subtracted themselves from modernity and capitalism's impetus, which could have brought salvation to them.

This interpretation is fallacious, for in truth these millions of people (i.e., the others) are victims of a raid by these rich countries, with their immense military, technological, financial, political, and ideological power. They raid the resources of the South, and in doing so, sacrifice the South's population as if it were coal for factories producing wealth.

People are increasingly more aware of this perverse situation, which is no longer accepted passively by groups who are more and more organized in the Great South, and who have gained global visibility in the World Social Forum (WSF). Unfortunately, this rebellious awareness constitutes one of the factors feeding the South's terrorism against the North. It is important not to forget that for centuries, it was the North who took terror to the peoples of the South, which was either colonized or subjugated. In our modern times, it is the North that suffers the terror that comes from its past victims, who retort with the same weapons used by its oppressors.

Nowadays terrorists do not occupy the physical territory of the United States of America, which is something proper to wars and guerrilla wars, but the minds and hearts of the population of the United States. The United States government, exploring patriotic feelings, imposed in the name of national security some clear limitations to freedom and human rights (i.e., the Patriot Act), but forgetting that these rights are unconditional and nonnegotiable. Islamic terrorism has generated the terrorism of the state (such as in the United States of America) and repressive dimensions in the security system of various countries, particularly in European nations.

To live hospitality within these dramatic conditions is to subscribe to the political cause of these poor majorities, who have been humiliated and ignored, so that they can be heard and included. Justice must be done so that they can reintegrate themselves to the human family. Such a change is impossible within the current global political scenario and with the kind of tyrannosauric globalization we experience. There is a need for a new paradigm of global relations that can overcome inequalities, inferiorization, and injustice against the Great South, where the majority of humanity lives. Otherwise, terrorism will reach new levels, eventually even to the point of using weapons of mass destruction (WMDs), such as chemical or biological weapons, or nuclear weapons (i.e., the so-called dirty bomb); this will force the rise of a new global political order. and (who knows?) of the humanitarian phase of globalization. When will the masters of life and death of the current phase of civilization understand this?

Eighth, the other may be someone whom we do not know, a *stranger*. A stranger is one who does not fit into a particular common social criterion. Strangeness can be caused by someone's different behavior or by someone's belonging to a different ethnic background that is not present in a society or by someone who speaks a different language or by someone who presents different ideas or understandings of the world uncommon to a cultural group. Every stranger causes a feeling of strangeness that is normally associated with uneasiness and fear. In order to safeguard itself, society may desire to expel the stranger either by persuasion or even by violent means.

The gospels bear witness that Jesus was considered a stranger by many people, even by family members. When Jesus left the home and wandered preaching, family members felt ashamed and tried to bring him back home; these family members said: "He is beside himself" (Mark 3:21). And Saint John writes: "He came to his own home, and his own people received him not" (John 1:11): this evokes the strangeness caused by Jesus in his listeners, and thus his rejection.

The stranger can provoke curiosity and the desire to establish contact in order to know him or her better, to know about his or her life and history. This can be a fecund relation to the extent that the stranger reveals another world or hidden dimensions of reality that had not been perceived before. To the extent that the stranger becomes known and an exchanging relationship is established, the stranger ceases to be a stranger and becomes, someone who is different, but still a member of the community.

In the beginnings of Christianity when someone converted and became a Christian, he or she ceased to be a stranger. Ethnicity or social class was not an issue, and wherever the converted went, he or she was received and welcomed as a brother or sister.

Hospitality toward a stranger involves openness, courage to face and overcome the strangeness that provokes fear, suspicion, disconnection, and even rejection of the other. Hospitality is to welcome the stranger just as the stranger presents itself, and without the need to place the stranger within the acceptable framework of the community.

Ninth, the other may be a *foreigner*, the representative of a different culture. This topic encapsulates a tragedy of global proportions, which was caused by the West's colonial, neo-colonial, and global-colonial expansions. It was here that the West revealed its limitations and its capacity for destruction. Let me identify the different kinds of foreigners, and how they were mistreated by representatives of Western culture.

The Destruction of the Cultural Other

The first front was against *Islamic culture* and against Islam. Since the eighth century CE Christians and Muslims have confronted each other militarily, with victories and defeats on both sides.

First of all, it is important not to forget the extraordinary culture that emerged from Islam wherever it established a dominion during its first centuries. For Westerners, the Islamic presence for seven centuries in Spain, with its great cultural centers, such as Granada, Seville, and Córdoba, is very important. Christian scholars went to these centers in search of sources of ancient Greece's philosophical and scientific treatises, as these manuscripts had completely disappeared from Christian countries such as France, Italy, Germany, and England. Thomas Aquinas, Duns Scotus, Alberto Magno, and Roger Bacon and others exchanged ideas with Arabic philosophers and sages, such as Averroes and Avicenna, and treated them with great respect.

But religious differences and the fact that Islam controlled the whole of biblical Israel, a sacred place for Christians, brought about successive crusades and a long and painful military front against Muslims.

Western intellectual circles of the Middle Ages tried to dismantle and to demoralize the religious message of Islam. Literature that was extremely injurious was spread among the people and *vade-mecums* (i.e., manuals) for travellers were published, where Mohamed was portrayed as a false prophet and Mohamed's texts as fables that are proper of a rude, ignorant, and infidel people.[5]

The Muslims, on the other hand, in those days and nowadays, see the West as arrogant, bellicose, intolerant, impious, materialist, and as a persistent violator of agreements.[6]

These prejudices from both sides endure in the collective unconscious of both parts. And these prejudices reemerge in every situa-

---

5. Cf. Jelloun, *Hospitalité française*, 115–16. Available in English as Jelloun, *French Hospitality*.

6. Cf. Maalouf, *The Crusades through Arab Eyes*.

tion of conflict between them. The military occupation of Iraq and of Afghanistan, and the permanent presence of the United States' military bases in Saudi Arabia are equivalent to a real occupation or takeover. The control that the West's great oil companies exercise over parts of the Middle East only feed prejudice, which is accompanied by anger and rebellion that are the very basis of Islamic terrorism that has impinged so much on global affairs.

If the humiliating and defeating conditions experienced by the Islamic world are maintained, then it is certain that those prejudices will never disappear. And thus, there will always be a live trigger ready to explode and cause new waves of terror and devastation.

Within this scenario there was no willingness from either part to demonstrate hospitality. However, it is important to mention that in the twelfth century the singular figure of Saint Francis of Assisi joined one of the crusades, went to the Middle East, and tried to dissuade Christians from fighting against brother Muslims. He went over the frontline and dialogued with the Sultan, who treated him with extreme hospitality. They understood each other on the basis of the heart and of a sense of humanitarian relations between Christians and Muslims to the point that the Sultan gave the custody of some holy places to Franciscan friars, places that are under their stewardship to this date.

The second front was against Black Africa. In this case, a direct relation of enslavement predominated, transforming entire African nations into merchandise to be sold to the sugarcane plantations in Brazil, the Caribbean, and the United States. Millions of people were turned into objects, treated like animals, and sold in slave markets. This is an eternal blemish on the West. The West was for centuries an advocate of slavery, and it never tried to make amends for this historical crime. It always refused to ask for forgiveness and to make any sort of compensation for the genocide it committed for centuries. Ironically, whilst the France of the French Revolution proclaimed the rights of men, the French troops in Africa decimated Africans as if they were mere flies, and without any concern for their humanity.

The third front occurred against the native indigenous cultures of the New World, in Latin America, the Caribbean, and the United States of America. The Iberians (i.e., the Portuguese and Spanish) who occupied and colonized the Americas encountered fine cultures, such as the Aztecs, the Mayans and the Incas, who possessed a sophisticated body of knowledge and complex urban organization. In Mexico, military confrontation, forced labor, and the spread by white settlers of diseases that were unknown in the Americas drastically reduced the native population from 22 million to merely 1.7 million over a period of only seventy years. This was the greatest genocide in the history of humanity. The cry of the victims still reaches the heavens, crying out for at least a minimum of justice, as many texts from the time bear witness.[7]

In Brazil, the arrival of Pedro Álvares Cabral on the 22nd of April 1500 was filled with great hospitality from both parties, Portuguese and Tupi native Indians, according to Pero Vaz de Caminha's narrative.[8] The first two Tupi native Indians that climbed on board Cabral's caravel were received with "much joy and feasting." The Portuguese gave them bread and cooked fish, pastries, honey, and dried figs to eat. Then the two native Indians "lay down on their backs on mats to sleep." Cabral gave order for pillows to be put under their heads and a blanket over them. And the two natives "consented and stayed and slept." One of the anonymous pilots of Cabral left an account that was published in Italy for the first time in 1507 by Montalboddo. In this account he says that the Tupi people after the first mass "danced and made music with their flutes," and that they accompanied the members of the fleet to the sea "until they were up to the waist in water, singing, playing and partying." The Portuguese also danced and played with them on the beach. Afterwards, the native Indians happily joined the Portuguese in gathering wood and fresh water for the fleet. As can be gathered, the relations were based on mutual hospitality and was a true idyll.[9]

Later however, when economic policies were introduced and with these an uncontrollable greed, violence became the norm. Why did this rupture appear—a rupture caused by Christians from the old European Christendom, from whom, given their faith, was expected welcome,

7. Cf. León-Portilla, *Visión de los vencidos: relaciones indigenas de la conquista*. This text is available in English as *The Broken Spears*.

8. Cf. Cortesão, *A carta de Pero Vaz de Caminha*,. Translation note: Pedro Álvares Cabral (1467–1520) was a Portuguese explorer and nobleman who discovered Brazil on the 22nd of April 1500. Pero Vaz de Caminha (1450–1500) was the registrar of the fleet that discovered Brazil; his letter to King Manuel is considered to be the most accurate and detailed account of the discovery of Brazil. The letter is available in English as: "Letter of Pedro Vaz de Caminha to King Manuel, Written from Porto Seguro of Vera Cruz the 1st of May 1500."

9. Cf. Leonardi, "Para além das raízes," 381–84.

co-living, and love? This rupture appeared because they understood native Indians to be nonpersons, to be inferior entities who could be lawfully enslaved. At this point, Aristotle spoke louder than Jesus Christ. According to Aristotle, who was pivotal in forging European ideas, the native Indian was a "natural slave" in the service of free man, who had been created to be in charge and to organize the world according to the canons of Western Christian white culture.[10]

This understanding was shared by the vast majority of colonizers and even by missionaries. In order to illustrate the gravity of the "destruction of the Indies," that is to say, the cultural annihilation of the cultural other as it was systematically denounced by Bartolomé de las Casas, the great defender of native Indians during the beginnings of the Mesoamerican colonization, I must refer to the famous Valladolid Dispute. In 1550 in front of the Spanish King Charles V, Juan Ginés de Sepúlveda, jester and educator to the royal family, and Bartolomé de las Casas, missionary of the Ordem de São Domingos in Mexico, confronted one another in a debate.

The question at hand was, is it lawful to wage a just war against native Indians by the fact that they resisted submitting to the Christian faith and to the king, who had been established by God as lord of the world?

Sepúlveda, without any scruples, repeats the traditional stance: Native Indians are inferior and brutish beings and "natural slaves." They lack in intelligence and practice religions that are the work of Satan, and this is the reason they resist to submit to the Christian faith. They must through force and for their own good be incorporated into the Christian faith. If they persist in their resistance, it is lawful to wage a just war against them and eventually eradicate them from the face of the earth. And we should not think that such actions are murderous or lack in love for the native Indians, for by refusing to accept the Christian faith and submission to the king, brought on themselves, they are guilty of their own destruction.[11] Sepúlveda argued a priori, and he had never seen or lived with a native Indian.

Las Casas, who had been an exploring colonist, and who had then become a Dominican friar, became famous for his missionary fervor to live with the native Indians, a fervor which was founded on respect and

10. Cf. Todorov, *The Conquest of America*.

11. Cf. Sepúlveda, *Tratado sobre las Justas causas de la Guerra contra los úndios*.

dialogue, and that opposed the violence used by colonists against the natives. The native Indians are rational beings, with culture and well-organized institutions, with religion and respectable traditions. They must be respected. It is up to us to try to establish a dialogue with them and to do so through gentle and peaceful means that totally exclude violence and invite them to join the Christian faith: the opposite stance to that of Sepulveda.

It is important to bear in mind that thirteen years before, in 1537, Pope Paul III wrote the first official document concerned with Latin America, his bull *Sublimis Deus*, where he reaffirms that the native Indians are "truly men and . . . are by no means to be deprived of their liberty or the possession of their property . . . . nor should they be in any way enslaved."[12]

This bull was never published in Latin America because the king had the power to veto its publication, and for this reason it was never practiced either. Sepúlveda's thesis triumphed politically and provided justification for the course of colonial practices: the most brutal domination of native Indians due to their resistance to the Christian faith, which in turn provided justification for their enslaving and for plundering their wealth, their gold and silver. Gold and silver were taken by the ton to Europe, and served as the material foundation for the rise of capitalism as the first expression of a global project, with all the perverse consequences that such a project brings to peripheral nations to this very day.

In Brazil colonization victimized native Indians in the same way. It is commonly held that there were about 6 million native Indians in Brazil at the time when the Portuguese caravels arrived in 1500. Their decimation, in uncountable ways, was so violent that nowadays only about thee hundred thousand survive. Especially perverse was the penetration of colonists in the Minas Gerais region. In 1808, given the resistance by natives who were the rightful owners of those lands, Dom João VI, king of Portugal, declared an open, aggressive, and massacring war against them and against their communities located between the basins of the rivers Doce, Macuri, and Jequitinhonha. Hunting natives was equated with hunting wild beasts. Natives were transformed into targets for soldiers' shotguns and rifles. The war was considered just because

12. Translator's note: Pope Paul III's encyclical *Sublimis Deus* is available online at www.papalencyclicals.net/Paulo3/p3subli.htm/.

the natives resisted royal orders, and because the war was understood to be the necessary solution that could guarantee the security of those who wished to build "civilization" inland.

The extermination was brutal and almost total. The cry of the victims still echoes in those valleys and mountains, and it reaches the heavens, crying out for at least a minimum of justice, and it will do so until the Day of Judgement that is to come.[13]

Curiously this willingness to exterminate those who are culturally different was also present in the recent colonization by Italians and Germans in the South of Brazil from the beginnings of the nineteenth century and into the twentieth century CE. Colonists penetrated regions that were inhabited by Kaingang and Xokleng native Indians. These were nomadic tribes that approached houses and settlements to take cooking pans, hoes and scythes, or clothes hanging on washing lines. As they did not have the concept of private property, they took those things innocently for their own use. Colonists understood the natives' actions as theft and felt threatened. The colonizing companies supported by the government organized squads to exterminated the *bugres*.[14] They were killed without any qualms as if they were wild beasts and not human beings, as corroborated by Pietro Brunello and Sílvio Coelho dos Santos in their respective researches.[15] One of the *bugre* hunters in an interview to Sílvio Coelho dos Santos said: "The assault was always at daybreak. First, we fired some shots. And afterwards we would do away with them using machetes. We would cut their ears off—we were paid by the pair. We had to kill them all as leaving survivors carried the risk of revenge."[16]

It was just like this that the "land was cleared" for the German and Italian colonists. It is exactly the same mentality displayed by the first Portuguese and Spanish colonizers in their fury to conquer Amerindian

13. Cf. Moreno, *A Guerra "justa" contra os índios* 92–127.

14. Translator's note: *Bugre* is a word that was used by European colonists to denominate individuals of various native groups of Brazil. The word is of French origin (Fr. Bougre) and it stands for "heretic." Its figurative meaning in English is something like "savage," "rude," "brutish," "impious." I have opted to keep the original Portuguese, i.e., *bugre*, in the English text—for no word in English can truly capture the meaning of this concept.

15. Cf. Brunello, *Pioneri. Gli italiani in Brasile e il mito della frontier*; Santos, *Os índios xokleng*; a short account also in Spedicato, "Anziosi di andare alla caccia del selvaggio," in *Suplemento Mosaico Italiano*, September, 2–3.

16. Santos, *Os índios xokleng*, 143.

wealth. It is the same murderous gesture displayed by the *homo sapiens* against the *Neanderthals* thousands of years ago. Neanderthals lived in Europe thousands of years ago; they had a conception of death and of immortality and performed funeral rites, which are signs of their humanity. Forty thousand years ago the *homo sapiens*, our ancestors, invaded Neanderthal territories, and hunted and exterminated its inhabitants, because about ten thousand years ago all signs of Neanderthals' inhabitation stopped.

Latin America continues to be an object of desire for global colonizers. In the Amazon region of Brazil, which borders many countries, biopiracy is commonly practiced. In the past it was the gold rush, now it is the genetic-and-pharmacological-resources rush, since these resources are strategic for future trade in the global market.

Within this scenario of systematic violence, any talk about hospitality falls on deaf ears or is mere prophecy. What becomes clear is the continuation of the West's barbaric attitude that insists on not recognizing the other. And after all these issues, the West has the arrogance to proclaim itself to be at the most advanced point of the *spirit of the world* and the sense of historical-social evolution, as was advocated by the philosopher G. W. F. Hegel (1770–1831).[17]

Last, the fourth front is between the West and the East. The East for the West was and continues to be a great rival. The East was not merely the main route for the trade in silk, spices, and exotic goods that were nonexistent in the West. In the East we find extraordinary wisdom, which is older than Christianity, and in the name of which the Chinese people decidedly refused to embrace the Christian faith of European missionaries.

Conversely, the West produced a systematic defamation of the East by calling the East despotic and without a God in an effort to disqualify their cultures and to dismantle the excellence of their wisdom, which much enchanted Jesuit missionaries such as Matteo Ricci (1552–1610) and his companions to China in the sixteenth century CE.

The awareness that the future of humanity lies in the East, particularly in China, grows steadily. China is viewed as the great oriental threat. Those who analyze global scenarios predict that not in a very distant future, there will be a great standoff between China and the USA, two core

17. Translator's note: I understand that Boff refers here to G. W. F. Hegel's views in his *Philosophy of Spirit* or *Philosophy of Geist*.

civilizations, due to a dispute over global influence and dominance over the process of globalization. The war will be preferably of an economic nature, but at some point it may have a military front so devastating that it might threaten the human global project, for both superpowers possess weapons of mass destruction (WMDs).

What kind of hospitality are we to postulate to those nations that still follow the old paradigm of the enemy and of war? Such a strategy destroys the preconditions of any kind of hospitality, and it can even destroy the whole of humanity.

Within this scenario hospitality emerges as the realization of an old dream, as one of the best dreams of humanity: the meeting between East and West. These would be like two brothers embracing and completing each other; completing each other with their own particular wisdom and spiritual traditions. The Tao and the Cross would establish a sacred and eternal alliance.

Such a deed would greatly enrich the process of globalization by allowing it to establish itself as the process of human globalization.

The New Others

Our modern times have seen the emergence of a diverse number of others, who are bearers of what could be dramatic dimensions. The *terrible other* is the one who possesses WMDs of all kinds, who is capable of putting an end to the human species and causing great damage to the biosphere and to all others who do not possess such weapons. Those who possess such destructive power ascribe to themselves the right to supersede international agreements and global organizations such as the United Nations, the World Trade Organization, and the International Court of Justice in The Hague, which judges crimes against humanity. Those who possess such weapons simply impose their will on the others and establish the directions to be followed by the process of globalization and by humanity, according to their interests.

This new wave of imperialist power reinforces the will to create a global empire founded on the conviction that Western civilization is the highest and most rational of all civilizations in history. And for this reason, and as the only visible option, it must be taken to all quarters of the earth as well as mold the process of globalization in accordance with its central canons.

The universal imposition of Western culture could cause, as I have pointed out previously, a terrifying standoff between the West and the rest of the world. If this occurs, there is a risk that humanity will end, or that humanity will recede to an archaic mode of living, surrounded by a devastated environment.

There is still another other who has always been here and that is progressively part of the collective consciousness, namely, nature and the Earth, which is to be understood as Gaia. During a great part of human history the Earth was always understood as something alive, and human beings as sons and daughters of the Earth; and sometimes human beings were understood as the Earth that feels, thinks, loves, venerates and cares. The relationship between the Earth and human beings was based on interactions marked by reverence and by respect, for the human beings felt themselves part and parcel of nature and of the Earth.

With the rise of instrumental and analytic reason and with the advent of technoscience, human beings' capacity to intervene in the rhythms of nature increased considerably. The Earth was thus seen as *res extensa* (Descartes), an object among others and a storeroom of inexhaustible resources to be used to satisfy human beings' desire for comfort and their consuming needs. The Earth was not respected as the great other. The Earth was attacked and subjugated just as theorists of modern science such as Francis Bacon and others had suggested: the Earth must be treated by us just as the inquisitor treats its inquisitee; we must torture the Earth until it gives up all its secrets, or we must submit the Earth to the torments of a Procrustean bed.[18]

This understanding of the Earth as the other who should be subjugated broke up the natural alliance between the human being and nature and the Earth. By breaking up this natural pact we placed ourselves above nature and the Earth and as such we are no longer with and within nature and the Earth. We have exiled ourselves from the Earth and we have separated ourselves from the community of life, of which we are but a link and a representative among others.

Something very dramatic is currently happening to humanity inspired by neo-liberalism, which privatizes everything, and as the outcome of the logic of the free-market, which transforms everything into merchandise and an opportunity for gain. Human rights are be-

18. Translator's note: Procrustes (the stretcher) is a figure of Greek mythology. A Procrustean bed is an arbitrary standard to which exact conformity is forced.

ing transformed into human needs, which can only be met with due payment. In this way drinking water is no longer considered a natural resource that is vital and irreplaceable for every human being and for all forms of life. Water is now considered a hydro resource, a commodity to be privatized, a commodity to be placed in the market and from which a great deal of money can be made. Whoever controls water controls life and whoever controls life has a considerable power for it has the power to grant or to deny access to water, it has the power over the lives or deaths of millions of people and over the chain of life that requires water to continue living. Behind this perverse commercial practice is a materialist perspective of the world that is insensitive to values and that destroys all social, cultural, spiritual and ecological sense of life. Water, on top of being part of life and thus access to it being a human right, is a free and cyclic gift of nature to life. It is formed by the evaporation of the oceans, it becomes dense and forms clouds, it travels through the atmosphere and falls as rain, penetrating the earth to guarantee the continuation of life and being taken into our bodies to satiate our thirst.

Moreover, our position of power-domination over the Earth caused us to lose the capacity to admire and be enchanted by the Earth's grandeur and turned us deaf to the messages the Earth continuously send us. We have become poor and alone, we are condemned to anthropocentrism and to the illusion that we are at the centre of everything and that creation only has meaning in relation to us, we have forgotten that we are but a moment in the greater whole. Danah Zohar, the quantum physicist, and Ian Marshall say something that is extremely relevant in considering the above perspective in their book *SQ: Spiritual Intelligence*: "The truth that you and the other are one, that there is no separateness, that you and the 'stranger' are two aspects of one life."[19]

The final outcome of this process of rupture was the emergence of modern industrialist societies that hansacked nature's resources, devastated ecosystems and compromised the future of the Earth as a whole. Today we realize that if we continue with this violence we can end up just like the dinosaurs.

As I have argued in chapter 2 of this book we cannot think about the human being as independent from the Earth. Human initiatives, even democracy itself, cannot only take into account human interests. These initiatives must take into account the whole chain of life and the

19. Zohar and Marshall, *SQ: Spiritual Intelligence*, 195.

interdependence of all beings so that we can guarantee a common future for all. The Earth is much more than a source of resources, which are always limited and some are not even renewable. The Earth is a living supra-organism, it is another *other*, it is the other with extreme differences but it is also the other who is very close to us for we are part and parcel of it.

If we recognize the Earth's alterity (i.e., otherness) then we can build a close relation and a relation of benevolence with it. Political agreements between nations and social pacts must have as their cornerstone the natural pact. Without the guarantee of the endurance and continuity of nature and of the Earth all other agreements and pacts are groundless and become impossible.

This situation is something new to humanity. Before we could hold that the Earth would always be there for us and that it would provide for all human projects. In our modern times this is no longer the case, for the future of the Earth is not guaranteed due to the human, *sapiens* and *demens*, capacity for destruction.

To conclude, I have demonstrated in this chapter that the West has a very negative balance with the various others. Western culture has always had serious difficulties in dealing benevolently with the other, and its strategy in dealing with the other, generally speaking, followed the following rationale: it either incorporated the other as a subaltern and in doing so negated the other's identity, or it enslaved the other, or it excluded the other by pushing the other to the margins of society, or it simply destroyed the other.

This strategy represents a pathological condition of identity and as such it must be considered carefully for it demands an urgent cure. As I shall demonstrate in the next chapter, the medicine to cure this infirmity is found in the West itself.

seven

Rescuing the Other: A Basis for Hospitality

If we find the poison that kills hospitality in the West, it is also in the West that we find the antidote for this ill. That is, the antidote is the centrality of the other that is proposed continuously in the biblical tradition.

The Centrality of the Other in the Judaeo-Christian Tradition

Within the Judaeo-Christian tradition the other and God, as the Great Other, are everything. There is a thread that runs through the Old and the New Testaments that can be summed up as "he executes justice for the fatherless and the widow, and loves the sojourner, giving him food and clothing; you shall not oppress a stranger, you know the heart of a stranger, for you were strangers in the land of Egypt" (Deuteronomy 10:18–19; Exodus 23:9, RSV). And the stranger must be welcomed and lodged as any of the house of Israel (cf. Leviticus 10:8, 10:13; 19:34).

The Judaeo-Christian faith on creation says that every thing was created out of God's Word. And for this reason He is the sole Lord. We are not owners of the earth, the earth is God's, and we are its "strangers and sojourners" (Leviticus 25:23). If we are sojourners, then in turn we must welcome others in an unconditional and limitless way. For each potential guest may hide God or one of his envoys, angels (Genesis 19:1). And because of this, the supreme Judge in the final moment of history on Judgment Day says: "I was a stranger and you welcomed me . . . I was in prison and you came to me" (Matthew 25:35–36).

To love God and one's neighbor are so insolubly linked that they form a sole commandment, the commandment of love (cf. Matthew 22:34–40). Saint Paul said that this commandment of love sums up all other commandments (cf. Romans 13:8) and fulfils all Law (Galatians

5:14). The commandment of love is simply "the royal law," and "if you really fulfil the royal law according to the Scripture, 'You shall love your neighbor as yourself,' you do well" (James 2:8, RSV).

Covenant is the central category of the biblical legacy, and it is established with God and with all other entities. And because of this, the other is, by virtue of covenant, not a stranger but an ally.

Most important is that the covenant with God is only valid if it is preceded by the covenant with the other. It is with reason that Jesus says: "if you are offering your gift at the altar, and there remember that your brother has something against you, leave your gift there before the altar and go; first be reconciled to your brother, and then come and offer your gift" (Matthew 5:23–24). The other has absolute precedence.

The New Testament affirms that God, by virtue of incarnation, became another in Jesus. It is in the other, therefore, that we find the utmost presence of God. This incarnated God, who is so close, wanted to identify itself with the extreme others, that is, with those who are naked, who are famished, who are thirsty, who are foreigners; with those that are called "my little brothers." As Matthew (25:31–46) says, "as you did it to one of the least of these brethren, you did it to me . . . As you did not to one of these, you did it not to me." Everything comes from the other; outside the other there is no salvation. Hell is not the other, as Jean-Paul Sartre affirmed; rather, the other I the pathway to heaven.[1]

Even for those who do not share biblical faith this tradition has a value in itself, and for this reasons it represents an important function in civilization, for this tradition ascribes a central role to loving the other and particularly to those in need. It should not be forgotten that the exclusion of the other is one of the factors causing modern terror—be this economic terror or military or attacks such as the one against the United States of America on September the 11th of 2001.

The relation with the other encourages responsibility. This is the eternal question posed by Cain, murderer of Abel: "Am I my brother's keeper" (Genesis 4:9)? The answer is yes; when faced with the other, with the other's face and begging hands, we cannot subtract ourselves: we must be responsible. This is what the word responsibility actually means: it means to give a response, to give an answer to the other.

---

1. Translator's note: Boff refers here to the famous line "Hell is other people" of Jean-Paul Sartre's play *Huis Clos*, or *No Exit*. Available in English in Jean-Paul Sartre, *"No Exit" and Three Other Plays*.

The other brings about ethics in us. The other either causes a welcoming attitude or an attitude of rejection. Ethics is the cornerstone of philosophy, to paraphrase the philosopher Emmanuel Lévinas.

The majority of Western philosophies are not centred on alterity (i.e., otherness), on the other, but on identity, on one's self. And for this reason ethics is never a priority. This deficiency took on, for instance, tragic forms in the philosophy of the well-known Martin Heidegger, for his philosophy is ethically very vacuous. For Heidegger, the human being is the "shepherd of Being" rather than "brother's keeper."[2] Heidegger joined the Nazi movement when he was elected rector of the University of Freiburg in 1933; later, when he was judged on this, he just said: "Once I wore the brown shirts of the Nazis, but this was a mistake."[3] Was this only a mistake?

Such a statement seems to be free from any sense of responsibility, and consequently, of ethical substance. What happened, in truth, was more than a mistake; what happened was a fault largely for tolerating the banning of Jewish professors from their chairs. Heidegger did little or next to nothing to save his teacher and supervisor, Edmund Husserl, when he could have.

The world is not just composed of people who make mistakes or who err. Tragically the world is also composed of people who are not ethical, and who are culpable, and who refuse to respond to the other with responsibility. And because of these people, tragedies have happened in human history.

The Judaeo-Christian tradition is a legacy of Western civilization that provides us with a solid basis for a hospitality that is possible and urgent in the current globalizing phase of humanity, a phase in which so many different cultures and millions of people meet, and must be welcoming to one another.

There are a number of conflicts all over the world. How can these conflicts be solved? There has been a major increase in the number of commentators and thinkers who state that these conflicts will not be solved through political agreements, rather these conflicts will be solved through the acceptance of a minimal ethical pact that is embraced by all

2. Translator's note: Boff refers here to Martin Heidegger's famous quotation from *Letter to Humanism*: "The human being is not the lord of beings, but the shepherd of Being."

3. Translator's note: Translated directly from the Portuguese.

parties. This pact will be founded on the adamant defense of life, on the preservation of the integrity of the planet Earth and of its ecosystems, on guaranteeing the necessary conditions for the preservation of life, and on the decision to permanently exorcize violence as a means of conflict resolution between peoples.

This minimal ethics presupposes welcoming the other as other, it presupposes respecting the other's singularity, and it presupposes a willingness to establish a long-lasting alliance with the other. These presuppositions are contained within the idea of an open and never-ending hospitality.

The Austrian-Israeli philosopher Martin Buber (1878–1965) provided us with one of the best philosophical characterizations of the ethics of the other and of a continuous dialogue with the other. In his book *I and Thou* Buber demonstrates that all human existence is dialogical and how the I emerges from the Thou, and that the I-Thou relation is at the heart of communal and social interrelations.

His statement is famous: if we live juxtaposed (*Nebeneinander*), we may end up opposed (*Gegeneinander*), and thus we must always try to be together (*Miteinander*), we must try to achieve some sort of agreement to live together.[4]

The Liberation Church, currently present in Latin America, Africa, and Asia, opted for the extreme others; that is to say, it opted for the poor and for the excluded, and it fights against poverty and exclusion. This is the manner through which it modernizes the Judaeo-Christian legacy of covenant and of hospitality. It does not do this through a paternalistic attitude of being there *for* the other; it rather does this by being *with* the other, and whenever possible by living *as* the other for this is the libertarian attitude.

The thought that emerged from this practice has been for some time a theology and an ethic of liberation. Its first categorical imperative is the following, and it has been formulated by the Argentinean philosopher Enrique Dussel: "Free the poor."

---

4. Translator's note: Boff refers here to the famous quote from Buber's speech "The National Home and National Policy in Palestine," 31st October 1929: "Das Nebeneinander zweier Völker auf dem gleichen Territorium muß aber, wenn es sich nicht zum Miteinander entfaltet, zum Gegeneinander ausarten." This passage is the translation of a Portuguese paraphrase of the speech.

Human Rights and the Culture of Peace

There is another Western school of thought that complements the one above and that, decidedly, is committed to rescuing the other's dignity. This is the noble struggle for human rights, in particular, the rights of those who have been wronged and humiliated throughout history.

The consciousness of human rights is a topic that is particular to Western civilization, which is strongly influenced by the Judaeo-Christian understanding as I noted in the previous section. The Magna Carta in England in 1215 and the Declaration of Independence by the American colonies on 1776 were influenced by this understanding.

In our modern times, and within the political sphere, we have seen a great impetus toward freedom and rights, but in practice we have not seen freedom and rights reaching all.

The most important documents on human rights, such as the Declaration of the Rights of Man and Citizen of the French Revolution, 1789; and the Universal Declaration of Human Rights of the United Nations, 1948; and all the other declarations of rights (e.g., of peoples, of minorities, of children, of culture, etc.) start from the ethical and political presupposition that the human being is an end in itself, and that it is never a means to an end.

These declarations serve as safeguards against tyrannical authoritarian powers that disrespect an individual's rights, or against those who overlook the rights of others and another people's culture so as to gain advantages or maintain privileges. Upholding human rights places limitations on despotism, and it also treats any trespass as a crime.

Reaching such a high consciousness about the dignity of the other represents a great advance in civilization for any culture. This consciousness is enlarged by the extent to which more dimensions of the other are perceived. The other is not only a different human being. The other can be any entity of creation: it can be a plant, an animal, an ecosystem, and even the planet Earth itself. When faced with any of them it is fit to hold the same attitude of recognition and of respect.

This is the very basis that allows us to overcome conflicting situations that are often taking place between power on one side and respect of rights on the other. Frequently what happens is that the interests of those who hold powerful positions prevail over respect for the other and over the other's dignity. Ideological justifications are often put forward to legitimize infringements: in the case of women, because they are more sentimental than rational; in the case of native Indians, because they are savages; in the case of Blacks, because of the color of their skin; in the case of Muslims, because they are potential terrorists. In this way, the distinction between the human and the pseudohuman continues just as it did during the great colonizations when it was possible to oppress without feeling guilty. During the Kosovo war in the 1990s, the Serbians castrated Muslim male prisoners so that they were not considered completely human but pseudohuman, so that it became acceptable to carry out ethnic cleansing against them without violating human rights.

We will only be able to cut this Gordian knot if we start with unconditional respect for all beings: for all others, for every form of life, and for every human being—independent of social, moral, and cultural status.

The rationale behind this respect is found in the fact that every being is part of a whole that has been evolving for billions of years. Everything is interdependent with every thing. Every being represents a link in the chain of life and deserves to continue to exist and live.

Thus the respect for human rights must start with the respect for every alterity (i.e., otherness), from the mineral to the vegetable to the animal to ecosystems to cultures to every single person. We will not respect the life of those who are similar to us if we do not respect life in all its diversity, if we do not respect every existing being.

If we lose the respect for the other, and if we exercise violence against nature, then sooner or later this violence will be turned against us.

Thus the culture of respect reveals itself as a culture of caring for others and for our Common Home; the culture of respect shows itself as a culture of co-responsibility for the common future of humanity and of the Earth; the culture of respect emerges as a culture of compassion for all those who suffer; the culture of respect discloses itself as a culture of cooperation and universal solidarity, for this is the very phenomenon that allows all to live within the same white-and-blue spaceship that is our planet Earth.

Infinite Democracy as the Inclusion of the Other

Another value that emerged in the West, and which has proliferated around the world, is the idea of democracy. Democracy functions as the remedy against all kinds of exclusion and against lack of hospitality.

Democracy is both an ideal and a reality. It is an *ideal* with all the characteristics of utopia, and for this reason it is always inclusive of and receptive to all the spheres where the other is found: it is found in the relation of man and woman, in the family, in the school, in the community, in unions, in social movements, and in governments. This *ideal* of democracy is a democracy that represents a universal value; it is an infinite democracy that is always being constructed. As it is a utopia, it is untiring; but it must always be arrived at through a refining process.

Democracy is also a historical *reality*, and for this reason it is always limited and conditioned to viable social circumstances. A play between the ideal and the real gives rise to the *process* of continuous development of infinite democracy; and this development occurs the extent to which civil participation increases and the extent to which society becomes more inclusive and empowers all its members.

The basic presupposition of all democracy is the following: what concerns all must be decided by all either through direct consultation or through representatives. The first expression of democracy is the choice of representatives through free elections.

In democracy everybody counts and everybody is important, and for this reason democracy does not admit the exclusion of the other. In a country like Brazil with fifty million excluded, democracy is tinged with unreality. Despite this problem, there is an impetus to construct an enriched democracy, which is not merely representative but also participative. Social movements have put forward the following ideal: *a society in which all can fit in, including nature*. Therefore, there is an endeavour toward an inclusive democracy with universal ideals, an infinite democracy as proposed by the Portuguese political thinker Boaventura de Souza Santos.[5]

The ecological aspect must be included in an expanded democracy. Democracy must not be confined to human beings, for this would be an-

5. Translator's note: Boaventura de Souza Santos is a prominent sociologist and professor of the University of Coimbra, who gained much popularity after his participations in the World Social Forum in Porto Alegre, Brazil.

thropocentrism. Anthropocentrism is a misunderstanding, for the human being is not the central point linking everything; anthropocentrism understands that all other entities only have value in relation to human beings. The human being is an important link alongside so many others in the chain of life. The human being is not isolated but always related to everything. Without being related to the biosphere, to the environment, to the physical-chemical preconditions of life, the human being would neither exist nor subsist. Important elements must be included in our current understanding of democracy, for ecological awareness has awarded rights to animals, plants, and the Earth itself. Democracy can no longer consider the social pact as dissociated from the natural pact. Rather, both pacts must be considered in relation to each other.

The natural pact stands for the relation of interdependence, co-living, and collaboration between the human being and nature. Nowadays it is imperative to guarantee the natural pact, because ecosystems and the Earth itself are being systematically affronted in their right to exist and in their alterity (i.e., otherness). If we do not guarantee the continuity of nature, then any other pact loses its meaning.

The social pact must encompass in its own constitution the natural pact. Human beings are not the only citizens; animals, trees, birds, landscapes, rivers, mountains, and ecosystems are also citizens. Could we imagine a city that did not aspire to have green areas, preserved rivers, clean air, protected animals, landscapes that are looked after, and protected mountains? It would not be a human city if it did not aspire to these.

Democracy must extend legal rights to all these beings, because they are subjects of rights and must be respected as such in their alterity (i.e., otherness) and in their co-living with us. These beings are citizens, are members, of a sociocosmic democracy. They are the others that should be respected and integrated into our social community. Peace would gain a new dimension: it would no longer stand for the peace between human beings, peoples, and cultures, but also for the peace with the Earth, which would be free from the devastation that has been inflicted on it for centuries. Only this kind of peace would stand for the perpetual peace dreamt of by the great German philosopher Immanuel Kant (1724–1804).

eight

Hospitality within the Context of Globalization

Modern hindrances on hospitality are vast. We do not even know how to exactly deal in a hospitable manner with the great global problems caused by migrations, migrations which are caused largely by wars or economic crises, and by the natural mobility between peoples and cultures. In spite of the fact that we do not know how to exactly deal with this situation, we must not give up on the ideal of hospitality, for it is at the very basis of our humanity and of our co-living in society. Without the ideal of hospitality we would regress to something similar to a pack of wild wolves; we would regress to that which is called a "state of nature."

If we are not sure about what policies we should concretely implement at a global level, we can at least encourage attitudes and behavior that embrace hospitality and that can give rise to a new kind of subjectivity in citizens.

Despite all these limitations, it is important to indicate some policies that could be implemented at a global level in human activity.

Hospitable Attitudes and Behaviors

The characteristics of hospitality, which I pointed out when I analyzed the myth of Philemon and Baucis could serve as a guide to us. Let me refer back to some of these characteristics of hospitality, characteristics which are pathways that can lead us to a process of globalisation that is truly human.

Unconditional Goodwill

If goodwill is not an attitude that is preset in everything that we think and do, then it is impossible to create common ground for all of us. If we are malicious in everything that we do, if I am suspicious about everything, and if I do not trust anyone, then how are we to build something that can bring everyone together?

To put this in a different way: only when everyone's goodwill is in place can we build something that is good for all. In moments of crises, goodwill is the main factor uniting everyone striving for a solution to the crises. Immanuel Kant (1724–1804), the most rigorous ethicist of modern Western thought, stated something that is of great relevance in his *Groundwork of the Metaphysics of Morals*: "It is impossible to conceive anything at all in the world, or even out of it, which can be taken as good without qualification, except a *good will*."[1] To put this in a simple way: the good will is the only thing that is solely good and that is not restricted in any way. Either the good will is entirely good, or it is not a good will at all. There is a truth in all of this that has practical implications.

This reflection impinges on any initiative of human cooperation, especially on the process of globalization, which is so deeply characterized by competition. If there is no goodwill on the part of the great majority of humanity, we will neither find a solution to the desperate social crises that tear apart peripheral societies, nor will we find a solution to the alarming ecological issues that threaten the planet Earth. There is no other way to achieve these solutions; no government, no charismatic leadership, can forge another potential and hopeful alternative for the social and ecological problems that the world currently faces.

Goodwill is the last option we have left for salvation. The current world situation is a calamity. We live in a permanent state of global civil war. There is nobody, not even the two holy fathers—the pope and the Dalai Lama—or intellectual and moral elites, or technoscience that can provide us with a solution for the global problems we face. The truth is that only we can help ourselves. Dostoyevsky wrote in his fantastic narrative "The Dream of a Ridiculous Man" (1877): "If only everyone wishes it, it will immediately happen."[2]

---

1. Kant, *Groundwork of the Metaphysic of Morals*, 59.
2. Dostoevsky, "The Dream of a Ridiculous Man," 24.

Brazil reproduces in miniature what happens globally. The social wounds produced by five hundred years of neglect toward the wider population are something horrendous. By and large, the Brazilian elite never sought a solution for the whole of Brazil; rather these elites only sought solutions for themselves. These elites are only engaged in safeguarding their privileges, rather than being engaged in securing rights for all. Through the use of various political maneuvers, and even through coup d'état, they manage to manipulate democratically elected governments so that these governments take on an agenda that is suitable to these elites and that make impossible, or at least delay, necessary social changes. In opposition to the majority of the Brazilian people, who have always shown immense goodwill, a great part of the Brazilian elite refuses to pay the debt of goodwill it has with the country as a whole.

If goodwill is something so essential, then it is important to encourage it in all. In dire situations, such as with the current state of the Earth that resembles the Titanic going down, all of us, even those who are mainly responsible for the current crises, must collaborate, with at least a minimum of goodwill. This is the condition for survival. Class struggle is something still very virulent, and it must be taken seriously, and in extreme situations it must be considered carefully. Everybody must act with at least a minimum of goodwill. If each one of us, in fact, wished that humanity moved forward and improved, then with everyone's goodwill this would happen.

Generously Welcoming

Generously welcoming stands for accepting the other joyously and without prejudice. Our situation has no alternatives: we are all on board a spaceship, the planet Earth. From the start, we cannot make any enemies. Wanting to or not, we must live together and accept each other. Contrary to what happened in the past, now there is nowhere to go to take refuge if one does not want to live alongside some people. It is now impossible for a country to completely close itself to the outside, as the process of globalization has turned this into an impossible option.

Welcoming must not be performed as a chore because we have no other option. We must joyfully welcome the other as if we saw in the other someone close to us, a companion, a brother or a sister, a member of the great human family, a family that was dispersed not very long ago and that now is becoming united in our Common Home.

Careful Listening

It is more important to listen with the heart than to listen with the ears. It is about opening oneself up cordially, it is about opening oneself up with the sentiment of one who feels the other, and who tries to see the other from the other's perspective and not from conceptions and preconceptions of one's own culture. I consider erroneous the following proposal put forward by some: that in order to comply with unconditional hospitality, that we should neither ask names, and nor should we ask where people come from. People are not numbers. People have names and origins. Without letting ourselves being contaminated by eventual prejudices associated with certain names or countries, we must call a person by their name and know where he or she comes from.

Through this very act we realize that each person has something to tell us. He or she tells us something simply by being present, through his or her face, gaze, hands, words, and way of dressing. To listen is to be willing to perceive facets of reality that are inaccessible to us, but that can be revealed to us by the other. So much wisdom, beauty, heroic sagas, creativity have been shown by different peoples and cultures. And also so much fighting, suffering, drama, and tragedy have other peoples and cultures endured through time. By listening we can learn, we deal with, we can absorb, we can perfect and enrich ourselves in our own identity, which is something that is not fixed in time but is a matrix that is capable of renewing itself and growing through experience of the other.

Truthful Dialogue

To dialogue is to enter into a relation of reciprocity and exchange. Every human being is a dialogical being, because its existence is always connected to coexistence and to interdependence, and for this reason we require each other to be human. The major issue of our modern times is dialogue between cultures, that is, intercultural dialogue.

Each culture shows a different way of being human that has its own limitations and vitalities. In intercultural dialogue we see the emergence of various pathways for the formation of identity; we see the various ways of dialoguing with nature; we see the various ways of naming the Divine and the Sacred; and we see the various ways of praying, of celebrating, of creating art and music. And at the same time we see the emergence of the various points in common that identify us as human beings, as members of the *homo-sapiens and -demens* species.

Dignity, respect, solidarity, care, participation, transparency, good governance, nonviolence, and reverence are values present in regional cultures, and in the new culture that emerges as the outcome of the process of globalization as a human phenomenon. All these values are slowly becoming more concrete and are becoming the basis for the convergence of all humanity in this globalized era.

The great risk at this point is that dialogical relations may become thing based, and therefore dialogical relations become more about exchanging goods and trading than about allowing people and cultures to be in contact and exchange ideas so that they can discover themselves as the great human family that is full of differences and rich in values.

Within this sociobiodiversity, the planet Earth appears as a complex mosaic of numerous ecological and social systems that by virtue of their interretroconnections between each and everybody embodies humanity. Each component must be recognized in its own identity and its own difference, and it must be perceived as part and parcel of a unique and diverse whole.

Honest Negotiation

Wherever there are conflicting interests, we must develop the willingness and the capacity for negotiation, for reaching the right measure and potential points in common within the logic of "everybody wins." Each part must have the courage of taking up commitments that attend to problems at hand, and that are always associated with the common good.

The phenomenon of the spread of humanity all over the planet and the emergence of the geosociety forces us to give center stage to the common good rather than the particular good. If we do not do this, then tensions and conflicts will endure, and these are hindrances to a more humanitarian globalization.

This attitude of open and honest negotiation must particularly prevail over mechanisms of power of hegemonic countries and of dominant classes, who make use of all means to preserve their powerful and privileged positions and their domination over other parts of the world and of society. For the majority of them, the process of globalization is the continuation of the process of Westernization of the world through the imposition of a Western lifestyle and parameters of culture and civilization.

Unrepentant Renouncing

To renounce one's own particular interests in favor of the common good constitutes a precondition for any strategy seeking consensus. To renounce in this case means the political aptitude of prioritizing that which is truly important to all. We do not lose out when we do this; rather we renounce to gain peace, sustainability, and cohesion around a common good. That is, to humanely live together within our Common Home.

Our collective responsibility increases in proportion to the risks we create for our own survival and for the continuity of life on the planet. And in the function of this supreme value, our survival and the continuity of life in the planet, which is the basis for all other values, it is imperative to renounce the particular so that we can save the universal.

Conscious Responsibility

It is not about denying one's own position and identity. What is required is that one must take conscious responsibility so as to avoid the particularities of each people, and even of each person, becoming obstacles to the materialization of the common good. When one's own difference is assumed within a collective cause, this difference can ascribe color to human coexistence. The affirmation of one's own difference does not necessarily implicate potential conflicts; rather, if one consciously affirms one's own difference in relation and always within the perspective of the whole, then this is valid and enriching to globalization.

The threat is the imposition of a single way of thinking, of cultural standardization, of the ironing out of differences, and of dissipation of experiences between people. These practices bring with it dissatisfaction, revolt, and bitterness, which are fertile soil for tensions and conflicts that hinder the implementation of the common good.

Courageous Relativization

To relativize one's own position and difference does not imply the re-nunciation of one's own values. It requires that one be courageous enough to stop understanding one's own values as the only ones that are valid and absolute since this could cause conflict. It is important to place one's own values in relation to the others' and to the whole. Within this perspective, one's own values emerge as one possibility among others of human development. Therefore, one's own values help to compose the polychromic mosaic of differences that embrace one another, that coexist together, that tolerate one another, and that assemble together the great confederation of peoples of the Earth, which was the greatest dream of the political thought of Immanuel Kant (1724–1804) and of other great modern thinkers.

Intelligent Transfiguration

Due to the fact that we are not only *homo sapiens*, but also *homo demens*, we are bearers of aggressive dimensions, we are always faced with vio-lence, violence which makes so many victims. Our challenge is not to eradicate these dimensions but to transfigure them. That is to say, to turn them into nondestructive dimensions. For instance, competition (which marginalizes and excludes so many people, classes, and weaker nations) must be transfigured through more benevolent forms of competition, such as sports, and cultural and artistic competitions and contests. Through such transfiguration, the dynamics of competition are chan-nelled into more acceptable ends that are not destructive, and that still preserve the social fabric.

If we pay close attention, this strategy has been used by humanity for many centuries in its search for positive solutions to conflicts and tensions. This strategy represents the passing from a "state of nature," where the right by force prevails, to a "civilized state," where the force of right is established.

This civilized strategy is usually followed by social movements that have not opted for the principle of extreme violence. However, these movements frequently transfigure extreme violence into symbolic vio-lence when they exercise pressure on society and on the state in their fight for the rights of women, blacks, ethnic minorities, and people who are discriminated against; and in their support for ecology and peace, and against wars. The means to achieve such ends is peaceful, for this is done through the exercise of democratic pressure, public debates, large rallies, and popular plebiscites.

The global phase of humanity will only consolidate when the culture of peace and renunciation of all physical violence grows to be a collective conquest and a common heritage of all peoples. Only then will all the conditions for a long-lasting peace between all tribes of the Earth be in place.

Possible Hospitable Policies

Attitudes and behaviors are at the heart of active citizens. It is always possible to implement changes at this level, because attitudes and behaviors depend solely on one's personal commitment and willingness to change a particular behavioral pattern. But this is not enough. It is also important to implement social changes that introduce improvements (reforms) or that introduce structural changes (alternatives). Let me demonstrate a few of these.

At Least a Minimum of Justice at All Levels

Inequalities are present in all quarters. These inequalities are usually identified as being economic in nature, but it is important to note that just as much inequality can be identified as cultural and religious in nature. According to Samir Amin, the well-known Egyptian economist, in his *Capitalism in the Age of Globalization*, a small part of the global elite controls five monopolies: technology, global finance, natural resources, communication and media, and the weapons industry. This elite control 83 percent of the global GDP, and this has implications for the levels of social inequality in the world. The gap between rich and poor doubled between the 1960s and the 1990s, which is a perverse social injustice and a true human catastrophe.

The current global socioeconomic system only serves one-third of humanity well. The remaining two-thirds, about four billion people, face a scenario of suffering and dire poverty. The current system does not possess the physical-ecological conditions to be universalized for the whole of humanity. If this were to become a possibility, we would need another four planets Earth, according to calculations made by the biologist Edward Wilson in his book *The Future of Life*, and this is something that is impossible.

There is very little solidarity between human beings. This makes injustice and inequality the most scandalous and incontestable features of our times. Injustice and inequality are not being overcome; rather they are being aggravated by the voracity of the kind of globalization process we experience—a process that is very excluding and that knows no ecological or ethical limits. The objective of this kind of process is to accumulate without end, and this is something done by those who have always accumulated for their own benefit.

Within the current global order economic issues are crucial in decision-making process. Politics is hostage to economics. And economics is guided by competition and not by cooperation. For this reason, from the start, economics introduces foundational conflicts between strong and weak, between creditors and debtors, between imperialist and reliant. The strong remain in the market, the weak disappear from the market. Within such a perverse scenario there is little space for just relations. A minimum level of justice depends on the implementation of just policies by three organizations that manage the current global economic order: the IMF (International Monetary Fund), the World Bank, and the WTO (World Trade Organization).

The IMF and the World Bank are concerned both with avoiding systemic chaos by submitting weak economies or economies in crises to its methodology that always guarantees the payment of a country's external debt to its international creditors, and with securing gains in the financial and economic global system for *the establishment*.

The WTO was structured in such a way that the largest part of commercial contracts are coordinated by the core economies, which control prices, tariffs, subsidies, and the circulation of goods and services.

Social injustice is on the increase, especially in peripheral countries. This kind of injustice has roots in the very history of these countries since these countries were once colonies and for many centuries experienced slavery. Such brutal facts made it impossible for self-development, and established relations of dependence between these peripheral countries and core countries continue to this day. By and large, the societies in these peripheral countries were organized so that the elite held social and political power and held the wider population hostage to its interests and privileges. Many of these countries were submitted to those guidelines imposed by the IMF—guidelines that protect the economic interests of the current global status quo. Often loans are given only if special clauses are accepted as part of the contract, special clauses that force countries to privatize state enterprises, even when these enterprises are concerned with vital, natural, and irreplaceable assets, such as drinking water.

Until these global institutions are permeated by at least a minimum sense of equality and of egalitarian participation, it will be difficult for the current level of social injustice to be overcome. Justice only lives up to its name if it redistributes wealth, and if it is able to share technological advances among all peoples. The United Nations (UN) could be the ideal organism for the implementation of strategic policies aiming at participation and equality, which are the basis for global social justice. But the five global superpowers (i.e., the USA, Russia, Britain, France, and China) hold an antidemocratic power that allows them to veto strategies within the UN that go against their interests; they can manipulate the UN in such a way that it makes it impossible for the UN to fulfil its mission.

Global articulations surrounding the idea of a "just and responsible world" aim at establishing global governance, and seek to implement at least a minimum of social and necessary justice.

This global governance requires another kind of social paradigm, a paradigm that is different from our current one, which contains so many contradictions. The new geosociety, as I have mentioned at various points in this book, must place, among other values, hospitality as a right and a duty of all peoples and of all citizens. Hospitality provides the basis for at least a minimum social justice and is the foundation for long-lasting peace.

The Majority as the Starting Point for Human Rights

I have previously touched on in this book the issue of human rights as a form of inclusion for all and for recognition of differences. I invite the reader to look back at what I have previously written about this issue in this book, especially concerning the rights of nature, of ecosystems, and of the planet Earth.

However, I want to emphasise here a particular point that is very important: the rights of the majority of humankind, which is impoverished and oppressed. If we do not give centrality to the rights of this majority, then human rights continue to be seen as a privilege that is present in some countries, or that is ascribed to certain groups that benefit from national or international systems. When we prioritize the majority, it becomes evident that we must place rights in a hierarchy. First and foremost, we have the right to life and to the means of life, which are guaranteed to all human beings; then, we have the other human rights, such as the right to come and go, the right of opinion, the right to one's own culture and religion, to mention a few.

If we think carefully, the great challenge for the vast majority of humanity is food, work, health, habitation and security. Even when these things are lacking, a person never ceases to reveal itself as a human being. And for this reason they demand to be recognized and respected, they demand access to culture, through which they will be able to elaborate the purpose of their lives, express their own singularities, communicate with others, and ascribe meaning to historical events and to the world.

This partiality in favor of the majority is the condition for universality. If we do not start with the inclusion of this vast majority, then human rights will never be universal—human rights will remain, in practice, the privilege of some.

The rights of these majorities are above the sovereignty of states. When human rights are violated bluntly as in the case of genocide of ethnic or religious groups (and I can cite as examples of this the genocide of Kurds in Iraq and Turkey, and the genocide of Muslims Serbia), the use of military force for humanitarian ends is justified (as it was approved by the UN) as is the pursuit of criminal proceedings for crimes against humanity in the International Court of Justice in The Hague, Holland.

The real content of hospitality is translated in our modern times as the creation of an atmosphere of collective dignity and respect and by the implementation of the kingdom of human rights and of the rights of nature.

Open and Improving Democracy

Full democracy constitutes another form of social inclusion and of concretizing hospitality as I argued in chapter 7 of this book, where I dealt with the issue of rescuing the other.

Any talk about democracy must start with a critical analysis. There is much talk about democracy, but the distorted nature of global societies and of the democracies in place demonstrate that core democratic values are being pushed aside—core values that are revealed by the famous trinity of the French Revolution: liberty, equality, and fraternity.

Historically, democracy appeared with the objective of fulfilling citizens' desire for participation and with the objective of creating social-historical conditions for the implementation of those core values (i.e., liberty, equality, and fraternity), and democracy aims at fulfilling these objectives by taking special care of the weak in society and by using limited means of coercion. Democracy was always understood to be a value, and for this very reason, as it is unlimited: a value to be lived within the family; within communities; within productive processes (though it, by and large, never got through the gates of factories); within institutions, civil society, and politics; and especially as a form of government. There are various types of democracy: direct, representative, political, cultural, economic, liberal, social, bottom-to-top, virtual, de facto, local, global and sociocosmic—this latter being that which I have postulated many times in this text.

However, in the current stage of the process of economic-financial globalization, democracy is being corrupted and is becoming a sort of ideological device for imperialist procedures that seek to deny democracy.

Representative democracy, even when it is well established, as it is in many countries of the world, has become insufficient for dealing with the new problems that emerged with the process of globalization. It can no longer limit itself to universal suffrage and to judicial proceedings whilst making decisions and trying to solve conflicts. The nation-state, which was the basis for representative democracy, has been greatly weakened by the power of multinational corporations. These corporations hold more power and have more economic weight than many countries with a medium-sized GDP. Acting beyond national borders, these corporations obey the capitalist logic and conform to the global market in their continuous pursuit of profit. These corporations are competitive and noncooperative; they privilege individual effort and favor the privatization of all possible assets, even those that are vital, such as water and health; and they have as their central aim the unlimited production of goods and services even when this foments social inequality and has damaging environmental impact.

Wherever these corporations establish themselves, they create serious social inequalities; for their objective is not inclusion but accumulation through the increase of private ownership of both assets and goods. For all these reasons they cannot be democratic. On the contrary, they reveal themselves to be deeply antidemocratic, because they destroy and make difficult egalitarian participation, freedom for all, a spirit of cooperation, and respect for the laws and the rules of the democratic game, which are indispensable values and procedures for the functioning of democracy. The freedom that liberal democracy preaches is the freedom for companies to set business up wherever they want in the world, to trade wherever they want, and to make all kinds of profit; and that all this should be done without any form of legal hindrance or upset, and by absorbing smaller companies and creating oligopolies even at the risk of putting national economies in a vulnerable and critical position.

These great transnational corporations avoid any sort of democratic control. They create a neocolonialist empire that is articulated at a global level.

In the face of this change of contexts, we must rethink democracy as part of a new platform. It is imperative to implement principles, values, and objectives that are capable of creating a new global democratic order and a legal system that is not hostage to great corporations and to superpowers with imperialist aspirations.

From the start, we must guarantee the ethical foundation of democracy, which is centred on valuing the human being as a being-of-relations, compassionate, generous with the construction of a common good and capable of living with others in cooperation and in peace, respectful of differences, caring toward the suffering of others, and conscious that it is a member of the human family and a link in the global community of life—sharing the same origins and the same destiny as the Earth, the Common Home, the Mother of all. All these ethical dimensions are loaded with a strong utopian component. If this feature is not to become an escape from reality, it is important to be aware that positive dimensions are always accompanied by negative ones, and democracy must strive against these negative dimensions on a daily basis and root itself within a process that takes into account the limitations and imperfections of personal and social human conditions.

Then, we must convince ourselves that only democratic citizens can guarantee a democratic society. Only a democratic society can generate and sustain a democratic state. Only democratic states can be propitious to a democratic process of globalization. Only a democratic process of globalization can found a democratic global administration, which stands neither for a supranational state nor for a confederation of states. The concept of a *state* (with territorial sovereignty) was expressed through the Treaty of Westphalia in the seventeenth century, a treaty that put an end to the religious wars in Europe. This created the theoretical and practical basis for the imperialism of stronger states over weaker states. This imperialism provoked conflicts and wars that caused great devastations in the European continent and in European colonies across the world.

Such a model is still in place; however, it is now considered outdated, for it perpetuates the idea that one country should desire to dominate another. What we should be aiming at is the implementation of a true and legitimate political power, which is guided by the principle of responsibility that is shared by all parties, and by the principle of interdependence. On the one hand, this political power will be *global*, and it will see to humanity's global demands; and on the other hand, it will also be *local* as it will do justice to cultural and regional differences without fearing pluralism within a global context—this will be a new phase for humanity. The new democratic power must thus be *"g-local."*

Last, it is important to understand that democracy cannot be imposed from the outside or via a top-to-bottom approach as it has so often been done by European countries on their old colonies, or by the USA on countries that are part of its sphere of influence. The imposition of democracy in this way negates the concept of freedom itself, which is the basis of any form of democracy. To build democracy, it is necessary to undergo a gradual pedagogic process through which people try out active citizenship and fight against individualism, against apathy, and against passivity, which are very much part of a consumerist culture. Democracy emerges as an open reality that is always in an endless process of improvement. Its meaning is to create the conditions to generate a participative and responsible human being who exercises creativity and freedom.

Is this mere utopia? Yes, it is. But this is its proper place, for its role is to present us with values and principles that stimulate alternative practices to the absolute irrationality of the current form of globalization and of the global political approach. It is only through the stimulation of alternative practices that the necessary conditions for a viable hospitality between all the tribes of the Earth will emerge.

Interculturation: a Challenge for Humanity

One phenomenon that is incidentally caused by the process of globalization is the following: the opportunity for all cultures to meet. Real time communication and exchange of information of all kinds have brought people physically together. This situation is a double-edged sword, for it can either rekindle ancient conflicts, or it can be an opportunity to overcome such conflicts. As I have previously mentioned, this represents a particular challenge to Western civilization, for it showed itself to be imperialist and with a desire to colonize; it imposed its vision of the world on other cultures; it exported its technoscience, its mode of production, its administrative model, its lifestyle, and its ideal of happiness that is founded on individualism, on accumulation of material goods, and on consumerism.

When faced with the Western steamroller, cultures feel wary of losing their identities. These cultures react by closing themselves up, by refusing to engage in an inevitable dialogue. This situation is fertile ground for the emergence of fundamentalism and terrorism, and the conditions for the rise of hospitality are considerably hindered.

It is important to consider the issue of culture—of reculturation, of enculturation, and of interculturation. Culture is the concrete framework of a person's and of a society's life (*Lebenswelt*). Culture furnishes people and society with collective dreams; it provides people and society with a meaning for co-living and for communal practices. Culture has two basic functions: it has an intrinsic function, which serves as the binding element, and which serves as a source of identity; and it has an extrinsic function, which serves as an element for differentiation and of dialogue with other cultures. On the one hand, culture roots people; and on the other hand, culture opens people up to the new.

If a colonial and imperialist process is in place, then the original culture is eliminated and is replaced by a foreign culture. A process of deculturation takes place with perverse consequences to people and to society. They lose their identity, they are uprooted, and they can even disappear. Or something else may take place: a cultural blending takes place, a blending in which elements of the dominating culture are assimilated by the subjugated culture. The dominating power imposes its core elements on the subjugated as a way to consolidate its power. This is something that occurred in Latin America and, particularly, in Africa.

In order for an enriching dialogue between cultures to take place, it is necessary, beforehand, that a reculturation of oppressed cultures take place. Through reculturation people and societies recover values, traditions, and identities, and take hold of their culture, and this is a pathway for their liberation and for their ulterior, autonomous development.

The process of globalization necessarily leads to the dialogue of every one with everyone, and enculturation is important for this. Values that are considered fundamental for co-living in a civilized way and for at least a minimum of peace must be assimilated to the matrix of every culture. These values are, for instance, open hospitality, human rights, the rights of the Earth and of ecosystems, democracy, co-living in peace, tolerance, active nonviolence, and good governance.

These values must be taken up by all as a prerequisite for the implementation and functioning of a process of globalization with a human face. These values can only be taken up through pedagogic processes of initiation, trial, and experimentation. And in assimilating these values it is fundamental to have referential figures. Every culture has inspiring characters, such as poets, painters, musicians, religious figures, politicians, and martyrs. Once these have been incorporated by the collective consciousness, they become the heritage of the whole of humanity, and are no longer the heritage of a particular culture. Enculturation is not enough, however. It is imperative to pursue interculturation. Interculturation is the result of the meeting of all cultures—with their own perspectives of the world, with their spiritual pathways, and with ethical and artistic traditions. This is a long and painful process, for it is also the meeting of contradictions, of challenging elements, and of the darker and inhuman dimensions of every culture.

In interculturation we find both complementarities and oppositions. These oppositions may generate conflict, may cause hindrances, and may yield not-very-successful compositions. For this reason it is necessary for a cultural catharsis to occur, a purification of those cultural elements that do not favor convergence with other cultures and that do not contribute to the construction of a peaceful process of globalization.

The issue of power reemerges at this point. We must be vigilant with the exercise of power so that it is not exercised as an imposition or as domination. This is a challenge faced by the West since the West holds the reins of power in the process of globalization. Will the West be willing to reevaluate its economic model that is the source of exclusions? Will the West be willing to reform its society so that it leaves behind its historical trait: that is, its arrogant and imperialist mentality? The West will change to the same extent that it is capable to dialogue with other cultures, some of which are older and wiser than the West. It is only in this way that we will be able to guarantee, along with all other peoples of the Earth, the sustainability of the Earth and Humanity's collective project.

Interculturation represents the great challenge for the whole of humanity, a humanity that marches toward a unity that becomes increasingly greater. This unity cannot stand for the standardization and for the homogenization of all, for this would reveal the domination of a particular culture over all other cultures. This unity is like a mosaic, in which each tessera has its origins in a particular culture. Despite the fact that each tessera comes from a particular culture, these tesseras fit together. They form a sole composition that is well conceived, colorful, diverse, complementary, integrated, and beautiful. Or we could draw another analogy, that is, interculturation is like a colorful material, in which each thread has color and texture. The intertwined composition of these threads produces a consistent, useful, and beautiful fabric.

Another Possible World: A New Paradigm of Civilization

We become increasingly aware that the possibilities and virtualities of the social paradigm that dominated the past few centuries is reaching its end. This paradigm was responsible for elaborating the project of technoscience, for creating the capitalist mode of production, and consequently for creating a culture based on capital and on the political order based on liberal democracy. These factors have been imposed on the whole world and constitute the kind of globalization we currently experience.

The current process of globalization is becoming increasingly destructive as it erodes its own foundations: nature and labor. It devastates nature and its resources in a frightful way, and it liquidates, impinges upon, or forgoes human labor, which is replaced by the computer or by the robot. The current process of globalization has exhausted its utopian reserves and is no longer capable of providing us with a future full of hope for all. On the contrary, its endurance gives rise to daunting scenarios. It has accumulated so much power that it could put an end to the human species and cause substantial damage to the biosphere. Therefore, it has become extremely irrational and dangerous.

It is imperative, it is extremely urgent, to replace it with a new paradigm of civilization if we want to continue to live and have a future. The point is: we either change, or we die. This is the crux of the problem and it has been formulated in the following way in the Earth Charter:

"We stand at a critical moment in Earth's history, a time when humanity must choose its future . . . The choice is ours: form a global partnership to care for Earth and one another or risk the destruction of ourselves and the diversity of life. Fundamental changes are needed in our values, institutions, and ways of living."[3]

What kind of changes are these? In truth, we do not know exactly. What we know is that changes must be global and not merely regional. These changes cannot be mere variations on the old paradigm, something which would prolong what has happened in the past. We must be innovative and produce something new by using the creative capacity of the human imagination and by making use of those historical experiential elements of various cultures that have been pushed aside or wasted. The emergence of the new is being slowly felt in various parts of the Earth.

Millions of people, those involved in grassroots movements for social change, such as we have seen in demonstrations in Porto Alegre (Brazil), Seattle (USA), Genoa (Italy), and Barcelona (Spain) are giving rise to a powerful global trend that demands substantial changes to the web of relations currently underlying globalization. This trend has gained a body in the World Social Forum (WSF).[4] In its fifth meeting in

3. Translator's note: see the Earth Charter online at www.earthcharteraction.org/.

4. Translator's note: The World Social Forum (WSF) is a response to the World Economic Forum (WEF). The WSF was created by various organizations arguing for an alternative process of globalization, and it has received great support and sponsorship

Porto Alegre (Brazil) in 2005, the World Social Forum demanded, for instance, a guarantee of food supply to populations; a moratorium on the privatization of water companies; the cancellation of the foreign debt of countries in the Southern Hemisphere; the dismantling of fiscal paradises; increased taxes on the arms industry and on companies causing the greenhouse effect; actions to tackle racism, sexism, and xenophobia; democratization of the United Nations; and a rigorous opposition to the use of violence and war in solving global problems.

If we pay close attention, we can see that at the heart of the new paradigm is an understanding of life as something diverse and sacred, rather than as a game for the increase of power or the accumulation of wealth. If the new world order does not give centrality to life, which must guide the economy, politics and education, then the new order will not put a stop to the eventual tragedy that has been caused by the old paradigm.

The postulation of life as the matrix that articulates everything can create the conditions for the emergence of an ethics based on care, on prevention, on protection, on responsibility, and on compassion. If all human beings, and the other entities of nature, have a guarantee to life, then hidden forces within themselves and within society will be freed up; hidden forces remain repressed or hidden away during the great effort for survival. As human beings become free from the obsession of always having to gain and accumulate, they will be able to channel their creativity and their capacity to mold the world and themselves.

Despite the inherent contradictions in the human condition, with its darkness and downfalls, life will be able to become that which it is called upon to be: a celebration and a feast. Life is the most beautiful and radiant fruit of the whole of the process of evolution, and it is the supreme gift of the Creator. Life can and must be collectively savored in all its artistic, cultural, and spiritual expressions from all ages and many different traditions.

The Earth will be able to become the garden of Eden, and it will no longer be condemned to be a place of endless quarrels, conflicts of interest, of pity, of sweat, and of tiredness. Such limitations will continue to exist but will be significantly more subtle. With the use of existing

from the Brazilian government and from other organizations. For more information, see: http://www.forumsocialmundial.org.br/. The Web site offers Portuguese, English, French, and Spanish.

technology, which is now democratized, we will all be able to liberate ourselves from the anguish of survival and to enjoy the generosity of nature and the benefits of culture.

The power to allow humanity and the Earth to achieve more advanced stages of interaction and of communion between every one with everyone, with the universe, and with the original Fountainhead of all Being, is in our very hands. However, the fact that a tragedy may occur for lack of awareness, for indifference, for loathing the sacredness of life and of our small and beautiful planet also remains a possibility. If this were to happen, then we would get to know the twilight of the human experiment and its slow and inevitable disappearance.

I anticipate that this will not happen, for the forces of life working along the process of evolution have always showed themselves to be more powerful than chaos and death. Life attracts life and not death— this is the purpose of the universe and the design of the Creator.

Conclusion

The fascinating myth of hospitality provided us with utopian aspects of this virtue, which must be the first one to be lived if the process of unification of the human family is to become a reality. This unification is a complex process that is not sufficiently consolidated yet. Various obstacles stand in the way of the implementation of open hospitality, and these obstacles are particularly found in those countries that have reached a higher stage of social and economic stability, such as the USA and the European Union.

These hindering forces do not invalidate utopia. Utopia continues to inspire motivating forces so that the spirit of hospitality may overcome impediments, prejudice, and hostility toward foreigners, and generally speaking, against migrating people. It is imperative to create an awareness of the urgency of hospitality as soon as possible. We have no alternative. This time the destiny of each people is inseparable from the destiny of all other peoples and from the destiny of the Earth also.

From now on, we will all be actors in the single history of the human species, which is unique and diverse. In order for all to feel actors in this history, hospitality, an open and reciprocal welcome, is essential. Hospitality creates the necessary foundation for other necessary attitudes that will be the object of my study in the two following books: co-living, respect, tolerance, and then communality, communion at the same table.

Hospitality is, from the start, a disposition of the soul, a disposition that is open and unrestricted. In principle, hospitality, just as unconditional love, neither rejects nor discriminates against anyone. Hospitality is simultaneously a utopia and a practice.

As utopia it stands for one of the greatest yearnings in the history of humanity, the yearning to always be welcome, independent of social and moral conditions; and to be treated humanely.

As practice it creates policies that make it possible for and provide guidance for welcoming. But because it is concrete, it suffers from the hindrances and the limitations of given situations.

It is not always possible to create the conditions for acceptable forms of hospitality. Long-term prejudices prevent this from happening. Nationalism, xenophobia, and fundamentalisms are on the rise, closing the doors to thousands of people, and increasing suffering due to rejection.

Nevertheless, it is always important to articulate utopia-ideal with concrete-real, unconditional solidarity with conditional solidarity, so that we do not resign ourselves to the current situation and become indifferent and stop believing in the improvement of the human condition.

It is present in the myth of Baucis and Philemon and in the ancestral memory of humanity: the idea that when one welcomes a foreigner, a pilgrim, a stranger, that one is welcoming God. Therefore, hospitality is intrinsically sacred. Hospitality allows us to meet, within the various ways in which it can be experienced nowadays, the Mystery that is hidden and revealed in everything, and particularly, the Mystery that is hidden and revealed in those human beings who are either close or distant to us. All human beings are potential temples in which we can welcome and anonymously serve the Lord of history and of the universe.

Thus, hospitality dignifies the human being and the divine and it can guarantee the foundations for co-living with at least a minimum of tenderness and friendship between all within the same Common Home, the planet Earth.

Bibliography and Further Reading

Allègre, Claude, J. *Introduction à une histoire naturelle. Du big bang àla disparition de l'homme.* Temps des sciences. Paris: Arthème Fayard, 1992.

Arruda, Ángela. *Representando a alteridade.* Petrópolis: Vozes, 1998.

Assis Carvalho, Edgard de, et al. *Ética, solidariedade e complexidade.* São Paulo: Palas Athena.

Aubert, Jean Marie. *Droits de l'homme et libération évangélique,* Paris: Le Centurion, 1987.

Barloewen, Constantin von. *L'Anthropologie de la mondialisation.* Translated by Olivier Mannoni. Paris: Syrtes, 2003.

Bártholo, Roberto dos Santos, Júnior. *Você e eu: Martin Buber, presença e palavra.* Idéias sustatentáveis. Rio de Janeiro: Garamond, 2001.

Beck, Ulrich. *¿Qué es la globalización?* Paidós Estado y Sociedad 58. Barcelona: Paidós, 1998.

———. *What Is Globalization?* Translated by Patrick Camiller. Malden, MA: Polity, 2000.

Ben Jelloun, Tahar. *Hospitalité française: racisme et immigration maghrebine.* Histoire inmédiate. Paris: Seuil, 1997.

———. *French Hospitality: Racism and North African Immigrants.* Translated by Barbara Bray. European Perspectives. New York: Columbia University Press, 1999.

Betto, Frei. *A obra do artista: uma visão holística do universo.* São Paulo: Ática, 1995.

Bitterli, Urs. *Die "Wilden" und die "Zivilisierten": Die europäisch-überseelische Begegnung.* Beck'sche Sonderausgaben. Munich: Beck, 1976.

Bobbio, Norberto. *The Age of Rights.* Cambridge: Polity, 1996.

Boff, Leonardo. *América Latina: da conquista à nova evangelização.* Campinas: Verus, 2004.

———. *Do iceberg à arca de Noé.* Visionautas. Rio de Janeiro: Garamond, 2003.

———. *Global Civilization: Challenges to Society and Christianity.* Translated by Alexandre Guilherme. Cross Cultural Theologies. London: Equinox, 2005.

———. *Ethos mundial: Um consenso mínimo entre os humanos.* Rio de Janeiro: Sextante, 2003.

———. *Global Civilization: Challenges to Society and to Christianity.* Translated by Alexandre Guilherme. Cross Cultural Theologies. London: Equinox, 2004.

———, and Virgil Elizondo, editors. *Ecology and Poverty: Cry of the Earth, Cry of the Poor.* London: SCM, 1995.

———, et al. *Direitos humanos, direitos dos pobres.* Petrópolis: Vozes, 1991.

Bolen, Jean Shinoda. *Goddesses in Everywoman: A New Psychology of Women.* New York: Harper & Row, 1984.

Brahic, A., et al. *La plus belle histoire de la Terre.* Paris: Seuil, 2001.

Brandão, Carlos Rodrigues. "Impor, persuadir, convidar, dialogar: a cultura do outro." In *Inculturação e Libertação*, by Carlos Rodrigues Brandão et al., 9–26. Coleção "Libertação e teologia." São Paulo: Paulinas, 1988.

Brunel, Pierre, editor. *Companion to Literary Myths: Heroes and Archetypes*. Translated by Wendy Allatson et al. London: Routledge, 1992.

Brunello, Pietro. *Pioneri: Gli italiani in Brasile e il mito della frontiera*. Rome: Donzelli, 1994.

Bruschi, L. C. *A origem da vida e o destino da matéria*. Londrina: UEL, 1999.

Buber, Martin. *I and Thou*. Edinburgh: T. & T. Clark, 1958.

Bücken, Hajo. *Das Fremde überwinden: Vom Umgang mit sich und den anderen*. 8–13. Offenbach: Burckhardthaus-Laetare, 1991.

Campbell, Joseph. *The Masks of God*. New York: Viking, 1959.

———. *Myths to Live By*. London: Souvenir, 1973.

Castells, Manuel. *La era de la información*. 3 vols. Madrid: Alianza, 2007.

Corcoran, Peter Blaze, editor in chief. *The Earth Charter in Action: Toward a Sustainable World*. Amsterdam: KIT, 2005. Online: http://www.earthcharterinaction .org/.

Cortesão, Jaime, editor. *A carta de Pero Vaz de Caminha*, by Pero Vaz de Caminha. Coleçao Clásicos e contemporaneous 1. São Paulo: Livros de Portugal, 1943.

———. "Letter of Pedro Vaz de Caminha to King Manuel, Written from Porto Seguro of Vera Cruz the 1st of May 1500." In *The Voyage of Pedro Álvares Cabral to Brazil and India*, edited and translated by William Brooks Greenlee. London: Hakluyt Society, 1938.

De Duve, Christian Rene. *Vital Dust: Life as a Cosmic Imperative*. New York: Basic, 1995.

Derrida, Jacques. *De l'hospitalité*. Petite bibliothèque des idées Paris: Calmann-Levy, 1997.

———. *Of Hospitality*. Translated by Rachel Bowlby. Cultural Memory in the Present. Stanford: Stanford University Press, 2000.

Di Sante, Carmine. *Lio' Ospitale*. Rome: Lavoro, 2001.

———. *Responsabilità: L'io per L'altro*. Terzo millennio 2. Rome: Lavoro, 1996.

Dostoevsky, Fyodor. "The Dream of a Ridiculous Man." In *Three Tales*. Translated by Beatrice Scott. London: Drummond, 1945.

Dussel, Enríque. *Ética comunitária*. Petrópolis: Vozes, 1987.

———. "Globalization and the Victims of Exclusion: From a Liberation Ethics Perspective." *The Modern Schoolman* 75 (1998) 119–55.

Eliade, Mircea. *Aspects du mythe*. Paris: Gallimard, 1963.

———. *Myth and Reality*. Translated by Willard R. Trask. New York: Harper & Row, 1963.

Elias, Norbert. *La sociedad de los indivíduos*. Historia, ciencia y sociedad 293. Barcelona: Península, 1990.

———. *The Society of Individuals*. Translated by Edmund Jephcote. Cambridge, MA: Blackwell, 1991.

Featherstone, Mike, editor. *Global Culture: Nationalism, Globalization and Modernity*, London: Sage, 1990.

Fiori, José Luis. *O poder americano*. Coleção Zero a esquerda. Petrópolis: Vozes, 2004.

Friedman, Jonathan. *Cultural Identity and Global Process: Nationalism, Globalization, and Modernity*. Theory, Culture & Society. London: Sage, 1994.

Fuchs, Ottmar. *Die Fremden*. Theologie zur Zeit 4. Düsseldorf: Patmos, 1988.

Gentili, Pablo. *Globalização excludente: desigualdade exclusão e democracia na nova ordem mundial*. Petrópolis: Vozes, 1999.

Goetz, Delia, and Sylvanus Griswold Morley, translators. *The Book of the People = Popol vuh: The National Book of the Ancient Quiché Maya*. Los Angeles: Plantin, 1954.

Gouast, René. *La poésie latine des origines au Moyen Age*. Paris: Seghers, 1972.

Gutiérrez, Gustavo. *Dios o el oro en las Indias, siglo XVI*. Colección Bartolomé de slã Casas. Lima: Instituto Bartolomé de las Casas—Rimac, Centro de estudios y publicacciones, 1989.

Habermas, Jürgen. *Theorie des kommunikativen Handelns*. 2 vols. Frankfurt: Suhrkamp, 1981.

———. *The Theory of Communicative Action*. 2 vols. Translated by Thomas McCarthy. Boston: Beacon, 1984–1987.

Havel, Vaclav. "The Need for Transcendence in the Postmodern World." Online: http://www.worldtrans.org/whole/havelspeech.html/.

Hawking, Stephen W. *A Brief History of Time: From the Big Bang to Black Holes*. Toronto: Bantam, 1988.

Held, David. *Democracy and the Global Order: From the Modern State to Cosmopolitan Governance*. Stanford: Stanford University Press, 1995.

Hobsbawn, Eric J. *The Age of Extremes: The Short Twentieth Century, 1914–1991*. London: Abacus, 1996.

Hollis, James. *Tracking the Gods: The Place of Myth in Modern Life*. Studies in Jugian Psychology by Jungian Analysts 68. Toronto: Inner City, 1995.

Huntington, Samuel P. *The Clash of Civilizations and the Remaking of World Order*. New York: Simon & Schuster, 1996.

Illich, Ivan. *Tools for Conviviality*. World Perspectives 47. New York: Harper & Row, 1973.

Jaulin, Robert. *L'ethnocide à travers lles Amériques: Textes ET Documents*. Paris: Fayard, 1972.

———. *El etnocidio através de las Américas*. [México]: Siglo XXI, 1976.

Jáuregui, Gurutz. *La democracia planetária*. Colección Jovellanos de ensayo. Oviedo: Nobel, 2000.

Kant, Immanuel. *Groundwork of the Metaphysic of Morals*. Translated by H. J. Paton. London: Routledge, 1993.

Kersting, Wolfgang. "Hobbes, Kant, a paz universal e a guerra contra o Iraque." *Fragmentos de Cultura* 14 (2004) 841–45.

Kohr, Martin. *Rethinking Globalization: Critical Issues and Policy Choices*. A Global Issues London: Zed, 2001.

Kristeva, Julia. *Stranieri a se stessi*. Translated by A. Sera. Milan: Feltrinelli, 1990.

———. *Strangers to Ourselves*. Translated by Leon S. Roudiez. New York: Columbia University Press, 1991.

Krugman, Paul R. *Pop Internationalism*. Cambridge: MIT Press, 1996.

Ianni, Octávio. *A era do globalismo*. Rio de Janeiro: Civilização Brasileira, 1996.

Jacquard, Albert. *De l'angoisse à l'espoir*. Paris: Calmann-Lévy, 2002.

———. *Lições de ecologia humana da angústia à esperança*. Epistemologia e sociedade 214. Lisbon: Lisboa Instituto Piaget, 2004.

Leonardi, Victor. "Para além das raízes." In *Entre àrvores e esquecimentos. Hístoria social dos sertões do Brasil*. Brasília: UnB.

León-Portilla, Miguel. *The Broken Spears: The Aztec Account of the Conquest of México.* Boston: Beacon, 1962.

——. *Visíon de los vencidos: relaciones indígenas de la conquista.* México: Universidad Nacional Autônom, 1959.

Lesch, W. "Alterität und Gastlichkeit. Zur Philosophie von Emmanuel Lévinas." In *Die Fremden,* by Ottmar Fuchs, 128–43. Theologie zur Zeit 4. Düsseldorf: Patmos.

Lévinas, Emmanuel. *Alterity and Transcendence.* Translated by Michael B. Smith. European Perspectives. New York: Columbia University Press, 1999.

——. *De l'existence à l'existant.* Paris: Vrin, 1978.

——. *Existence and Existents.* Translated by Alphonso Lingis. Boston: Kluwer, 1988.

——. *La traccia dell'altro.* Napoli: Libreria Pironti, 1979.

Loenhoff, Jens. *Interkulturelle Verständigung: Zum Problem grenzüberschreitender Kommunikation.* Opladen: Leske-Budrich, 1992.

Longair, M. S. *The Origins of our Universe: A Study of the Origin and Evolution of the Contents of Our Universe: The Royal Institute Christmas Lectures for Young People 1990.* Cambridge: Cambridge University Press, 1991.

Lovelock, James. *Gaia: A New Look at Life on Earth.* Oxford: Oxford University Press, 1979.

Maalouf, Amin. *The Crusades through Arab Eyes.* New York: Schocken, 1985.

Maïla, Joseph. "Des conflits identitaires à la cohabitation interculturelle." *Foi et Développement* (2004).

——. "Enjeux stratégiques mondiaux: Des conflits indentitaires à la cohabitation interculturelle." *Foi et Développement* (2004).

Melucci, Alberto. *L'invenzione del presente: movimenti sociali nelle società complesse.* Stdui e riserche 281. Bologna: Il Mulino, 1991.

——. *Nomads of the Present: Social Movements and Individual Needs in Contemporary Society.* Edited by John Keane and Paul Mier. Philadelphia: Temple University Press, 1989.

——. *Passagio d'epoca: Il futuro è adesso.* Milan: Idee Feltrinelli, 1994.

——. *Vivencia y convivencia: teoria social para una era de la información.* Madrid: Trotta, 2002.

Melville, A. D., translator. *Metamorphoses,* by Ovid, with an introduction and notes by E. J. Kenney. Oxford: Oxford University Press, 1986.

Metz, Johannes Baptist. "Das Christentum und die Fremden. Perspektive einer multikulturellen Religion." In *Schwierige Fremdheit,* edited by Friedriche Balke, 154–73. Geschichte Fischer. Frankfurt: Fischer, 1993.

Mieth, Dietmar, and Lisa Sowle Cahill, editors. *Migrants and Refugees.* Concilium 1993/4. London: SCM, 1993.

Moltmann, Jürgen. "Die Entdeckung des Anderen: Zur Theorie des kommunikativen Handelns." *Evangelische Theologie* 50 (1990) 400–414.

Moreno, Cézar. *A colonização e o povoamento do Baixo Jequitinhonha no século XIX: A Guerra "justa" contra os índios.* Coleção Testemunho Jequitinhonha 4. Belo Horizonte: Canoa das Letras, 2001.

Morin, Edgar. *L'identité humaine.* Méthode 5. Paris: Seuil, 2001.

——, and Anne Brigitte Kern. *Terre-patrie.* Paris: Seuil, 1993.

Morris, Richard. *O que sabemos sobre o universo: realidade e imaginação científica.* Rio de Janeiro: Zahar.

Mourão, Ronaldo R. de Freitas. *Do universo ao multiverso: uma nova visão do cosmos.* Petrópolis: Vozes, 2001.

Moutappa, Jean. *Dieu et la révolution du dialogue: L'ère des échanges entre les religions.* Paroles vives. Paris: Albin Michel, 1996.

Müller, Robert. *The Birth of Global Civilization.* Anacortes, WA: World Happiness and Cooperation, 1991.

———. *O nascimento de uma civilização global.* São Paulo: Aquariana, 1993.

Novello, Mário. *Le cercle du temps: un regard scientifique sur les voyages non conventionnels dans le temps.* Atlantisciences. Biarritz: Atlantica, 2001.

Ntabona, Adrien. "L'Interculturalité, avenir de l'humanité." *Foi et Développement* 1–4 (2001–2002).

Oller i Sala, M. Dolors. *Ante una democracia de "baja intensidad": La democracia a construir.* C. F. (Barcelona) 56. Barcelona: Cristianisme i Justícia, 1994.

———. "Un futuro para la democracia: una democracia para la gobernabilidad mundial." In *Cuadernos Cristianismo y Justicia* 115 (2002) Barcelona.

Paris, Ginette. *Pagan Meditations: The Worlds of Aphrodite, Artemis, and Hestia.* Dallas: Spring, 1986.

Pearson, Carol S. *El héroe interior.* Madrid: Mirach, 1991.

———. *The Hero Within: Six Archetypes We Live By.* San Francisco: Harper & Row, 1986.

Pureza, José Manuel. *O património comum da humanidade: rumo a um direito internacional da solidariedade?* Saber imaginar o social. Porto: Afrontamento, 1998.

———, editor. *Para uma cultura da paz.* Andamimes do mundo 1. Coimbra: Quarteto, 2001.

Ramírez, Salvador Vergés. *Derechos y libertades hoy: evolución y progreso.* Nuevo diálogo 15. Madrid: San Pablo, 2000.

Ricouer, Paul. *Oneself as Another.* Translated by Kathleen Blamey. Chicago: University of Chicago Press, 1994.

Robertson, Roland. *Globalization: Social Theory and Global Culture.* Theory, Culture & Society. London: Sage, 1992.

Saad, Gabriel. *Signes et rites de l'hospitalité dans la traduction.* Clermont-Ferrand: Presses Universitaires Blaise Pascal, 2001.

Sahtouris, Elisabet. *Earthdance: Living Systems in Evolution.* San Jose, CA: iUniverse.

Santos, Sílvio Coelho dos. *Os índios xokleng, memória visual.* Florianópolis: UFSC, 1997.

Sartre, Jean-Paul. *"No Exit" and Three Other Plays.* Translated by Stuart Gilbert and Lionel Abel. New York: Vintage, 1958.

Schmitt, Carl. *The Concept of the Political.* Translation, introduction, and notes by George Schwab. Chicago: University of Chicago Press, 1996.

Schüssler Fiorenza, Elisabeth, and M. Shawn Copeland, editors. *Feminist Theology in Different Contexts.* Concilium 1996/1. Maryknoll, NY: Orbis, 1996.

Sella, Adriano. *Globalização neoliberal e exclusão social.* Temas de atualidade. São Paulo: Paulus, 2002.

Sepúlveda, Juan Ginés de. *Tratado sobre las justas causas de la guerra contra los índios.* México: Fondo de Cultura Económica, 1979.

Ska, Jean Louis. *Abramo e suoi ospiti: il patriarca e i credenti nel Dio unico.* Collana Bíblica. Bologna: EDB, 2003.

Souza Santos, Boaventura de. *A crítica da razão indolente: contra o desperdício da experiência.* São Paulo: Cortez, 2000.

————. *A crítica da razão indolente. Contra o desperdício da experiência.* 3rd ed. São Paulo: Cortez, 2001.

————. *Pela mão de Alice: o social e o político na pós-modernidade.* Biblioteca das ciências do homem: Sociologia, epistemologia 18. Porto: Afrontamento, 1994.

Spedicato, Paolo. "Anziosi di andare alla caccia del selvaggio." *Suplemento Mosaico Italiano* 15 Setembro 2004.

Swimm, Brian, and Thomas Berry. *The Universe Story: From the Primordial Flaring Forth to the Ecozoic Era—A Celebration of the Unfolding of the Cosmos.* San Francisco: HarperSanFrancisco, 1992.

Tarter, Sandro. *La riva di un altro mare. Alterità, soggettività, giustizia a partire da Lévinas.* Pubblicazioni di scienze filosofiche e politiche 14. Pisa: ETS, 1995.

Teilhard de Chardin, Pierre. "La formation de la 'noosphère.'" In *The Future of Man*, 149–78. Translated by Norman Denny. London: Fontana, 1968.

Todorov, Tzvetan. *The Conquest of America: The Question of the Other.* Translated by Richard Howard. Norman: University of Oklahoma Press, 1999.

————. *Nós e os outros: A reflexão francesa sobre a diversidade humana.* Rio de Janeiro: Zahar, 1996.

Touraine, Alain. *¿Poderemos viver juntos? Iguais e Differentes.* Petrópolis: Vozes, 1999.

Toynbee, Arnold. *Experiences.* London: Oxford University Press, 1969.

Ward, Peter. *The End of Evolution: On Mass Extinctions and the Preservation of Biodiversity.* New York: Bantam, 1994.

Whitmont, Edward C. *Return of the Goddess.* New York: Crossroad, 1997.

Wilson, Edward O. *The Future of Life.* London: Abacus, 2003.

Woolger, Jennifer Barker, and Roger J. Woolger. *The Goddess Within: A Guide to the Eternal Myths That Shape Women's Lives.* London: Rider, 1990.

Zaoual, Hassan. "Pour un dialogue des civilisations." *Foi et Développement* (2002) 1–5.

Zohar, Danah, and Ian Marshall. *SQ: Spiritual Intelligence; The Ultimate Intelligence.* London: Bloomsbury, 2000.

book 2

Co-living, Respect, and Tolerance

Preface

This is the second book in the series Virtues: For Another Possible World, and it is titled *Co-Living, Respect, and Tolerance.*

To tell the truth, respect and tolerance are contained within the virtue of co-living, which is a core category of the global phase of humanity. I have decided, however, to give separate attention to these as they are connected to complex issues.

I shall follow the same methodology used in book I, the volume on hospitality, and therefore I shall introduce the topic through the use of narratives sourced on emotional intelligence. In this way the reader will be able to grasp the virtue firsthand before analyzing the concept. After concepts are fully given, they will serve as instruments for a proper understanding of these virtues as well as for understanding the articulations of virtues with other dimensions of human existence within the context of the process of globalization. However, understanding a virtue is not enough in itself. It is necessary to apply it to life so to make life virtuous—this is the important point.

I am convinced that the crisis, something which is characteristic to paradigm changes, will meet a satisfactory solution if we are able to illustrate a new ethics that is intelligible to the greatest possible number of people and that can be implemented immediately.

We do not have much time. As the Earth Charter warns us, "The foundations of global security are threatened. These trends are perilous—but not inevitable."[1] Our Common Home (*ethos* in Greek) requires an ethic that is able to maintain an integrated human family, that minimizes the risk of an eventual devastation of life, and that guarantees a future of hope for humanity and the chain of life: thus the importance of the virtues of hospitality, co-living, respect, tolerance, and communality.

1. Translator's note: See the Earth Charter online: http:// www.earthcharterin action.org/.

At a time when our destiny and the destiny of the Earth have been placed on our hands, these virtues are fundamental to a common outlook based on values that will provide sustainability to a new conception of civilization.

Petrópolis, 1st January 2006

nine

Co-Living

Hospitality opens the door and welcomes in; co-living allows for sitting together and to coexist and to exchange. Co-living is just as important as hospitality for these virtues extend and complement each other.

Normally, hospitality is for a determinate period. Nobody remains permanently as someone's guest. When it becomes permanent, such as in the case of political refugees or those who immigrate for economic or ethnic reasons, the individual becomes part of the society to which it has immigrated. It is at this point that the issue of co-living becomes apparent; co-living is pertinent to a situation of permanent or long duration.

At any rate, co-living must be fully understood so that it can reveal all the richness hidden in it. I shall make considerable effort to theorize and properly explicate the virtue of co-living as well as trying to draw a distinction between this virtue and other forms of being together.

The issue of co-living raises some questions:

- Why live together?
- How to live together?

Before tackling these questions and following the methodology already used in book 1, I shall relate an experiential narrative about co-living, which is one of the most notable in the history of cultural ethnology and anthropology. It occurred in Brazil, but its meaning is universal.

Co-Living: The Midwives of a People

In this experiential narrative we are confronted with a special meeting between the Christian faith and a particular native Indian culture. Normally, the propagation of Christianity is done by the various churches through announcing the message of Jesus, which is collected in the four gospels. This announcement is always done from a particular cultural perspective and from churches' institutional models.

There is the Catholic model of evangelization, which aims at the implementation of the Church with dioceses, parishes, communities, catechism, sacraments, liturgical feasts, centers for the formation of clergy, charitable institutions, hospitals and schools; and all these have as a central and common reference the figure of the pope in Rome, who guarantees the unity of the doctrine and of the organization.

There is the Protestant (i.e., Lutheran, Presbyterian, Baptist, and others) model of evangelization, which creates, wherever they establish themselves, Christian communities with celebrations, welfare institutions, and schools, that are connected to the mother community in the country of origin but with relative autonomy. And there are other models, but these are not relevant here.

All these models embody power and are easily aligned with other social and political powers in their pursuit for the implementation of the Christian faith. In this way, during the times of colonization in Latin America, Africa, and Asia, the throne and the altar, the colonizer and the missionary, forged a single project and together implemented the new political and religious order. The gospel of power, and not the power of the gospel, reigned. This strategy to evangelize from a position of power was dominant for centuries and can still be seen in the strategic policies of the central government of the Roman Catholic Church in the Vatican, and to some extent in all other major historical churches. This is an imperialist perspective of the evangelic mission, for the objective is to incorporate new Christians into the Christian history of those core countries where Christianity first established itself.

This strategy was dominant, but by no means was it the only one. Some missionary figures showed themselves to have a sensitivity to cultural differences. These missionaries tried a different pathway for their missionary work, and this is something meaningful even nowadays, for it represents a different paradigm, a paradigm which is not connected to power. A missionary belonging to this tradition is Saint Francis of Assisi in the thirteenth century and his attitude toward Muslims. Another is Bartolomé de las Casas in the sixteenth century and his attitude towards native Indians of Mesoamerican cultures. These figures approached other peoples of different races, languages, and religions through a peaceful, fraternal, and loving attitude of co-living. They tried to preach the gospel without the apparatus of power and only through love, dialogue, encounter, entry into the host culture, and an exemplary life.

In our modern times, this method was resurrected by Brother Charles de Foucauld (1858–1916), a French clergyman with a deep spirituality, who went to live with Muslims in the Algerian desert at the beginning of the twentieth century. His aim was not to announce explicitly the gospel but simply to share life with them and to embrace the difference of culture and religion within the spirit of Jesus, who sees all as brothers and sisters visited by divine grace. This experience was interrupted when Brother Charles was murdered due to internal quarrels within the Muslim community. He remains a source of inspiration and an example.

He was the inspiration and the example for the Sisters of Jesus, who are followers of Brother Charles. Their Algeria was the northeast of the Brazilian state of Mato Grosso in central Brazil, an area close to the Araguaia River, where the native Indians of the Tapirapé nation faced serious difficulties.

In October 1952 the Sisters were advised by some French Dominican friars who were missionaries in the region that the Tapirapé faced extinction. The original population of fifteen hundred people was now reduced to forty-seven people due to wars with the Caiapó nation (who were their longstanding enemies), due to diseases brought in by white settlers, and due to a lack of women in the tribe. Following the spirit of the teachings of Brother Charles, the Sisters decided to go and live with the Tapirapé, not to convert but to share in the fate of this people.

When they arrived, Sister Genoveva, a pioneer who still lives with the tribe, heard the following statement from *cacique*[1] Marcos: "The Tapirapé will disappear. The white people will finish us. The land has value, the game has value, the fish has value. But the native Indian has no value whatsoever." The Tapirapé had internalized that they were not worth anything and that they were condemned to disappear. They had resigned themselves to their fate, their tragic end.

By being faced with such a tragedy, the Sisters decided humbly to ask permission to stay with the tribe so that they could live with them,

1. Translator's note: *Cacique* is a word from Aruaque, a language spoken by various native Indian tribes in Latin America. It can be translated in English as "chief."

and who knows, help to change the awaited tragic end. They were welcomed without any reluctance. At the beginning, the Sister decided not to live in the *taba*, in the communal hut. They decided to live close by in a wood cabin, and they constructed a little chapel in one of its corners. They started to live the gospel of fraternity with the Tapirapé by helping them in the orchards, by enduring with them as they strived for their daily meals, by learning their language and by encouraging their culture, customs and religion. This was a charitable pathway, which did not seek returns.

As time went by and trust was gained the Sisters were incorporated into the tribe. Despite being different the Sisters opted to become equal to, and became equal through living with, the Tapirapé. And they are treated as such by the Tapirapé even today.

Slowly, the Tapirapé regained their self-esteem. Thanks to the Sisters mediations, women from the Karajá, another native Indian tribe, accepted to marry with Tapirapé men and this guaranteed the continuation of the tribe. From 47 people they now amount to over 500 people in 2005.[2]

In 50 years the Sisters did not convert a single member of the tribe. But they managed much more: they became the midwives of a people, and they did this in the light of the teaching—"I came that they may have life, and have it abundantly" (John 10:10).

In October 2002 I had the privilege of being invited to the festivities marking the 50th year anniversary of the Sisters living with the Tapirapé in Santa Terezinha, state of Mato Grosso, close to the Araguaia River. Dom Pedro Casaldáliga (poet, prophet, and defender of the rights of native Indians and of peasants), who always supported the sisters and who always encouraged the Sisters to live with the Tapirapé, was also present at the festivities.[3]

On that occasion, I noticed whilst looking at the face of a typical young Tapirapé Indian girl and that of Sister Genoveva, that if Sister Genoveva had died her grey hair with local vegetable die (as the Tapirapé do) then she could have easily been mistaken for a Tapirapé woman. Through living with the Tapirapé she became physically similar to them,

2. Cf. Künsch, *O renacer do povo Tapirapé.*

3. Translator's note: Dom Pedro Casaldaliga was born in Spain and has lived in Brazil since 1968. He is the bishop of São Felix de Araguaia, Mato Grosso, Brazil. He is often called "a militant of hope."

and this is so because she incorporated the soul of the Tapirapé culture. In fact, she fulfilled the prophecy of the founder of her order when she sent the Sisters to live with the native Indians: "The Sisters must become Tapirapé, so that they can go to and love others. But they will always be Tapirapé."

This is an example of co-living and of living the gospel without any connection with power, where power is understood as word, or reason, or theology, or church, or any other instance of social, political or cultural power. This is an inspiring example for human attitudes if we want to meet the challenges that yield from humanity's global phase.

How Are We to Live with Those Who Are Most Different?

Following my methodology of presenting some sort of narrative, metaphor, or myth to introduce and illustrate the virtue of co-living, I wish to refer here to a beautiful parable of Jesus that demonstrates, concretely, how we should treat those who are most different and distant from us. It is commonly known as the Parable of the Good Samaritan. I shall place it within its historical context so that it is better understood.

The land of Israel encompassed two kingdoms, one in the North the other in the South. The books of the Old Testament inform us that the capital of the Northern kingdom was Samaria, and that the capital of the Southern kingdom was Jerusalem.

Due to internal conflicts that are not relevant here and therefore will not be analysed, the two kingdoms became separate. The Northern kingdom was composed of ten of the twelve tribes of Israel. However, its capital, Samaria, was conquered in 722 BCE by the Assyrians, and thirty thousand Samaritans were deported and were replaced by foreigners of various backgrounds. In very little time the population became mixed-raced.

Such facts caused Jews to build a strong prejudice against the Samaritans. This prejudice was particularly noticeable in the inhabitants of Jerusalem, who had very strong feelings about the purity of their race and religion. And therefore, there were notorious hostilities between Jews and Samaritans (cf. John 4:9; 8:48).

The prejudice worsened when the Samaritans decided to accept only the Pentateuch, the first five books of the Bible, and so reject all other books, such as the books by prophets and sages; and moreover, relations deteriorated when the Samaritans built their own temple on Mount Gerizim, which rivalled in importance the temple in Jerusalem (cf. John 4:20).

This was the situation met by Jesus. However, he did not share in the prejudice held by Jews towards Samaritans and vice versa. So much so that he held a private conversation with a Samaritan women close to Jacob's well (cf. John 4:4–8), despite this being a scandalous situation for the time, and cured ten Samaritan lepers (cf. Luke 17:16), and most importantly, told the story of an anonymous Samaritan who, when found the victim of a robbery, filled himself with compassion and a caring attitude and helped the victim with no prejudice.

Jesus made this gesture of the good Samaritan a fundamental criterion for the true attitude towards the other, and in particular when the other is someone that is not close to us, someone whom we do not know, and in the case of the parable, someone who is in need. In the language of the Bible, someone in need is the very definition of someone who is our neighbor (cf. Luke 10:30–38). Therefore, the parable is about living with the other, and in particular with those who suffer and are in need.

Let me now refer to the text of this parable for this will allow me to explain further the issue of living with the other and with the different within an ethnic and religious context. This parable is narrated by the evangelist, Saint Luke (10:30–38). Here is the text:

The Story of the Good Samaritan

"Teacher, what should I do to inherit eternal life?" He said to him, "What is written in the law? How do you read?" And he answered, "You shall love the Lord your God with all your heart, and with all your soul, and with all your strength, and with all your mind; and your neighbor as yourself." And he said to him, "You have answered right; do this, and you will live." But he, desiring to justify himself, said to Jesus, "And who is my neighbor?"

Jesus did not provide a theoretical explanation, which is not always convincing; rather, he narrated a story, the story of the good Samaritan. As it happens in every story, the meaning of the narrative is told, explained and revealed with much emotion and passion. This narrative is similar in beauty and tension to the myth of Baucis and Philemon, which is provided in the first book of this trilogy.

Let me continue with the narrative.

"A man was going down from Jerusalem to Jericho, and he fell among robbers, who stripped him and beat him, and departed, leaving him half dead. Now by chance a priest was going down that road; and when he saw him he passed by on the other side. So likewise a Levite, when he came to the place and saw him, passed by on the other side. But a Samaritan, as he journeyed, came to where he was; and when he saw him, he had compassion, and he went to him and bound up his wounds, pouring on oil and wine; then he set him on his own beast and brought him to an inn, and took care of him. And the next day he took out two denarii and gave them to the innkeeper, saying, 'Take care of him; and whatever more you spend, I will repay you when I come back'. Which of these three, do you think, proved neighbor to the man who fell among robbers?" He said, "The one who showed mercy on him." And Jesus said to him, "Go and do likewise."

Let me now explain this narrative. What attitude should we assume when faced by someone who has been robbed, beaten up, and left for dead?

Co-Living: Approaching, Seeing, Having Pity, and Taking Care

The first attitude we can identify in the parable is a totally uncaring attitude. The priest and the Levite see the other in need, but are not concerned. They pass by completely untouched.

The priest descends from the sacerdotal family of Zadoc, he belongs to the higher sacerdotal cast; he presides over worship and is versed in the doctrines, which he teaches others. He knows well that (within the Jewish tradition, and particularly the tradition derived from the prophets) true worship of God, the worship that most pleases God, is to help the poor, the widow, the orphan, the needy and not the offering of bulls and lambs, incense and prayers (cf. Isaiah 1:10–17). But all this wisdom did not help him. He did not help the needy on the road. Perhaps, he has some sort of excuse: he must take part in an important feast at the Temple and he cannot be late.

The Levite, of the ancient sacerdotal family of Levi, belongs to the lower sacerdotal cast. He helps at the temple, he looks after furnishings and utensils, he keeps holy places clean, and he helps in the sacrifices of bulls, lambs and birds. He also saw the man "stripped, beaten, and half dead," but he was not touched. Certainly, he also must have had some sort of excuse: there are many tasks at the temple that must be done, the altar must be prepared and floors must be cleaned of the blood of the sacrificial animals. Perhaps, he was also running late. He must not lose time and thus he leaves the needy unattended on the road.

Both of the members of the chosen people of sacerdotal lineage did not approach the other because they did not go close to the needy and denied the needy the minimum of co-living.

The second attitude is of someone who sees, is touched and changes his or her plans. This attitude shows hospitality and care. This is the attitude of the Samaritan, a mixed-raced Jew who is considered a heretic and with whom one should not have contact. Therefore, the virtue is demonstrated by he from whom, according to the understanding of the time, one could not except anything good, for the Samaritan is outside the divine law.

What does the Samaritan do? The narrative is very detailed. He is travelling and when he sees the "stripped, beaten and half dead" man he puts his travels on hold. He does not make any excuse, he does not say he is running late, he does not say that he risks being robbed by thieves. He puts obvious and prudential concerns aside and focus solely on the other. He overcomes all distances for he "went to him." He forgets about himself and about his voyage when he "saw" the other. He does not see the other in a 'cold manner', as a journalist who, due to his or her profession, must be objective with his camera so that he can relate truthfully what he or she saw. The Samaritan sees with the eyes of the heart for he fills himself with "compassion."

Compassion, according to the Buddhist tradition, a tradition which lives and explains this attitude so well, implies two moments. The first moment is a moment of stripping and of detachment. Stripping and detachment involves forgetting oneself and forgetting one's interests so that one can concentrate solely on the other. It is important to "see" the other as the other and not as an extension of oneself or of one's I-sphere.

The second moment is a moment of care. Care is expressed through departing from oneself in the direction of the other, and this gesture is translated as solidarity in the service of and in welcoming the other. Compassion means to assume the same 'passion' of the other. That is to say, to suffer with whoever suffers. But it also meant to be joyful with whoever is joyful. It is important to make communion, to walk together, to live together, to mutually offer one's shoulders and one's hands.

The text emphasizes that the Samaritan "went to him," to the most different, because he was "stripped, beaten and half dead." The Samaritan did not ask, as Jesus' interlocutor did: "And who is my neighbor?" My neighbor is not a given and definite reality, such as for instance, a relative, an inhabitant of my own town, or someone of my own religion, or a professional colleague. My neighbor is anyone whom I approach.

Thus, this invalidates any good reason for thinking to oneself and wondering: "there are so many "important" things to do, just as many that require my attention, I have no time to waste"; or "there are risks in helping." Whoever still thinks like this, has not comprehended the creative force of love and compassion and is not capable of overcoming prejudices, personal interests and fears. Within this scenario, the other continue to be the other, alone and helpless, enduring his or her pains, fallen at the side of the road.

However, the Samaritan "went to him." It was up to him, to the Samaritan, to make the other into his neighbor. My neighbor is whomever I approach. I define myself through the inclusion of the other and by giving priority to the other. The other represents a challenge to me, the other yells a screeching noise, the other puts his hand forward searching for help. When I bend forward towards the other that is when I see the emergence of my neighbor. As we know, one's attitude when faced by the other gives rise to ethics. The Samaritan acted ethically, and for this reason, he became known as "the good Samaritan."

The Samaritan concretely lives the proximity of the other for he "bound up his wounds." Moreover, if we update the parable into modern speech: "the Samaritan placed him in his cart and took him to the closest hospital"; in short, "the Samaritan took good care of him." The Samaritan took good care of him not only in this first instance, but later also as he left a good sum to cover expenses and even said: "and whatever more you spend, I will repay you when I come back." He was consonant with the utmost form of co-living and with unconditional hospitality to the very end.

It is at this point in the parable that Jesus asks: "Which of these three, do you think, proved neighbor to the man who fell among robbers?" And the answer to Jesus question was crystal clear: "The one who showed mercy on him."

This answer does not need to be explained. It is self-explanatory.[4]

Therefore, I am responsible for turning the other into my neighbor, or not. Each and every person who is in need and who crosses my path is my neighbor if I approach him or her. It does not matter his or her religious, social, or ethnic background. The important thing is my own attitude of approach to him or her, whoever he or she is. When I do this I make him or her my neighbor.

This attitude of openness and of co-living constituted the very trade mark of early Christianity (and perhaps also of other spiritual pathways and social institutions); but then Christianity associated itself with worldly powers and this changed Christianity dramatically. This change can still be spotted in our modern times: Christianity includes and excludes, it draw limits and for this reason it has victimizing characteristics, particularly with reference to issues connected to gender, family morals and sexuality.

We find in Origen of Alexandria (185–254 CE), who is perhaps the foremost theological genius of early Christianity, an example of peaceful and tolerant co-living. He lived in Alexandria, in the North of Egypt, and then in Caesarea, in Israel, in a very free intellectual environment, which placed Christianity as a singular spiritual movement that was not enclosed and was always in dialogue with other intellectual pathways, such as Neo-Platonic, Aristotelian, and Gnostic. For this reason he did not make dogmatic statements or professions of faith; rather, he employed a discourse founded on dialogue that searched truth through processes. He believed that revealed truth has a singular logic, which articulates with the logic of other knowledge spheres and with other spiritual pathways, for the Holy Spirit works through all of them. Thus, Origen was very articulate in his use of reason and produced a very eloquent discourse in advocating the reasonableness of the Christian proposal without negating the validity of other proposals. Hundreds of people, even non-Christians, attended his courses. Many of these non-

4. There is a vast literature on the exegetic explanation of the parable of the Good Samaritan. I consider the following titles good sources: Marshall, *The Gospel of Luke*, 444–50; Monseleweski, *Der barmherzige Samariter*; Sellin, "Lukas als Gleichniserzähler," 166–89; "Lukas als Gleichniserzähler," 19–60; Eulenstein, "Und wer ist mein Nächster (Lk 10,25–37)," 127–45.

Christians decided to convert to Christianity, but others did not feel this urge though they felt edified. But they held much respect for each other. This rational and dialogical movement gave birth to theology as a rational pathway for the Christian faith that is always open to new enquiries and new interlocutors.

In the fourth century and within the context of the Roman Empire, however, orthodoxy condemns Origen's approach for considering it dangerous and even heretical. This orthodoxy sought and constructed the unity and security of Christianity through creating dogmatic formulations that must be imposed and believed by all and that challenges the doctrines of other religions and of other spiritual pathways. As this is not always easy and viable, religious power made use of the political and imperial power of the time to reach its objectives. Then again imperial power, which was in decline, made use of Christianity to strengthen its position, and declares Christianity to be the official religion of the Empire and thus the state itself starts to impose those dogmas on all its inhabitants. This strategy was explicitly used by the Emperor Constantine and later by the Emperor Justinian.[5] Due to this, co-living becomes something forced, the famous *compelle intrare*, that is to say, "forced to enter," and this is in opposition to the very nature of co-living since it is based on the respect for alterity (i.e., otherness) and on the search for points in common.

What Is Co-Living?

Now that I have provided this lengthy introduction sourced on a narrative about the *reality* of co-living, I can progress and put together the *concept* of co-living. This will be a theoretical effort aiming at providing the foundations for the practice of co-living.

It is important to understand the concept of co-living not as an enclosed definition but as a clearly outlined understanding, as an understanding that is the final result of a process of approximation and of attaining knowledge of the other and of the different. This process has various stages which are described below.

5. Cf. Fürst, "Identität und Toleranz in frühen Christentum," 26–31.

Steps toward Co-Living

From the beginning, the other always represents a challenge either because of the feeling of strangeness that it provokes in us or because the other is not someone from our own sphere. As such the other always represents a challenge that must be comprehended and deciphered.

Some questions arise when we first meet the other: Where does the other come from? What does the other want here? How long is the other staying? What are we to do with the other? How are we to approach the other? Is it possible to live with the other? These questions may seem inappropriate and compromising to the unconditional character of hospitality and co-living, but they arise spontaneously when we are confronted with the foreigner and the stranger.

To understand the other presupposes the possibility of overcoming the distance that separates us from him or her. This is about establishing a bridge between two people who consider each other as different. When I dealt with the issue of hospitality I argued that welcoming, listening to the other, dialoguing with the other, among other things, as ways of understanding the other at an intellectual, but also practical, level. When mutual strangeness is overcome and initial fears subdued, a pathway for a living and real understanding is open.

To understand implies, inevitably, forming a representation and a conception of the other and this is a process that has to do with conceiving. To conceive always involves two people, who exchange between themselves and who intertwine their lives. And from conceiving something new is born, something that is the fruit of two people. The French verb for 'to know', *con-naître*, translates well this phenomenon of mutual collaboration: to know is equivalent to 'to be born together'.

It is not possible, however, 'to be born together' if prejudices and cultural preconceptions prevail. Prejudices and cultural preconceptions are crystalized conceptions that impede the creation of a new conception that is born out of the encounter between two people. Prejudice is an obstacle and a hindering force, and it is not always easy to overcome, and impedes the attaining of true knowledge. Albert Einstein said with irony: "It is easier to disintegrate an atom than a prejudice."

The biblical precept "do not make images of God" has a great pedagogical value for human inter-relations. If an image in made, then the opportunity for a living encounter has already been lost as it has been replaced by an iconic representation. The biblical imperative is "to rise and to lift up your eyes," "to welcome the hungry, the thirsty, the migrant, and the naked." In doing so, we free ourselves from images and we are able to see the other as the other and welcome him or her.

If this attitude is assumed, then a new phase of *participative and committed observation*, which is always a two-way street, starts. One has an interest in the other, and vice versa. One presents oneself to the other, and vice versa; reciprocity takes hold.

Language is important in this new phase. To know the other's language is to know the other's soul. In a globalized world, the continuation and the teaching and learning of a language allows a people to maintain its own living identity and culture. This also creates the conditions for exchange. To learn a language is to open a universe. A language is a sort of metaphysics, that is to say, an interpretation of the world, of the human being and of God. There will always be a *lingua franca* through which people are able to establish communication more easily, even if missing out on the singularities that can only be expressed in one's own language. However, a people's language is irreplaceable and represents one of its greatest assets.

To know implies understanding the *symbolic universe* of the other. A great part of communication is symbolic. Symbols are loaded with meaning and resonance which are not always easily grasped for they preserve and communicate seminal experiences of a people. It is through symbols that a people identify and ascribe cohesion to itself. As symbols usually have an archetypal foundation that is connected to the collective unconscious, a symbol speaks for itself and communicates directly with the innermost part of the other. Symbols establish a form of communion that goes beyond words. Symbols speak and give food for thought. Symbols reveal that which is presupposed in all communication between different people: for the more different that people and groups are, there is a common substratum to them. Without this common substratum it would be impossible to communicate and to understand. This common substratum is *humanitas*, humanity, the fact that we are beings with language, that we are beings of words, of relation, of creativity and of openness to the other and to the mystery of the world, which is also called God.

When this stage is reached then we take another step towards approximation: this stage implies an *alliance* with the other, who from being a stranger becomes an ally in a common cause. This implies a level of *identification* with the other, despite the fact that this can never be complete. One starts to learn the history of the other, its beauty, the grandiosity of its heroes, its sages and wise men, its festivals and its folk-lore, and vice versa. Sympathy (i.e. to tune in with the other) emerges, and this must become empathy (i.e. to identify with the other in most possible ways).

This empathy can and must evolve into authentic love. It is the eyes of love that unveil hidden dimensions in the other. The adage of trans-cultural tradition is appropriate: we love others not because they are in-teresting and beautiful people, on the contrary, they are interesting and beautiful people because we love them. This is the highest point in an encounter with the other and with others, that is, the emergence of a liv-ing reciprocity that knows no limits. At this point, along with concepts and forms of communication so finely studied by Jürgen Habermas in his *The Theory of Communicative Action*, enters the concept of *life context (Lebenswelt)*.[6] This is a context that follows a logic of cordiality that is encompassing and that is not merely rational but also inclusive of meaningful things in life, of symbolic, religious, artistic, recreational realities, amongst others. We thus reach co-living, the most encompass-ing experience in relating to the different other.

What Exactly Is Co-Living?

The category co-living emerged, curiously, in Brazil and it is the outcome of two niche experiences, and this is something identified by commenta-tors such as Sundemeier in *Konvivenz und Differenz*.[7]

The first niche experience is connected to the pedagogue Paulo Freire (1921–1997) and especially to his works *Pedagogy of the Oppressed* and *Educação como práctica de liberdade* but also with other texts such as *Pedagogy of Hope* and *Pedagogia da tolerância*.[8] The second niche experience is connected to the emergence of *Comunidades Eclesiais de Base*, i.e. Base Communities, in Brazil, which signified a true ecclesio-

---

6. Cf. Habermas, *The Theory of Communicative Action*.

7. Cf. Sundemeier, *Konvivenz und Differenz*, 48.

8. Cf. Freire, *Educação como prática de liberdade*; *Pedagogy of the Oppressed*; *Pedagogy of Hope*; *Pedagogia da tolerância*.

genesis, a re-invention of the Church that had its starting point in the faith of the people and in social movements.

Paulo Freire starts with the conviction that the dichotomy teacher/student is not original, is not something that happens at the beginning. What is original is the community of learners, where every one has a relation with everyone and where everyone learns with everyone by exchanging. To learn is much more than an intellectual act of appropriation of knowledge that has been customized and accumulated. To learn is a vital act, is a communion of lives, of interests and of destiny, it is a play of personal and social relations in which all dimensions of life emerge and articulate with each other, sometimes with some tension, sometimes in harmony, but always within a dynamism of exchanging in all directions.

Paulo Freire always insisted that the illiterate are illiterate only insofar as writing is concerned, they are not illiterate with respect to oral traditions or life learning experiences. Freire constantly repeated that reading the world precedes reading the word. It is within this horizon of understanding that the concept of *co-living* (which is something life creating) emerged.

As the philology of the word *co-living* clearly suggests, this concept is about living life always with the other and never without the other. To live does not here mean something psychological, a movement of the psyche or of human subjectivity. To live involves psychological features but it goes beyond these for living encompasses all dimensions of the human being.

Thus, to live is seeded in co-living and in coexisting. Co-living and coexisting are "ways-of-being" that are encompassing and inclusive. To live is an outcome of life, of life taken in all its complexities, of life shared with others, of coexisting with others and of sharing dynamically in others' lives, of sharing others' way-of-being, of sharing others' struggles, quests, defeats, and victories. It is within this co-living that real learning takes place, real learning as a collective effort for knowledge, as a vision of the world, as values that guide life and as a utopia that maintains the future open ended.

Co-living does not erase or nullify differences. On the contrary, co-living is the capacity to welcome differences, of allowing for differences, and at the same time, to *live with* these differences and not to *live in spite* of these differences. Co-living only emerges when differences are relativized in favor of common points, and this allows for the rise of necessary converging points that form the concrete basis for a peaceful co-living, despite the continued existence of some levels of tension due to genuine differences.

The second niche experience that gave rise to the category *co-living* emerged from the vast chain of Comunidades Eclesiais de Base—CEBs—i.e., Base Communities, which is a typical phenomenon present in the churches that opted for the poor, their culture and their world. This phenomenon has its starting point in Brazil and it first appeared in the 1950s, but later it spread throughout the Church.

Base Communities are characterized by the fact of being communities, that is to say, they are a reality formed by immediate, egalitarian, inclusive, charitable and fraternal relations. They are called *base* because, by and large, they have sprung up from the "lower strata" of society and of the Church, that is, they appeared in popular contexts, in the context of the poor, of the excluded, of low-paid workers, of the working-classes and of sub-employed people. In short, Base Communities emerge from the meeting of those who are pushed to the margins of the current dominant social process. They are also called *base* in an ecclesial sense for they have their starting point in laymen and laywomen, in those who do not hold power in the Church, in those who compose the mass of faithful and who are guided and encouraged by clergy.

These two niches, and with this dual base, managed to form communities in which faith and life are lived in common. Where life—with its problems, happiness, dramas—is shared and enlightened by the Words of the Scriptures. The pages of life meet the pages of the Bible and from this meeting new reflections and different prayers emerge, and most importantly, practical decisions that seek to improve the lives of all participants are made.

It is the co-living of every one with everyone that brings life and dynamics to the Base Community. As social and religious commentators identified, Base Communities can represent a true ecclesio-genesis, that is to say, the genesis of a new way-of-being Church, a new way-of-being that is more horizontal, fraternal, participative, egalitarian, inserted in popular culture and libertarian. The traditional roles of the bishop, priest, religious men and women, and even of theologians are not suppressed. Much to the contrary, they are required. But when these are inserted into the Base Community they assume new functions. They participate in the community's journey and live with the community, they assume an encouraging role, they become allies in the construction of a new model of church that is less pyramidal and more communitarian, a new model where the word flows within the group, where celebrations are shared and where decisions are made collectively.

As one may gather, co-living springs up spontaneously within this new way of living the Christian faith in the web of Base Communities that are supported by thousands of small Bible study groups, and prayer and action groups.

There are three pillars supporting co-living: participation, communion and celebration.

The *participation* of all is essential. This means that all participants feel they are responsible agents in the community. They distribute among themselves tasks that range from sharing the word, celebrations, religious services to conducting concrete works within the community, works which have been decided by the whole community, usually in articulation with other Base Communities. Participation always implies mutual help in the various dimensions of life, which is generally marked by all kinds of needs. Partnerships are established between members and between groups, such as groups associated with human rights, health, education, women, ecology, landless people, homeless people, and unions. Once again, participation forces us to seek convergent points and to put aside differences—be this religious, ideological, and class differences, among others.

Co-living is deepened by *communion* of minds and of hearts. That is to say, co-living is not merely the result of converging points sought by groups that coexist and that pragmatically strive for common objectives. Something more profound may happen: people become involved, connections are established, people grow to be friends, and love emerges. Minds and hearts vibrate together. This is a unifying force that can only be expressed by the category *communion*. Communion encompasses concrete dimensions such as solidarity, mutual help, a feeling of belonging together, and this goes beyond simple participation. Communion allows groups, despite being geographically distant, to feel that they are on the same journey, that they are going in the same direction, that they are dreaming the same dreams. Thus, for instance, the Sami people in Northern Scandinavia feel solidarity for the Yanomamis native Indians in Brazil, and exchange signs and symbols of communion representing their same struggle and in their same hope. The black ring made of Tucum coconut that many bishops, and even cardinals, theologians, laymen and laywomen, pastoral carers, social scientists, anthropologists, and others, use on their hands has become a distinct sign of a communion with the cause of the oppressed and excluded of the world (i.e., native Indians, black people, women, minorities, people who are prejudiced against for one reason or another), a sign of communion for their liberation and for a new inclusive world.

It is clear that co-living within this concrete dimension involves an undeniable spiritual resonance that ascribes real magic to life.

This feeling of communion that involves spirituality, love and affection, usually, is not included in sociopolitical analysis, in those studies by those who approach the subject from a critical, structural and systematic perspective. This perspective perceives the functioning of the system but it does not perceive concrete actors, who are loaded with emotions and feelings, and without whom the system would not function. It is at this level that the phenomenon of communion becomes relevant as the most concrete manifestation of co-living.

The Christian tradition finds in mystics the foremost example of co-living as communion. Firstly, because they understand the Ultimate Reality as eternal co-living and as the absolute communion of the three loves, Father, Son and Holy Spirit. Secondly, because they perceive a person's pathway as co-living and as communion with God with such intimacy that it allows for the fusion of God and person but with the identity of the parts preserved. The mystic Saint John of the Cross observes that co-living and communion mean that "the loved (i.e. the soul) is transformed in the Loved."

The Buddhist tradition speaks of compassion, i.e. *Karuna*, and of loving kindness or unconditional love, i.e. *Metta*, as ways of co-living with the other, especially those who are alone and suffering.

Lastly, co-living emerges as a concrete reality and as a unifying force in *feasting and celebrating*. A community does not live only for struggles and coexistence, but also for parties and celebrations, and communities are very rich and creative in this respect.

It is part of the magic of parties to trim differences, to tolerate diversity, to bracket issues, to stop conflicts for a moment and to strengthen the feeling of belonging and of being part of the family.

A party is not a place for discussions and for the elaboration of strategies and tactics. A party is a world of excellences, it is a moment of celebrating life, struggles, victories and just the fact of being together. As Nietzsche commented, to celebrate and to rejoice is to be able to say: "all things are welcomed."

It is at this moment that co-living can become more radiating, that co-living can assume a magic aura that powers up the meaning of community life and strengthens reasons for co-living, for walking together, for building together a world in which it is worth living.

Co-Living: A Psychosocial and Cosmic Dimension

The category of co-living, which I have just characterized by taking as my starting point those two niches that gave origin to it (i.e. communitarian pedagogy and Base Community), serves as a paradigm for a universal co-living between all tribes of the Earth, tribes which now find themselves forced closer together in our Common Home. There is no other alternative: we either learn to live together and in doing so we have a future, or we isolate ourselves in our particular differences and excluding identities and in doing so we meet the worse. There is a saying by Hegel that is very true: "we learn from history that we have learned nothing from history except suffering."

It is neither wise nor prudent to have to learn from suffering in an age in which so many suffer deeply and in which adding to suffering may mean a dead end for us. However, for those peoples who consider themselves to be superior perhaps the only possible pathway is to learn by suffering. Maybe this is the only way for them to learn, to learn through ecological disasters that affect them, learn through decimation of parts of their populations through epidemics, or learn through catastrophes caused by their own irresponsibility or by violent reactions from a nature that has been systematically abused. Who knows?

This reflection opens up new dimensions for co-living. Co-living cannot be reduced to an anthropocentric perspective of reality, a perspective that is present by and large in the majority of commentators on this issue. The human being does not exist without nature, without the community of life, without being inserted in the universe; in the universe with all the energies that penetrate and entwine the human being.[9]

9. Cf. Abdalla, *O princípio de cooperação.*

It is imperative to establish a new way of co-living with nature. Since Neolithic times (about 10.000 years ago) and more systematically from around the time of the Industrial Revolution in the seventeenth century to our modern times, nature has been explored without any respect for its alterity (i.e., otherness) as a depository of resources which now face exhaustion. The paradigm of industrialization, of the society based on knowledge and information which are increasingly used in the exploration of nature, modifies our daily lives, has made our lives easier, and has brought us longevity. However, all these benefits have a high price, that is, a high level of social inequality and environmental costs that are perverse. This model can no longer guarantee our future as it destroys nature and relations between peoples. As various commentators on world affairs have warned us: "we either change or we will perish."

The psychosocial effect of this dramatic situation is revealed in the currently held low expectations for the future by the common citizen in the street. Everybody is increasingly aware that everything is worsening on a yearly basis: wages, health services, social welfare, transport, churches, religion and the quality of life in general.

From a society of exploration we must become a society of cooperation; from an excluding and self-affirmative society we must become an integrated society in its entire wholeness; from a means of production that is costly to nature to a model of co-living and synergy with nature. The result of this form of co-living is a geo-society sustaining life in all its forms.

Peoples must learn to live together and with the planet Earth, Gaia, with ecosystems, with their most immediate surroundings, with the water, the air, the earth, plants, animals, birds, and not least, with the realm of micro-organisms, bacteria, fungi, viruses, on which life is dependent. For this reason, I have emphasized that democracy must be limitless, it must be bio-cracy, it must be socio-cosmic, and citizenship cannot be only human but also planetary and terrestrial.

Co-living must be extended in the same way, it must be extended to cosmic dimensions as I argued in chapter 2 of book 1. We are the result of an evolutionary process that has lasted billions of years. Energies that sustain the cosmos have acted in us, energies which sustain each cell of our bodies and every vibration of our minds and hearts. To live together with the cosmos is to enter into a subtle synchrony with it, with its grandiosity and complexity, with its terrifying beauty and integrity.[10] It is interesting to note here that the ancient Stoics observed: *membra sumus corporis magni.* That is, "we are limbs of a great body," we are part and parcel of the cosmos. Co-living can reach such levels.

We must also live together with our dark dimensions that may be personal, factional or collective. As well as being *homo sapiens sapiens* we are also *homo demens demens.* We are bearers of excluding and loathing dimensions that live together with inclusive and loving dimensions. Both of these always coexist inside us.

It is fitting for the civilizing working of every people within its own culture to keep control of those dark dimensions, to stop destructive mechanisms gaining the upper hand and producing destruction and death. It is important to increasingly create space for the dimensions of light so that they can impose limits on those dark dimensions, despite the fact that we should be aware that we can never repress those dark dimensions completely. We must live with our demons but also with the gaze of our guardian angels. This means that there will always be tensions and conflicts in every instance of co-living. Co-living is never something given but something that must be constantly built. This characteristic never does away with ruptures, but forces us to continuously seek the construction of more civilized and non-violent forms of relating to each other.

The resulting peace of this process, as it was so clearly stated in the Earth Charter, is: "created by right relationships with oneself, other persons, other cultures, other life, Earth, and the larger whole of which all are a part."[11]

Lastly, it is important to live together with our infinite desires. The human being is rooted on Earth and in the universe. But a human being's desire goes beyond these. The human being discovers itself directed towards the infinite that devours his inner being. This infinite feeds the human being's imagination with increasingly ample perspectives and sophisticated utopias. By its very nature utopia always remains utopia, that is, something nonrealizable. But utopia unsettles us, it always causes us to move in a direction, and to allude to Saint Augustine's understanding of the human condition, it makes us *restless (inquietum est cor nos-*

10. Cf. O'Murchu, *Evolutionary Faith.*

11. Translator's note: See the Earth Charter online: http://www.earthcharterin action.org/.

trum donec requiescat in te, that is, *our heart is restless until it finds rest in You*).[12]

To live together with our interior fire and with our infinite project allows for a geo-society that is less dogmatic and more flexible, that is less self-centred and more open, less materialist and more spiritual, it allows for the geo-society to become a human space in which love and the joie-de-vivre is easier.

Just as the Sisters of Jesus became the midwives of a people, the Tapirapé nation, we also can become midwives and midhusbands of the new global society, of the new Earth over which a rainbow of divine benevolence and human good will stands.

12. Translator's note: Boff refers here to the famous words of Saint Augustine in his *Confessions*, bk. I, chap. 1. The text is available online: www.newadvent.org/fathers/1101.htm/.

ten

Respect

Along with hospitality and co-living it is imperative to have respect for every human being, for other peoples, for other peoples' cultures, traditions, and religions, and for every being. We can find many common points and we can take co-living to high levels but there is always something to be ironed out, perspectives and dimensions of the other that we either do not understand or that we have difficulty in accepting or that simply cause in us a feeling of strangeness that we find disagreeable.

It is when this happens that it is imperative to have respect for differences and tolerance as core attitudes so that we can be together in our Common Home.

A Parable about Infinite Respect

I will refer to a case sourced in the early Christian community where the apostles, the most immediate followers of Jesus, were still active. The apostles learned this lesson from the master and later emphasized that respect is of extreme importance.

We know that the orthodox Jewish culture of the time of Jesus was not very forthcoming in respecting differences and in religious tolerance. On the contrary, it was very rigorous insofar as it was concerned with dealings with strangers. In the times of Jesus it was inconceivable to establish friendship with someone who was not a Jew, and it was forbidden to visit someone who did not profess Judaism.

Christianity represented a rupture with this kind of prejudice, which is nothing more than lack of respect for the other. From its very beginning, Christianity was born universal, and therefore, it respected all without exception. Saint Paul well understood Jesus' practice of unconditional love, which broke all barriers. I quote: "God shows no partiality" (Galatians 2:6) for "there is neither Jew nor Greek, there is neither slave nor free, there is neither male nor female; for you are all one in Christ Jesus" (Galatians 3:28).

Jesus' disciples themselves, who were all Jews, had to learn this lesson, sometimes the hard way. Saint Peter provides us with a somewhat surreal narrative that has been passed onto us in the Acts of the Apostles, where the topic of respect, supported by heaven, appears (cf. Acts 10:9–16).

In the narrative a Roman centurion named Cornelius, who was religious and who gave alms to the poor, showed an interest in the Christian religion and was willing to learn more about it. He invited Peter to his home because he wanted to gather close friends and relatives there so that they could discuss the issue.

Peter was reluctant for he wanted to respect the tradition and as such did not want to visit a pagan's home. Peter confessed: "You yourselves know how unlawful it is for a Jew to associate with or to visit any one of another nation" (Acts 10:28). He felt torn apart as he was unsure whether he should observe the tradition or accept the invitation by the Roman centurion. He had a vision.

The narrative says that Peter, whilst praying, "fell into a trance and saw the heaven opened, and something descending, like a great sheet, let down by four corners upon the earth. In it were all kinds of animals and reptiles and birds of the air" (Acts 10:10–12). And he heard a voice saying: "Rise Peter; kill and eat" (Acts 10:13). And Peter replied: "No Lord; for I have never eaten anything that is common or unclean" (Acts 10:14). And the voice said again: "What God has cleansed, you must not call common" (Acts 10:15); and "this happened three times, and the thing was taken up at once to heaven" (Acts 10:16).

Clearly, the sheet here refers to the gospel and to Christianity itself. The many beings that are in the sheet, all of which are edible, symbolize taboos of the Jewish religion. According to Jewish law it was unlawful to eat certain kinds of meat, for they render the person who eats them unclean. Those forbidden animals in the sheet represent those people whom the Christians, who broke away from the Jewish tradition, had to respect and to enter into communion (which is the spiritual equivalent of eating). In this way, all are pure, all come from God, all must live together and with no exclusions. Christians must be bearers of this universalism, a universalism that knows neither prejudice nor lack of respect.

Peter became baffled by this vision. But he connected 'ecstatic' vision to the invitation by the Roman centurion. There was a lesson to be learned here and he acknowledges: "God has shown me that I should not call any man common or unclean . . . truly I perceive that God shows no partiality, but in any nation any one who fears him and does what is right is acceptable to him" (Acts 10:28; 10:34–35; cf. Galatians 2:6 and Deuteronomy 10:17). In short, prejudice and disrespect are unworthy to God; rather, universal respect is worthy.

Convinced by the celestial vision, Peter went to the Roman centurion's house, in Caesaria, which was an important city in Israel at the time. And when Peter was in Cornelius' home he started speaking with much enthusiasm about Jesus' deeds, about "how he went about doing good and healing all that were oppressed by the devil, for God was with him" (Acts 10:38). Peter was both emotional and happy as he told those present how Jesus had been misunderstood, persecuted and crucified, and how he had resurrected. He, himself, and the other apostles who had eaten and drunk with Jesus were witnesses to this wonderful fact (cf. Acts 10:39-41). And Peter stated: "every one who believes in him receives forgiveness of sins" (Acts 10:43).

These words were very encouraging to Cornelius and to his guests. Whilst Peter was still speaking, suddenly the Holy Spirit descended upon all those who were present, Jews and pagans. And the same phenomenon that had happened in the day of Pentecost when the Holy Spirit descended upon the community of apostles and upon the representative of various peoples (Medes, Parthians, Romans, etc.) who were present (cf. Acts 2:1–13) occurred again. And "they were filled with the Holy Spirit and began to speak in other tongues" (Acts 2:4). And on this occasion they also started to speak in tongues and to glorify God.

Peter was completely astonished for something completely unexpected happened: the Holy Spirit descended upon all those who were present, even those who did not belong to the Christian community as they were not even baptized. Normally, the Holy Spirit only communicated after a person had converted and was baptized. On this occasion, God's liberality was demonstrated: the Holy Spirit descended upon all, pagans and Christians, without any precondition. And thus, Peter, with this sanction from the heavens, baptized all those present, and incorporated them into the community of faith.

Peter took a courageous step, which was not without consequences for the new understanding of Christianity as a universal religion that goes beyond the boundaries of religion, race, and social status. So much so that later Peter was questioned in Jerusalem by his brethren, who, despite being disciples of Christ, held on to Jewish tradition of not mixing with foreigners.

Peter simply cut them short by saying, "If then God gave the same gift to them as he gave to us when we believe in the Lord Jesus Christ, who was I that I could withstand God" (Acts 11:17)?

God does not discriminate, but respects all. Every one is a son or daughter of God. God pours over all his Spirit of life. Whoever shares this universality shown in the descent of the Spirit must receive the sign of belonging to the community. Whoever shares this experience is worthy of being baptized, which is the official sign of belonging to the community.

Thus the statement "there is neither Jew nor Greek, there is neither slave nor free, there is neither male nor female; for you are all one in Christ Jesus" (Galatians 3:28) becomes true. In short, every one must be respected and welcomed.

This narrative yields important lessons for the issue of respect. First, the search for a meaning in life and of existential truth gains fundamental centrality, as it was shown with reference to the Roman centurion. Religions are at the service of this search, and for this reason it must always be respected. This search takes precedent over any religion, prejudice, or taboo.

Second, existing religions, and their doctrines and rules, are efforts to translate a meeting with God and with existential truth. As such, they are cultural creations that are subject to historical changes.

Third, God is infallibly found "in every nation . . . who fears him and does what is right" (Acts 10:35).

Fourth, the Spirit cannot be monopolized by anyone, by any religion, or by any church. The Spirit shows itself always free from religious organization, doctrines, rites, and interdictions. The Spirit gives itself to all without any discrimination—it is enough for one to be open and to be in an authentic search to meet the Spirit. The Spirit enters wherever it is allowed to enter.

Fifth, there is the religion of the Spirit that "blows where it wills" (John 3:8). The Spirit's worshipers are found anywhere, in any religion, in any religious place (it does not matter if it is Jerusalem, as the Jewish people want, or in Gerizim, as the Samaritans did, or in the Vatican, as Roman Catholics do, or in Moscow as the Russian Orthodox want), provided that the God-Father-and-Mother is worshiped "in spirit and truth" (John 4:23).

Such an understanding instigates respect for each and every pathway; "in spirit and truth" is a pathway that takes us to the heart of God. Thus, they possess an intrinsic value; they must be recognized, respected and positively valued.

What Is Respect?

This narrative and its practical consequences provide us with elements that help us to understand respect. From the start, respect presupposes recognizing the other in its alterity (i.e. otherness) as well as perceiving the other's intrinsic value.

Recognizing the Other

To recognize the other as the other: this attitude represents a great challenge to every one and to every society. The other, as I have argued in detail in Book I, cannot be reduced solely to the other *human*. The other is every and each other, every and each not-I, that appears to me.

The first other, the most immediate other, for we are immersed in it, is the world around us, it is nature. Historically, there have been various kinds of human relations with nature, some that are more respectful and cooperative, others that are more aggressive and functional. It is a fact that since the emergence of the *homo habilis* and the invention of the instrument around 2.3 million years ago, the process of human intervention in nature with the use of force and aggression also started. And alongside this human intervention in nature also emerged the risk of human being's losing respect for nature and negating nature's alterity (i.e., otherness). Human beings have even started to understand and manipulate nature only in its usefulness to human beings, disregarding nature's own intrinsic value.

Anthropocentrism obliges us to believe that all other beings only possess value in reference to human beings, who can make use of other beings as they see fit. We must remember, however, that the great majority of beings existed before the emergence of the human being. It is only when 99.98 percent of the history of the Earth had already passed that the human being appeared in the evolutionary process. Therefore, nature did not require the help of the human being to organize its immense complexity and biodiversity. The proper thing to do would be for the human being to understand itself in communion with the community of life already established, to understand itself as a link in the great chain of life, as a singular link, for it is an ethical and responsible being.

Respect implies recognizing that other beings may be older than us and that, with reason, warrant existence and coexistence with us. We must respect them by imposing limits on our self-centred and despotic nature. In the past, unfortunately, such limitations have been pushed aside.

In *The Future of Life*, Edward Wilson, a well-known commentator on biodiversity, depressingly concluded, whilst taking stock of the respectful/disrespectful relationship between human beings and nature, the following: "Eden occupied was a slaughterhouse. Paradise found was paradise lost. Humanity has so far played the role of planetary killer, concerned only with its own short-term survival. We have cut much of the heart out of biodiversity. The conservation ethic, whether expressed as taboo, toteism, or science, has generally come too late."[1]

We have reached a crucial point. We must recover an attitude of respect to limit our capacity to destroy and as a condition for the preservation of nature and of our survival.

After nature, the other that is more close to us is the other human being. Human being—who is bearer of consciousness and of dignity, and who is an end in itself. When faced by another human being we must stand with reverence and respect, for each human being is unique in the world, each human being represents the simmering of evolution and is a revelation of God. No cultural or religious end or purpose is superior in dignity to a human being. A human being can never be used or downgraded to a means to an end, to a means of production, to means to war, to a means of scientific experimentation. The human being is the apex of the evolutionary process, at least till now. And since its appearance, the human being has creatively intervened, interacted, and helped with the unfolding of the evolutionary process.

1. Wilson, *The Future of Life*, 102.

Thinking within these parameters the Second Vatican Council (1962–1965) stated beautifully in the *Gaudium et Spes*: "everyone must consider his every neighbor without exception as another self, taking into account first of all His life and the means necessary to living it with dignity."[2] And it goes further and states: "Respect and love ought to be extended also to those who think and act differently than we do in social, political and religious matters."[3]

Unconditional Respect to Consciousness

However, there is another 'other' that is the closest of all: personal consciousness. This is the most sacred item of the human being. And thus, an attitude of unconditional respect is an imperative when faced by consciousness.

What is consciousness? It is that interior voice that always accompanies us, that never quiets, that directs us towards doing good and advises us against doing evil, that bestows upon us grace for the good we have done and that casts upon us guilt for the evil we have practiced. The figure of Cain in the Bible stands for the evil that exists inside each of us and that seeks to escape, even if it is not being chased, for it wants to free itself from the weight of consciousness. But consciousness is always present because there is no refuge, no hidden place, no secret, that consciousness does not know. Consciousness brings light to everything; and light brings us joy and forces us to cover our eyes.

The existence of consciousness places us before a mysterious instance, for it is above us despite being inside us. We can neither manipulate it nor can we quiet it. It is simply always there. We can disobey it but we cannot destroy it. Every person knows, in its own heart, the good and the evil it does and that it does not.

Those spiritual traditions that understood consciousness as the living presence of God with us, in us and alongside us were right. Because it is absolute, we must respect it, we must hold total respect for it. *Gaudium et Spes* says, "consciousness frequently errs from invincible ig-

---

2. *Gaudium et* Spes, n. 27. Translator's note: *Gaudium et Spes* is available online at http://www.vatican.va/archive/hist_councils/ii_vatican_council/index.htm

3. Ibid.

norance without losing its dignity," and for this reason the requirement for respecting it stands.[4]

Such respect is in place when consciousness freely defines its relation with God and with sacred things. In doing so it projects an ultimate and personal meaning to its short passage in this world. Respect for religious freedom is defined by the Second Vatican Council in its *Dignitatis Humanae* as: "All men are to be immune from coercion on the part of individuals or of social groups and of any human power, in such wise that no one is to be forced to act in a manner contrary to his own beliefs, whether privately or publicly, whether alone or in association with other, within due limits."[5]

In our modern times, they are not few who suffer discrimination and prejudice because of their consciousness. Saint Peter wrote in his first letter: "for one is approved if, mindful of God, he endures pain while suffering unjustly" (1 Peter 2:19). However, these afflictions are, and will always be, illegitimate.

Respect and the Secular State

In our modern age, particularly because of the globalisation process, the state was required to become secular so that religious consciousness was safeguarded. There were times when the state professed a particular religion as official (e.g., Roman Catholicism, Islam, Anglicanism, to mention a few). Those who professed to be of other religions or spiritual traditions suffered certain public distress. But with the advent of democracy, the secular state prevailed in almost all countries. No religion is imposed as official, and all religions are respected—the state remains impartial to all of them. This impartiality does not mean that the state does not know the eventual spiritual and ethical value of religiousness, which is something always beneficial to society as a whole. However, because of the state's respect for its citizens' consciousness, the state does not favor one religion over another. The state guarantees religious pluralism and respect to minorities.

---

4. Ibid., n. 16; cf. *Gaudium et Spes*, nn. 16 and 28; and *Dignitatis Humanae*, n. 2. Translator's note: Both texts are available online at http://www.vatican.va/archive/hist_councils/ii_vatican_council/index.htm.

5. *Dignitatis Humanae*, n. 2.

Because of this impartiality (and this is something ethically contentious) the secular state is not allowed to impose behavior derived from a particular religion's rules and dogmas even if this religion is the dominant one. The same is true for State employees who are religious. When they enter the political sphere and take up posts with the state's apparatus, they are not required to renounce their religious convictions, they are asked to argue and demonstrate good reasons for their views on issues in open dialogue with others. The only thing that is required of them is that they neither intend to impose their views on all nor that they try to translate as universal laws their own particular understanding. Secularism forces all to exercise communicative reasoning; to overcome dogmatism in favor of peaceful co-living; to find points in common; and when faced with conflicts, to be open to negotiations and to resolutions.

Humanism underlies secularism—the basis for democracy. Humanism holds unconditional respect for the human being, understands that each and every life has an intrinsic value independent of ethnic, economic, or social condition, for life is a bearer of dignity and of rights. This is about having faith, not in God as in the case of religions, but in the human being itself.

This faith is expressed through recognizing the legitimacy of pluralism in cultural and religious manifestations, and by all co-living peacefully. This is not, and will never be, easy. Whoever is convinced that one's position is the true one, will be tempted to publicize it and to win followers. Respect for a human being's consciousness and convictions, however, stops one imposing one's views on others through absolute and coercive means as this is a feature of confessionalism and fundamentalism, which are religious deviations.

Radical secularism is also a deviation. It stands for a political view of the world that, for some reason, intends to eradicate religion from society, and to give space only to secular and rational values. Such an attitude holds no respect for religious people and so fractures co-living in peace.

Respecting the human being and all beings establishes a minimal ethical attitude that must be taken on by all. Otherwise, there is no way of establishing a situation of peaceful co-living between citizens that are so diverse and of finding resolutions for conflicts. Democracy itself is not confined to the rule of the majority as it also implies the adequate integration of the minority—certainly, to the extent in which it is a minority.

This minimal ethical attitude can be resumed by the following principle from the Earth Charter: "Care for the community of life with understanding, compassion, and love."[6] This principle encompasses basic values, a minimal ethical attitude, that will support humans co-living within our Common Home, the planet Earth.

The function of the secular state is, therefore, to maintain an open space and an atmosphere of freedom of expression for all creeds, and only interfering when the established official laws are broken.

For instance, a religion injures the secular nature of the state when it advises ministers of the state and judges who profess this religion to disobey laws that have been legally approved by the state's legislature, such as in cases of decriminalization of abortion or acceptance of homosexual civil unions, among other such cases.

Political action aims at the realization of a common good that is concretely possible within the constraints of a given situation and departing from a common state of collective consciousness. Certainly, what may happen is that the realization of the best common good is concretely unachievable due to polemical issues. And in these situations it is reasonable to embrace a lesser common good or to tolerate a lesser evil so as to avoid a major setback. Such an attitude is derived from the democratic spirit that must be encouraged in all.

A society that intends to be authentically democratic must take on secularism as a foundational dimension. It is only through secularism that two fundamental values join together, namely, the respect for freedom of consciousness and judicial equality.

Secularism ascribes the same level of dignity to all religious citizens. It allows them to overcome differences without giving up their own distinctiveness, and in doing so it allows them to respect consciousness. And at the same time, it implements the principle of equality for all are recognized as equals.

This reflection is not only applicable to religions but also to other perspectives and understandings of the world that are present in a secular society. The Second Vatican Council called this in the *Gaudium et Spes* the "autonomy of earthly affairs."[7] Politics, economy, sciences have a value in themselves and are derived from the mystery of the good cre-

6. Translator's note: Read the Earth Charter online: http://www.earthcharteraction.org

7. *Gaudium et Spes*, n. 36.

ation of God. Their value is not dependent on faith but on reason and thus they have a composition and self-sufficiency that is particular to them.

In reality what happens is that the majority of modern secular societies are dominated by the culture of capital. Generally speaking, questionable values such as individualism, reverence for private property, exaggeration of media celebrities, laxity of traditions, and magnification of pleasure (especially erotic pleasure) prevail in this culture. Means of mass communication, the majority of which is privately owned by powerful people, are used in their search for profiting from trends. 'New Gods' are created, 'New Gods' that are connected to money, to credit, to pleasure at any cost, 'New Gods' that are liturgical expressions of this 'secular religion'. 'Secular religion' venerates infinite progress and idolizes the use of technology in our daily lives, but as we know this practice is political and ecologically false for it implies the continuous exploration of nature and the exclusion of the majority of peoples. This is an attack against democracy and against the secular statute of society.

But it is important to emphasize the positive aspect of secularism in modern societies and citizens. Eugenio Scalfari, a well-known Italian intellectual and founder of the important Italian newspaper *La Repubblica*, says in the *Adista*: "Those who profess to be secular have, by definition, no pope, no emperor, no king, no bishops, no prince-bishops. They have as their lords their own consciousnesses—the feeling of responsibility. The principles of freedom, equality and fraternity are cardinal points of orientation . . .We are neither relativists nor are we indifferent. We suffer just as the weak, the poor, the excluded . . . We preach our own Sermon of the Mountain. We want good to overcome evil, the many evils that ravish the individual in its own basic subsistence and which hinders the affirmation of individual consciousness, rights and duties."[8]

The Intrinsic Value of Every Being

Respect implies recognizing the value of other beings, alive or inert. Every being has an intrinsic value because it exists and, by existing, it expresses something of the Being and of the original Fountainhead of energy and of virtualities, which is the place where all beings come from

8. Scalfari, "Perché non possiamo non dirci laici," 4. Translator's note: This passage is translated directly from the Portuguese.

and to where all beings return. This can be expressed within the religious perspective as: each being expresses the Creator itself.

Existence is a mystery, an inexhaustible source of admiration and of joy. Why is there being and not nothingness? This is a question that has plagued philosophers since time immemorial. This question is the source of mysticism, of enchantment and of contemplation. Ludwig Wittgenstein says in his *Tractatus Logico-Philosophicus*: "Not *how* the world is, is the mystical, but *that* it is."[9] When faced by the mystical and by the mystery it is appropriate to have respect and veneration. These are the highest values of human experience. They found the kingdom of excellences, that which has an intrinsic value and that imposes itself in an irrefutable manner.

Every entity, and in particular living beings, is a bearer of this excellence, that "has value regardless of its worth to human beings," as it is clearly expressed in the Earth Charter.[10] When we perceive that beings have an intrinsic value a feeling of care and responsibility towards them arises in us so that these beings can continue to exist and to evolve.

Respect and veneration, care and responsibility, are present in all civilizing processes. Ancient cultures attest their veneration for the majesty of the universe and respect for nature and for each of its representatives.

Buddhism, which does not present itself as a faith but as a form of wisdom, as a way of life in harmony with all things and with the Whole, teaches deep respect for every being, especially for those who suffer—it teaches compassion. Buddhism developed a path for the integration of all the elements of nature, the wind, water, earth and space—this is the famous *feng shui*, which always involves respect and unconditional welcome.

Hinduism, in a similar fashion, lives this dimension of respect and of non-violence (*ahimsa*) as a pillar of religious experience, which was found in Gandhi, one of its most modern and convincing expressions.

Christianity recognizes Saint Francis of Assisi (1181–1226 CE) as an exemplary figure. His original biographer, Thomas of Celano (circa 1200—circa 1260–1270 CE) writes in *The First Life of St. Francis*:

9. Wittgenstein, *Tractatus Logico-Philosophicus*, 6.44.
10. Translator's note: www.earthcharteraction.org/.

What gladness thinkest thou of beauty of flowers afforded to his mind as he observed the grace of their form and perceived the sweetness of their perfume? . . . And when he came upon a great quantity of flowers he would preach to them and invite them to praise the lord, just as if they had been gifted with reason. So also cornfields and vineyards, stones, woods, and all the beauties of the field, fountains of waters, all the verdure of gardens, earth and fire, air and wind would he with sincerest purity exhort to the love and willing service of God. In short he called all creatures by the name brother, and in a surpassing manner, of which other men had no experience, he discerned the hidden things of creation with the eye of heart, as one who had already escaped into glorious liberty of the children of God.[11]

And as a consequence of this, continues Celano, St. Francis walked respectfully over stones, as a sign of reverence to Christ, who had been called stone; Saint Francis carefully collected worms from the ground so that they would not be stepped on; St. Francis provide sweetened water to bees during the winter so that they would not die from the cold and from lack of food.[12]

Here we find another way of inhabiting the world: that is, living with these entities, co-living with these entities, and not living over and above these entities, not dominating these entities.

Arthur Schopenhauer (1788–1860) developed a unique ethical system founded on respect and compassion towards all beings in the universe. Also Albert Schweitzer (1875–1965), whose philosophy is very fashionable these days, elaborated a substantial ethical system based on respect for all beings and for life in all its forms. Given that such an ethical system is extremely relevant for the future of the Earth and for humanity it is appropriate for me to provide a brief account of Schweitzer's views.

An Ethics of Respect for All Beings

Albert Schweitzer was originally from the Alsace. He demonstrated a precociousness from a very young age. He became a famous biblical exegete with a vast number of publications, especially in respect to questions connected to the possibility, or not, of a scientific biography of

11. Thomas of Celano, *The Lives of S. Francis of Assisi*, 81.

12. Cf. Thomas of Celano, *The Lives of S. Francis of Assisi*, 165.

Jesus. He was also an accomplished organist and performer of Bach's works.

Due to his research on Jesus's message, especially Jesus's Sermon of the Mount, which is centered on the poor and the oppressed, Schweitzer decided to abandon everything and to go and study medicine. In 1913 he went to Africa to work as a physician in Lambaréné, Gabon (then part of the French Equatorial Africa territory), he went to areas that had been dominated and thoroughly explored by European colonizers. Schweitzer says explicitly in a letter: "what we need is not to send missionaries to those parts to convert Africans; rather what we need is to send people who are willing to make for the poor what needs to be done—if the Sermon of the Mountain and the words of Jesus are of any value. If Christianity does not do this, then it has lost its meaning. After a long reflection on this issue, it became very clear to me: my life is neither science nor art, but to become a simple human being who, in the spirit of Jesus, makes a difference, even if a very small one."[13]

In his hospital in the middle of the tropical jungle in equatorial Africa, and in between patients' appointments, he reflected upon the fate of culture and of humanity. He considered the lack of a humanitarian ethic as a serious crisis in modern culture. He dedicated many years studying ethical issues, which were published as various works—the most important of these, however, is *Ehrfurcht von dem Leben*.[14]

Everything within this humanitarian ethic is founded upon respect, veneration, compassion, responsibility, and care for all beings, especially those that suffer.

Schweitzer's starting point is sourced on the basic foundation of our existence, that is the will to live, which is expressed in *Wie wir überleben können* as: "I am life that wants to live among lives that want to live."[15] Nietzsche's will to power (*Wille zur Macht*) is in direct opposition to Schweitzer's will to live (*Wille zum Leben*). I quote from *Wie wir überleben können*: "The key-idea of goodness is to preserve life, to develop life, and to elevate life to its maximum value; evil consists in destroying

13. Schweitzer, *Wie Wir Überleben Können*, 25–26. Translator's note: This passage is translated directly from the Portuguese.

14. Cf. Schweitzer, *Ehrfurcht von dem Leben*. Translator's note: This is available in English as *Reverence for Life*.

15. Schweitzer, *Wie Wir Überleben Können*, 73. Translator's note: This passage is translated directly from the Portuguese.

life, in damaging life and hindering the development of life . . . This is the necessary, universal and absolute principle of ethics."[16] For Schweitzer, existing ethical approaches were incomplete because they were only concerned with a human's behavior towards other human beings, forgetting to take into account other forms of life. The respect that we owe to life "encompasses everything that is meant by love, donation, compassion, solidarity and sharing."[17] In short, "ethics is unlimited responsibility for everything that exists and lives."[18]

As one's life is a life with others' lives, the ethics of respect for life must always be a co-living and a co-suffering (*miterleben und miterleiden*) with others. This is concisely expressed by Schweitzer in *Was sollen wir tun?* as: "you must live your life co-living and preserving life— this is the foremost commandment in its most elementary form."[19]

Schweitzer argues that compassionate and caring behavior emerges from this ethic based on respect for life. He challenges all in a sermon where he states: "Keep your eyes open so not to lose the opportunity to be a savior. Do not pass by, without realizing that, a little insect struggles in water and risks drowning. Get a little stick and remove it from the water, dry its wings, and experience the marvellous feeling of saving a life and the happiness of having acted with the support and in the same way of the Most-Powerful. That young insect that has lost its way in a dry and hard road and cannot make a nestling-hole—take it and place it on the grass. "Whatever you do to the little ones, you do to me"—this message of Jesus does not apply solely to human beings but to all creatures, even the smallest ones."[20]

Schweitzer's ethics of respect combines emotional intelligence and heart in an effort of turning ethics into a safety net for all things and of recovering the idea that every thing has an intrinsic value. The major problem for this ethic is the dampening of sensitivity, lack of awareness and ignorance, which make us lose sight of the gift of existence and of

16. Ibid, 52 and 73. Translator's note: This passage is translated directly from the Portuguese.

17. Ibid, 53. Translator's note: This passage is translated directly from the Portuguese.

18. Schweitzer, *Wie Wir Überleben Können*, 52; and *Was Sollen Wir Tun?* 29. Translator's note: This passage is translated directly from the Portuguese.

19. Schweitzer, *Was Sollen Wir Tun?* 26; Translator's note: This passage is translated directly from the Portuguese.

20. Ibid., 55; Translator's note: This passage is translated directly from the Portuguese.

the excellence of life in all its forms. The human being is called upon to become the guardian of every human being. When the human being fulfils this mission, the human being reaches the highest level of humanity.

I shall conclude this chapter by recalling an observation I made in Book I: we either have unconditional respect for every being, especially for every living being and more so for every human being, or we lose the foundations that support our efforts for human dignity and for human rights. If we do not respect every human being then we will end up not respecting the human being, who is the most complex and mysterious being of creation. But the human being is also the most vulnerable, when it is poor, sick and discriminated against. Without respect and veneration we also lose sight of the Sacred and of the Divine that interweave throughout the universe and emerge in human consciousness.

eleven

Tolerance

Co-living, respect and the inevitable pluralism that emerges from the encounter of cultures within the process of globalization do not do away with conflicts and tensions between persons and peoples. Not everything pleases every one. Not all philosophies of life and religions are successful in providing answers to the anxieties of people and communities. There are some cultural dimensions of other peoples that are not merely different from ours, they are contrary to ours, especially with reference to family customs, to the treatment of women, and to views on sexuality.

How are we to behave when confronted by such differences? Historically, these differences have provoked conflict and even wars. This pathway has never brought us peace nor has it brought us understanding between peoples. Rather, this pathway has left a trigger of bitterness and the will for revenge. Thus, it is important, now more than ever, for the spirit of tolerance, otherwise, we will witness the rupture of the social fabric of the world with dire consequences for co-living and for mutual respect.

As I have done previously, I will illustrate the attitude of tolerance with an exemplary story.

A Parable about Tolerance

There is a story about Jesus of Nazareth that concerns the tolerance we must nourish when confronted by the other, even the other who is our enemy, and generally speaking, when confronted by the evil that lacerates history. This story will provide us with the elements for a more well-rounded understanding of tolerance.

The Gospel of Matthew (13:24–30) provides us with the following parable:

> The kingdom of heaven may be compared to a man who sowed good seed in his field; but while men were sleeping, his enemy came and sowed weeds among the wheat, and went away. So when the plants came up and bore grain, then the weeds appeared also. And the servants of the householder came and said to him, "Sir, did you not sow good seed in your field? How then has it weeds?" He said to them, "An enemy has done this." The servants said to him, "Then do you want us to go and gather them?" But he said, "No; lest in gathering the weeds you root up the wheat along with them. Let both grow together until the harvest; and at harvest time I will tell reapers, Gather the weeds first and bind them in bundles to be burned, but gather the wheat into my barn."

The meaning of the parable is clear but Jesus insisted in explaining it (cf. Matthew 13:36–43).

The field is the world and God sows the wheat. The weeds are sown by *diabolos*, by *fiends*.[1] The wheat represents the children of God and the weed the children of the Malignant. They live together in the same field until the day of harvest. The harvest is the historical time when good and evil will be separated. The weed, the evil, will go to the fire, the wheat, the good, will go to the barn. "And they will gather out of his kingdom all causes of sin and all evildoers, and throw them into the furnace of fire; there men will weep and gnash their teeth. Then the righteous will shine like the sun in the kingdom of their father" (Matthew 13:41–43). It is important to bear in mind that the field is also to be found within each and every person, for good and evil coexist inside each and every one of us.

In short, not everything has merit in this world. Good and evil will know different fates. The victim will not have the same destiny as the assassin.

---

1. Translator's note: Boff uses the Greek word *dia-bolos*, which is akin to the Portuguese word *diabo*, and which means *devil* in English. The origin of the word is *dia*, which means "across" and *bolo*, which means "to throw," so it stands for "to throw across," "to slander." I opted to keep *diabolos* in the English text and to add *fiend* to the translation.

Chaos and Cosmos, Order and Disorder, Are Intertwined

This story is not only applicable to the human being. In truth, it represents a structure that intertwines reality, cosmos and the human being. It is most evident in vital processes and in human interrelations. It is within such an understanding that we can better appreciate its spectacle.

In modern language we would say that the original chaos becomes the cosmic order and that human *sapience* is undeniably connected to *dementia*. These are opposing poles of the same unique and dynamic reality. They are polarities that cannot be suppressed. Every effort to suppress them ends up in terror; be this in the case of the wheat—the terror of those who presume to hold the truth and who seek to impose this truth upon others; or be this in the case of the weed—the terror of those who foment old prejudices and visceral hatreds.

That which comes together in reality, e.g., good and evil, wheat and weed, cosmos and chaos, cannot be separated through the use of force by the human being. The human being must learn to distinguish one from the other and then make a choice. In doing so the human being reveals itself to be an ethical being because it takes responsibility for its acts and for the consequences of its deeds.

Someone could raise the question: is everything allowed then? Isn't there a difference then? That is not it. I am neither saying that everything is allowed nor am I saying that the differences are blurred. The distinction remains: the weed is weed, and it is not wheat; and the wheat is wheat, and it is good for human nourishment as it is not weed. The human being must not confuse one for the other and equate them. The human being must discern them and make a decision: the human being must either take the weed side or the wheat side.

It is at this point that tolerance becomes relevant. Tolerance is the capacity to positively maintain a difficult and tense coexistence of two opposing forces by knowing that these are opposing each other but that are part of the same and unique reality at the same time. They are like the two sides of the same body, the left and the right. They confer dynamism to the history and to the life of each and every person despite the tribulations that they may cause.

Intolerance constitutes a permanent challenge. It diminishes reality for it takes one side by negating the other side. It coerces all to take the same standing. It is through intolerance that fundamentalism and dogmatism are born. When one turns something into an absolute truth, one is condemned to be intolerant and not recognize and respect the other's truth. One stops accepting the coexistence of differences and oppositions. The first thing that one does in these cases is to suppress pluralism and to impose a single way of thinking. The following step is for one to organize strategies for the restoration of traditions and doctrines that fit in with one's interests. It is in this way that conservatism emerges, whose most radical expression is fundamentalism. When fundamentalism emerges dialogue with the other and listening to the other have already been terminated and a situation of using force to repress the other and to impose one's views on the other is in place.

The immediate consequence of this scenario is social rupture. A generalized distrust involving betrayals, accusations and claims of religious or ideological purity emerge. People lose their feeling of belonging and no longer feel a part of a group and/or religion. Many distance themselves in bitterness and others leave their society for good. There is no longer joy and a good atmosphere, which are something so important for co-living even when faced by serious issues.

Dogmatists and fundamentalists are usually impatient as well as being very sad and having no understanding of bliss—this stops them from being able to contextualize issues. They are not capable of waiting for the appropriate historical moment as they want to resolve issues within the shortest possible time. Thus, they resort to violence, which is something considered by them as the quickest and most efficient means of achieving the solution to their problems. Very often violence degenerates into religious, ideological, or economic war, and as has been suggested, it can lead to a clash of civilizations with dramatic consequences for the future of humanity and for the planet Earth.

The gospels are witness that this attitude existed even among those who were closest to Jesus. The gospels refer to a case in which some of the apostles, because they were not welcomed in a Samaritan village, said: "Lord, do you want us to bid fire come down from heaven and consume them" (Luke 9:54)? Jesus, however, "rebuked them" (Luke 9:55). Jesus encouraged fundamental tolerance, just as the celestial Father who "makes the sun rise on the evil and on the good, and sends rain on the just and on the unjust" (Matthew 5:45). And Jesus advised: "For he that is not against us is for us" (Mark 9:40).

With these reflections I have provided the core elements for understanding the value of respect and of tolerance. As this is a difficult issue it is important for me now to clarify it further.

What Is Tolerance?

Conceptually, there is two kinds of tolerance: passive and active.

Passive tolerance represents the attitude of one who accepts the existence of the other not because one desires the other to exist but because it cannot do anything about it. One's will in this case is to marginalize and even to exclude the other. And one does this for certain reasons: either because one feels ambivalent with regards to the other, that is the other has no value; or because one feels weak when faced by the other and avoids conflict; or, lastly, because one fears that one's position will be jeopardize if one shows oneself to be intolerant.

This kind of tolerance, *passive tolerance*, emerges out of three faults: indifference, cowardice, and convenience.

- *Indifference*: One does not see in the other anything of worth or of interest. This attitude impoverishes one because if one embraced differences then one could learn from and enrich oneself from them. This attitude also diminishes the other who feels like a shadow, who does not raise interest, respect and love in others. Sigmund Freud demonstrated that the opposite of love is not hate, but indifference. Indifference psychologically 'kills' the other. The different become indifferent to each other. This attitude can generate resentment and bitterness, which are a source of tension and revenge.

- *Cowardice*: This attitude emerges from the feeling of fear when confronted by the other, who is considered superior or stronger. One fears a relation with the other because one thinks that one will have to submit to the other, that one will lose one's freedom or that one will become dependent on the other. Possessing self-esteem and the awareness that the other is also a human being and thus a brother or sister, a possible ally, would lead one to establish a relation of dialogue and exchange.

- *Convenience*: Every relation implies changes in the way of seeing and behaving. Every relation implies that something is gained and that eventually something is lost. Those who are complacent, who are satisfied with their situation, avoid contact with others who are different so that they can continue in their sameness and do not have to undergo processes of adaptation and change. In doing so, they lose the opportunity to grow and to know themselves and others better or to know other ways of being human that are distinct from their own.

Let us now consider *active tolerance*. *Active tolerance* consists in the attitude of one who positively co-lives with the other because one respects the other and accepts the multifaceted richness of reality. One is able to see dimensions that one would never see without the other, one perceives possibility for co-sharing and for partnership and in doing so one enriches oneself through the contact and exchange with the other.

There is something that is irrefutable: in the universe, in the system of life, and in people, there are always differences. One is never equal to another. Every one has something that differentiates. For this reason, we can talk about multiverses, parallel universes, which exist according to the String Theory and Superstring Theory.[2] Even within the same universe there exist different galaxies, different stars, and different planets that are formed by different chemical-physical elements (about 100 different elements). And consequently, there exist millions of forms of life. This is also valid for the human sphere—in this case the differences demonstrate the richness of the single and unique humanity.

The differences we find in nature are irreducible and, curiously, all these differences coexist and co-live even if there are tensions and contradictions. There exists an active and creative tolerance that is manifested as a vital and cosmic dynamism; this dynamism is present even when chaotic mechanisms arise and when one devours the other, and when intolerance seems to be in place. Intolerance is relative, is limited and it is present within universal tolerance, for there is always a dynamic equilibrium between life and death, between order and disorder. If this was not the case things would reciprocally destroy each other and there would be no synergy, no interdependence of every thing with everything, there would be no guarantee of a future for all.

The human being is inserted within this dynamism for the human being is part and parcel of the whole. It is appropriate for the human

2. Translator's note: String theory and superstring theory are theories in theoretical physics.

being, for the human being is singular as a rational and ethical being, to take on this dynamism and to transform it in a subjective and conscious project. The human being should be tolerant just as the whole of reality is.

However, the human being is a free being: it can take on intolerance as a project. Such an option represents something negative and it must be considered as such for it produces destructive effects on differences.

As I shall demonstrate below, there are limits to tolerance, limits that are not born out of intolerance, but from the right to guarantee differences and the co-living between these differences.

Levels of Realization of Tolerance

Tolerance is from the start an ethical requirement. It represents a right of every person that must be recognized. This right has been expressed in all humanistic traditions, which prescribe: "do unto others what you would have them do unto you"; or put negatively: "do not do unto other what you would not have them do unto you." This ethical precept represents an obvious existential condition and does not require further explanations.

First, the central point expressed by tolerance can be resumed as: each person has the right to live and to co-live with the planet Earth. Each person is an expression of the Earth and has the right to be here with its own particular differences. This right precedes any expression of life, such as understandings of the world, religions, ideologies, aesthetics, and desires. Societies should organize themselves in such a way so that all are, by right, included and able to continue to exist on Earth.

Second, tolerance is also linked to the very nature of truth. We can concede that there exists a single truth. This single truth, however, is communicated under very different forms and facets. It is humanly impossible to capture truth from all angles. We are limited by space and time, by rationality, by words, and by other means of communicating. We are constantly moving towards new perspectives of truth and in doing so we increase our involvement with the truth. But truth itself does not consent to being captured exclusively by a particular language or group of people. Only God has the capacity to capture, in a single glance, the totality of the manifestations of truth.

Differences constitute the usual pathways of revelation of various dimensions of truth. And for this reason it is important to be tolerant of all differences. Without differences, we lessen ourselves and we diminish our involvement with truth. Whoever rejects or diminishes or avoids getting to know the other on purpose impoverishes itself and deprives itself of dimensions of truth that could increment its freedom and development.

Truth is like a light. It reaches everyone: it illuminates the stone on the path, it reflects in the waters, it is changed by plants through the process of photosynthesis, it causes us to open our eyes and our minds to a complex and multifaceted reality. As I have said above, only the Deity can see everything and everyone from all sides simultaneously and in a single glance. Despite possessing this capacity, the Judaeo-Christian tradition affirms that the deity is absolutely tolerant because " [God] makes the sun rise on the evil and on the good, and sends rain on the just and on the unjust" (Matthew 5:45).

Third, tolerance is the axial virtue of pluralist and democratic societies. Pluralism is a given, that is, it is a fact that imposes itself on societies, even in those societies that are rigorous and fundamentalist. Within these societies we can verify tendencies, and as a consequence, the formation of groups that differentiate themselves from other groups and from their very beginnings seek to break away from the rigidity which is characteristic of fundamentalism.

Tolerance is fundamentally the virtue that underlies democracy as a way of organizing society and of structuring government. But it is also a universal value to be lived at all levels, so that democracy becomes integral. Within the democratic spirit all, in principle, are citizens and subjects of rights because all are equal before the law and have the same dignity.

Democracy only functions when there is tolerance towards political, ideological and other kinds of difference. Along with tolerance comes the will to seek a common ground through debate and through the commitment to forge a peaceful and civilized way of resolving conflicts and disagreements.

All proclamations on human rights start from this presupposition: the recognition that all human beings are equal and must be treated humanely. This presupposition precedes all subsequent forms of categorizing or differentiation by ethnicity, gender, religion, understanding of the world, and even other forms such as being a criminal or honest citizen. The criminal is never only a criminal. The criminal never ceases to be a man or a woman with all the dimensions hidden in his or her life. Because the human being is an end in itself and can never be exhausted by a single form of manifestation, the human being requires respect and to be welcomed.

Last, tolerance represents a universal pedagogy. Tolerance is reciprocal. Each different other gives good reasons for being different to others who are also different, and who in turn also give good reasons for being different. What unites them is trust in reason, is the capacity to formulate persuasive arguments. To persuade the other is not the same as to defeat the other; it is rather to encourage the other to see dimensions that were hidden prior to meeting and dialogue. This is something that works both ways. Differences continue to be differences but the reasons to embrace these and for mutual growth increases and become very apparent through tolerance.

In the West we can cite an exemplary case, the case of the Franciscan Raimundo Lúlio (1232–1316 CE),[3] who in his monastery in Miramar in Majorca, Spain, maintained a permanent dialogue with representatives of the three Abrahamic religions: Jews, Christians and Muslims. In his work *Book of the Gentile and the Three Wise Men* he demonstrates the complete tolerance of the three religions.[4] He affirms that that which is truthful in each of these religions cannot be outside the truth.

According to Lúlio that which is truthful is demonstrated through the virtues that each of these three religions produces and by the ways in which these religions tackle faults. Each of these religions is at the service of truth. By dialoguing with the other, with righteous intentions and with a joyful heart, it causes us to respect and to be tolerant towards the other for we realize we are all bearers of truths that are a reflection of the truth. Hence there is no point in making enemies because others follow different pathways. All paths, in their own way, lead us to the summit of the mountain where we all meet God.

What is valid to the religious discourse is also valid to different perspectives of the world and to diverse political projects. All these are expressions within a common framework: we are all on the planet Earth, we are all bearers of consciousness, feelings, intelligence and love. We

---

3. Translator's note: Raimundo Lúlio is also known as Ramon Llull, Raymond Lully, Raymond Lull and Raimundus or Raymundus Lullus.

4. Translator's note: cf. Ramon Llull, *Selected Works of Ramon Llull*.

are all challenged to find ways of being together in our Common Home for we have no other to inhabit.

The Limits of Tolerance

Everything has limits, even tolerance. Not everything is allowed in this world. Past and current prophets sacrifice their lives because they have the courage to raise their voice and say: "you are not allowed to do this or to do that." There are circumstances in which tolerance stands for complicity and collusion with crime, culpable omission, complacency or social and ethical insensibility. Let me provide some examples of this.

We should not be tolerant towards those who hold the power to eradicate humanity from the planet, to destroy a great part of the biosphere, and of throwing the system of life back millions of years. In this case, instead of tolerance, it is important to implement a strict control and to implement international treaties against the production of every kind of weapon of mass destruction, something which is already present in the statutes of the United Nations.

We should not be tolerant towards those who murder innocents, sexually abuse children, and traffic in human organs. We must maintain due respect to the human person but we must also firmly apply national and international laws in these cases.

We should not be tolerant of those who undoubtedly enslave minors by seeking to produce cheaply for their own benefit. To tackle this crime there are international laws that aim at the protection of children and teenagers.

We should not be tolerant of those who commit terrorist acts and implement fundamentalist actions in the name of a political project or of a religion, and in doing so affect and kill thousands of innocent people. In this case we must set in motion lawsuits against heinous crimes in international tribunals.

We should not be tolerant of those who in their eagerness for profit damage life and cause the death of thousands of people. Let us not forget those pharmaceutical companies who created and/or falsified medicines that are harmful to health, or politicians who, instead of looking after the common good, squander public assets. In this case the punishment prescribed by the laws of each given country represents the limit of tolerance.

We should not be tolerant with the mafia gangs, dealing in armaments, drugs, and prostitution, who also engage in kidnappings, torture, and assassinations. There are clear punishments prescribed by national and international legal codes for these crimes.

We should not be tolerant of practices that, in the name of tradition or culture, cut the hands off robbers and submit women and children to sexual mutilations. Such cases go against human rights and should be dealt with by international criminal tribunals.

In these cases and in so many others, we must not be tolerant but act firmly, rigorously, and severely. This stands for the virtue of justice rather than for the vice of intolerance. If we do not act in this way then we have no principles and we become accomplices in evil.

Tolerance without limits ends in intolerance just as freedom without limits leads to the tyranny of the stronger. Both freedom and tolerance require the protection of the law. Otherwise, we witness the dictatorship of a single understanding of the world and the negation of all other understandings. The result of this is hatred and the desire for revenge which foments all kinds of intolerance and terrorism.

Where are the limits of tolerance? I understand that there are three immediate ones. The first limit is the suffering of the other. Wherever there are people being humiliated, discriminated against, and dehumanized, tolerance finds its limits. Nobody has the right to inflict unjustified suffering on the other. It is worth mentioning here the case of those cultural traditions, however ancient these are, which sexually mutilate women—such as the case of some African nations; or that discriminate against women—such as the case of some Arabic and Chinese cultural traditions.

Another limit is imposed by the United Nations' Human Rights Charter of 1948, which was signed by all nations. All cultures, and differences, must meet with the precepts and values established in the charter and without exception. There is no way of justifying practices that implicate the violation of a human being's dignity and systematic humiliation. Human rights only make sense if they are absolutely universal. They provide us with the basis for a common human culture that requires us to treat all human beings humanely.

The third limit is imposed by the Earth Charter, which is concerned with the dignity of Mother Earth and with the rights of all ecosystems and all representatives of these systems. The Earth Charter was approved by UNESCO in 2000 and if embraced by the United Nations it will be added on to the Human Rights Charter. We will then have a more encompassing perspective, that is no longer anthropocentric, of the rights of each and every being, and of the community of life. Each and every aggression against nature, such as the systematic deforestation of tropical forests, polluting the atmosphere, poisoning and destruction affecting the quality of human life, all these will be intolerable and will incur the prescribed sanctions.

Lastly, it is important to ask, Can we be tolerant with the intolerant? History has demonstrated that tacking intolerance with intolerance leads to an escalation of intolerance. And this leads us to a situation with no way out. Pragmatically speaking there are limits indeed. If intolerance implies crimes and losses to others then it is important to refer to the limits imposed by the law. The freedom of all must never be sacrificed because some desire freedom to be eliminated.

Due to these limits imposed by the law we must be tolerant with the intolerant. The intolerant is free to express its views; but in doing so, the intolerant encounters the reality of those who are different and who share the intolerant's common space. This encounter, if genuine, will lead to dialogue and will encourage the intolerant to think about the contradictions of its stance. The universal precept "do unto others what you would have them do unto you" is also applicable to the intolerant.

Dialoguing at all levels is a requirement of the new global phase of humanity, for humanity must seek, by all means, a way of co-living that is peaceful and with the minimum possible of social conflict.

Should We Be Tolerant with Fundamentalism and Terrorism?

My reflections in the previous sections lead us to the challenging problem of fundamentalism and terrorism, which are serious issues at the dawn of the third millennium.

Fundamentalism: Sickness of Doctrines

The niche of fundamentalism is historically found in the Protestantism of North America in the nineteenth century, when the USA experienced a modernizing impetus, not merely technological but also through the democratization of the means of communication and in the liberalization of social customs. This scenario cause a strong reaction in those more traditional and Protestant quarters of the North American society, quarters which were faithful to the ideals of the 'founding fathers', who were all strong and rigorous advocates of Protestant ethics.

The term *fundamentalism* is connected to the series of books titled Fundamentals: A Testimony of Truth, which was published by Princeton University through the initiative of Presbyterians. This series of books proposed an antidote to modernity: a rigorous and dogmatic Christianity that is founded on a literal reading of the Bible, which is considered infallible and flawless in each and every word, for those are the words of God. These books opposed any form of exegetical interpretation of the Bible and any updating of the Bible's message for current contexts.

This fundamentalist trend has been part of North American society and politics ever since. It gained religious expression in the so-called electronic church, those churches that make use of modern means of communication and that cover the USA from coast to coast. These churches fight against liberal Christians, against those who hold a more scholarly interpretation of the Bible and against those who accept feminists, homosexuals, decriminalization of abortion. All these are interpreted by Protestant fundamentalism as the works of Satan. Its political expression is particularly enrooted in the Republican Party, in President George W Bush, who was once alcohol dependent, later converting to the Evangelical Church.

The political and religious strands united around the ideological idea of 'manifest destiny'. This idea emerged in the United States after the Mexican American War (1846–1848) when the United States incorporated Mexican territory (i.e., Texas, California, Nevada, Utah, and parts of Colorado, Arizona, New Mexico, and Wyoming). This idea declares that the United States has a divine call to take enlightenment, concept of private property, democracy, free market, and human rights to all peoples, as it was affirmed by the second president of the United States, namely, John Adams. Americans consider themselves to be "a new chosen people" who are destined to take all to "the land of Emmanuel, site of the new and unique Kingdom, which will be given to the Saints of the Highest."[5] This religious-political conjunction gave rise to the arrogant and unilateral attitude that successive American governments have

5. Cf. Armstrong, *The Battle for God.*

shown in international relations. By the fact that they feel themselves to be chosen by God they feel they do not require to pay attention to international organizations, such as the United Nations, or signing up for international treaties. They think that the legitimization of the policies come from the heavens rather than from human laws.

What is fundamentalism? Fundamentalism is not a doctrine but an attitude and a way of understanding and of living a doctrine. The fundamentalist attitude emerges when a truth is understood as absolute and as the only one that is legitimized—this attitude excludes all other truths, which are understood to be erroneous, and for this very reason, relinquished from their right to exist. Whoever believes that his understanding is absolute and the only one that is legitimized is condemned to be intolerant when confronted by the other. This enclosed attitude is characterized by being demeaning of other, by prejudice, by violence and even by wars.

Fundamentalism is not solely an occurrence in religions; rather, fundamentalism is an occurrence in all fields of human activity where a particular perspective of the world, theory and/or practice, is considered to be the only valid one for all. An example of this is the current technical-scientific fundamentalism, which understands that the modern way of doing sciences and developing techniques is the only form of attaining knowledge and of establishing a proper relation with reality. Other examples are free-market fundamentalism, which is considered as the only possible expression of economy; or neoliberal fundamentalism concerning globalization, that is, that sees the current process of globalization founded on the financial system, on the market and on multilateral corporations as the only one that is legitimized and effective; or political fundamentalism, which is particular to the West, and which intends to impose on all peoples its way of organizing society (i.e., representative democracy) and State. The same can also be seen in the arts, literature, cinema, and other fields of knowledge when a school of thought presents itself as the bearer of a single, final and unique methodology, disqualifying all other ones.

The final outcome is always the same: causing prejudice, tensions, aggressions and wars, be these just virtually or in reality between groups and peoples.[6]

6. Cf. Ali, *The Clash of Fundamentalisms*.

However, there is a kind of old fundamentalism that is at the heart of many modern conflicts that are both religious and political in nature. This is the fundamentalism of the children of Abraham; Jews, Christians and Muslims.

Their fundamentalist streak is based on the belief, on the tribal myth, that they are God's "chosen people," and as such they enjoy the special privilege of being apart from and above all other peoples. To reinforce this mythology they present their inspirational Book: the Torah for Jews, the Bible for Christians, and the Koran for Muslims. They believe these texts contain the revealed truth, which was exclusively confided to them but that it is meant to reach all peoples of the Earth. They believe they are the chosen ones for they are meant to take the message to all quarters of the Earth and to convert all to God.

This understanding, which is so embedded in Jewish, Christian and Muslim consciousness, is founded in a very questionable characterization of God. It confuses the understanding that the tribe (and thus, the reference to tribal mythology) has of God with God itself. The characterization of true God is only proper if conceived from within their understanding, which is something clearly arrogant and false.

The concept of God implies that its divine nature is beyond any limitations and that it can never be completely framed by a person's or religious organization's understanding. When someone or when a religious organization make such claims, it either composes an idol, which is a false representation of "God," or it provides a naive characterization of what we humans understand of God and what God is in itself. God is similar to a rainbow: it overshadows and visits with its light and grace all peoples. All peoples are 'chosen peoples' and this is something that the prophets of the Old Testament had already intuited.

Moreover, fundamentalism goes against the Scriptures that are common to Jews and Christians. In its first eleven chapters it narrates the history of the peoples of the Earth, peoples who are all understood to be peoples of God, all of whom are under the covenant established with the act of creation, a covenant which was renewed after the devastations of the great flood. It is only in the twelfth chapter that the expression 'chosen people' with reference to Abraham is used. The 'chosen people's' mission is to stimulate in all peoples the long lasting memory of the only God. And therefore, this is not about segregation, it is rather about the union of all in the same holy memory of the only God, Creator and Provider of all, and Lord of history.

What is problematic in fundamentalism is not that it affirms the inspiration of the Book, but that it maintains that inspiration is restricted to *this particular* Book, something which negates all other texts of other religions. Departing from the nature of God itself, Creator of all, we must affirm that God inspires all so that when they read their respective Books they are inspired to live in accordance with God.

It is important to overcome the obsessive understanding of inspiration as something that is reached to justify that we have a sacred and inspired book in our possession. Rather, the book is inspired because it inspires us to live according to God. The book is not pure and simply, literally speaking, the Word of God. If it was so, then there would be a divine dictionary and grammar. The book contains the Word of God witnessed in various words and in various ways of saying different things in different cultures.

All peoples are under the domain of divine inspiration. Each and every people's books, sages, scholars, prophets helped and still help peoples to walk their pathways in accordance with divine inspiration. These are sacred pathways leading to the encounter with the Spirit.

The three Abrahamic religions, Judaism, Christianity, and Islam are the most manifestly fundamentalist amongst all religions. Only their most enlightened segments are capable of overcoming this old tribal limitation and of ecumenically embracing the works of the Spirit unfolding in history. The Roman Catholic Church, in spite of the various reforms and *aggiornamentos* that were promoted by the Second Vatican Council (1962–1965), has showed, here and there, traces of fundamentalism in the syllabus used in the formation of the clergy.

Fundamentalism represents a chronic disease of Abrahamic religions and of any other religion that considers its doctrines and spiritual pathway absolute, and in doing so, negates a concrete and rightful pluralism of pathways leading to God. This is the main reason, but not the only one, for Abrahamic religions being the most bellicose and warmongering religions in history. There was and there still is much violence connected to Abrahamic religions: persecuting those who profess other religions, inquisitions that condemned people to be burned alive, countless religious wars that were extremely cruel. Violence is not only present in instances of doctrinal control and of repression. Violence is also present in the mentality, in the tradition and in the culture. For instance, the Church for centuries encouraged the impious and cruel idea that causing pain and even killing the enemies of the faith during a religious feast constituted a dignified way of honoring God or of honoring the Saint who was being celebrated. Not to mention the cases when Jews were violently grabbed from their ghettos and killed in a 'sacred' frenzy by Christians.

Terrorism and the Conquering of Minds

The topic of fundamentalism is directly connected to another, which is a nightmare at the dawn of the twenty-first century, namely, terrorism. Terrorism constitutes the major threat to the current global order as it can strike in any part of the world.

There are various kinds of terrorism. In many Latin American societies such as Colombia and Brazil the terrorism caused by the drug mafias is frightening. These mafias control whole areas and can even bring important parts of a city (e.g., Rio de Janeiro) to its knees for hours by demanding shops and schools to close their doors or by suspending all kind of public transport in the area. The wars between the drug mafias can cause more deaths in a year than the wars in Afghanistan and Iraq.

More worrying is political terrorism, something engaged in by groups who conduct great attacks that upset the whole of humanity and force powerful states, such as the United States, to change their national and international political strategies.

The terrorist attack of September 11th in 2001 against the United States was paradigmatic. Within an hour the major symbols of capitalism were hit. The Twin Towers in New York, which are the symbol of capitalism at the economic level, the Pentagon in Washington DC, which is the symbol of capitalism at the military level, and the White House also in Washington DC, which is the symbol of capitalism at the political level (though the plane destined to hit the White House was brought down).

Since that date fear has struck many Western countries. Fear destabilizes people and the status quo. Thus, for instance, an Arab man in New York asks for information from a policeman and ends up being arrested, for the policeman imagines that he is a terrorist; later, it is confirmed that the Arab man is just a common citizen. Or the case of a plane that takes off from Houston and is destined for Dallas; some passengers imagine that there are some armed men on board; this is enough for alarm bells to start ringing and fighter planes, F-16s, to be scrambled to escort the plane back to Houston. The government of the United States has frequently scared the entire nation by announcing that terrorist attacks are imminent. In spite of the fact that these attacks have not materialized, such announcements end up feeding a generalized paranoia.

This analysis demonstrates a particularity of terrorism: to keep minds busy. In common wars and in gorilla wars it is imperative to occupy physical space in order to triumph. This is not the case with terrorism. It is sufficient to occupy people's minds and to activate the imagination of people through the threat of new attacks and through the fear that is thus internalized in people and institutions.

The United States has physically occupied the Afghanistan of the Taliban and the Iraq of Saddam Hussein. But Al Qaeda has psychologically occupied the minds of Americans. Al Qaeda has turned the United States into a nation, from the common citizen to the government, that is hostage to fear.

The prophecy made by the mastermind of the attacks of September 11th, Osama bin Laden, made on the 8th of October 2001, unfortunately came true: "The United States will never again feel secure, will never again have peace." To keep people's minds busy, to keep people emotionally destabilized, to cause people to mistrust a single gesture, foreigners or strangers, this is the aim of terrorism and this is its very essence.

In order to reach its objective of domination from the inside, terrorism adheres to the following strategy:

1. Terrorist acts must be spectacular, otherwise they do not cause generalized commotion.

2. Terrorist acts, despite being hideous, must provoke admiration for the sagacity employed.

3. Terrorist acts must suggest that they were painstakingly prepared.

4. Terrorist acts must be unexpected so to give the impression that they are uncontrollable.

5. Those who committed terrorist acts must remain anonymous for the more suspects there are the more terror will be created.

6. Terrorist acts must provoke an enduring fear.

7. Terrorist acts must distort one's perception of reality so that any thing out of the ordinary will cause terror. It is enough to see an Arab man to imagine that he is a terrorist; or a shantytown dweller well dressed to imagine that he is a drug dealer.

In short, terrorism could be briefly formalized as: it consists in every act of spectacular violence that is practiced with the purpose of keeping minds busy with fear and terror.

The important thing is not the violence per se, but its spectacular character, which is able to dominate everybody's minds and hearts. It is in the terrorist's interest that images portraying their acts are shown—those planes that hit the Twin Towers, the twisted trains in Madrid, shredded bodies, dead people lying all over the place, hundreds of injured people being taken into hospital, the nervous behavior of hundreds of policemen, the public confusion and the agitation and the mobilization of all the powers of the state.

It is important to understand that terrorism is not a phenomenon caused by wars; it is rather caused by politics and by the failure of politics. When all possibilities of dialogue and of exchange are exhausted, violence emerges. Terrorism emerges from this standoff; it emerges loaded with resentment, bitterness and hatred. For this reason to combat terrorism through the use of military force as the sole means of tackling it is a foundational mistake, it is to make use of the same logic that feeds terrorism in the first place.

More important than knowing who committed and commits terrorist acts is to know why they have resorted to doing so. One resorts to terrorism when politics fails, when there is no dialogue, when negotiations have ceased. When all these fail, one resorts to desperate and punitive measures, and terrorism emerges ferociously.

In our modern times, the greatest terrorist threat comes from Islamic fundamentalist groups. Why does this threat come from Middle Eastern Islam? Because behind each and every terrorist act is hatred, bitterness, frustration, and the desire for revenge. Every day Arabic television stations, particularly Al Jazeera and Al Arabiya, show the violence suffered by their Palestinian brothers due to the brutal actions of Israeli governments who want to consolidate the state of Israel, and if possible to expand the state of Israel to the size it had in the times of King David (i.e., a thousand years before our common era) and who do not accept the establishment of a Palestinian state for it could become a threat to Israel. Repressive actions and the military occupation are done with the use of the most modern war mechanisms and with great brutality and victimizing children, the elderly and innocents. Moreover, such actions also destroy the material and institutional basis for a future Palestinian state. This strategy counts on the explicit and unilateral support of the United States and with the indifference of all other Western countries, who with resignation watch the almost daily killing of people. Such images feed old prejudices between Muslims and Westerners. Since the eighth century Christians and Muslims had alternate victories and defeats. In the nineteenth century and up until the First World War Westerners occupied the Middle East and dreadfully mistreated local populations.

Adding to this is the fact that Arab Muslims are clearly conscious that they hold the blood of the global system of production, trade, and technology—that is, oil. No car moves, no plane takes off, very few things function without oil and its derivates. And they, Arab Muslims, holders of this key to wealth feel manipulated by Western powers, marginalized and ignored insofar as decisions defining global affairs are concerned. Moreover, they are considered to be backwards, despotic, and fanatical. This prejudiced reading that the West has of the Muslim world is a factor that feeds the desire for revenge. Terrorism finds its matrix within this cultural scenario.

Perhaps terrorism is the only possible "war" for a globalized world, for a war in the strong sense of the word would not be possible anymore as it would destroy the human species and part of the biosphere. Perhaps terrorism is the only possible 'war' in which the weak and marginalized are able to win.

How are we to defend ourselves against someone who decided to sacrifice its own life and to turn its own body into a bomb that can be set off anywhere? There are not enough mechanisms of control that are capable of monitoring every single square meter. For this reason, if the current situation endures then terrorism seems to be invincible. Terrorism will last until another kind of relation prevails, another kind of relation that dissolves the hatred and loathing that underlies and feeds terror, and that includes all within our Common Home, where all are able to live with differences that do not present a risk to this new global social pact.

Tolerance and Interreligious Dialogue

Interreligious dialogue is one of the most urgent imperatives in the global phase of humanity. Modern fundamentalism and terrorism are deeply rooted in religious convictions. Only motivations founded in a radical and transcendent view of life provide the necessary courage for people to sacrifice themselves and kill others, who are seen as enemies. This view of life is, generally speaking, the outcome of religions. Behind the main conflicts at the end of the twentieth century and at the dawn of the new millennium there is a religious backdrop, such as in Ireland, in Kosovo, in Kashmir, in Afghanistan, and to some extent in Iraq, where Sunnis and Shiites violently confront each other.

It is not without reason that Samuel P Huntington, one of the sharpest commentators on the process of globalization, wrote in an article entitled "If Not Civilizations, What? Samuel Huntington Responds to His Critics," in *Foreign Affairs*, whilst answering various criticisms that were raised about his views that

> In the modern world, religion is central, perhaps the central, force that motivates and mobilizes people . . . What ultimately counts for people is not political ideology or economic interest. Faith and family, blood and belief, are what people identify with and what they will fight and die for.[7]

In fact, despite the process of secularization and the eclipse of the sacred with the rise of critical thinking since the time of Enlightenment in the eighteenth century, religion has survived all attacks. Moreover, in the last decades we have seen a powerful come back of religious and mystical facets in all societies. This comeback was caused mainly by the suspicion and by the devastatingly critical arguments against religion by masters such as Marx, Freud, Nietzsche, Popper, and others. Like it or not, religion is the common cosmos-vision of the majority of humanity. It is in religion that the majority of humanity finds guidance and the source for ethical attitudes. Ernst Bloch, the Marxist philosopher who insightfully pointed out the profound meaning of religion, rightly said: "wherever there is religion, there is hope." And where there is hope we find numerous ways for fighting, for dreaming, for designing utopias of salvation, and for ascribing a meaning to life and to history.

7. Huntington, "If Not Civilizations, What?" 191–94.

Thus, our starting point must be religion, or better said, religious pluralism. There are as many religions as there are cultures. Because religion works with an ultimate meaning and with values that guide life, religion is permanently risking falling into fundamentalism, viewing itself as absolute and better than others. This attitude, as I maintained previously, is only one step away from religious wars and this is something that has occurred and still occurs today. Religions must know each other, establish dialogue, and search for at least a minimum of common points that allows them to co-live in peace.

Firstly, it is important to recognize religious pluralism. This is an irrefutable fact and as such it must be accepted. The question is if this religious pluralism is and can be rightful? There is considerable divergence on this point, especially within the hierarchies of the Roman Catholic Church, of other Christian churches and of other religions. These hierarchies hardly hide traces of arrogance and of fundamentalism for they understand themselves to be the exclusive bearers of divine revelation and the sole heirs to God's act of salvation.

But it is important to defend the rightfulness of plurality. In order to legitimate this right it is important to refer to an internal feature of religions: no religion can fully frame God within its discourse and rites. If this was the case, God would be just a piece of the world, God would be within reality, God would be an idol. God would completely lose its transcendence from human objectivity. God is always beyond and above us. And consequently, there is space for other ways of expressing and other forms of celebrating God that are not exclusively connected to a single and particular religion.

The Judeo-Christian tradition itself has an internal feature that can aid churches to overcome this narrow-minded aspect: the first eleven chapters of Genesis. Before speaking of Israel as the chosen people, Genesis refers to all peoples of the Earth as the peoples of God. All peoples are part of the first covenant with God, the covenant of creation. God is overshadowing all peoples like a rainbow, the rainbow of the renewed divine covenant after the Great Flood. The biblical scriptures are precise: "When the bow is in the clouds, I will look upon it and remember the everlasting covenant between God and every living creature of all flesh that is upon the earth" (Genesis 9:16).

It is only later that Genesis speaks of the family of Abraham, father of the people of Israel, chosen not to be above others but because "in you all the families of the earth shall be blessed" (Genesis 12:3).

The theology of those first eleven chapters of Genesis continues to be relevant. It reminds us that even today all peoples are peoples of God, all live upon the Earth, garden of God, and compose the single Human Family, which is formed by many families and traditions, cultures and religions.

What is more, religion is to be understood as part of a process of integral ecology. We are all in favor of biodiversity: the more species of plants, animals, birds exist, the more different people exist, the better for the whole. Why would it be any different with regard to religion? The more religions and churches that exist, the more we will be able to appreciate the beauty of God and of Jesus's legacy. It would be a mistake to say: there should be only one kind of life, and this is scorpions; or, there should be only one species of tree, and this is Araucaria trees. This would represent an intolerable impoverishment of biodiversity. Why then say with respect to religion: there should be only one kind of religion, only one creed and only one way of celebrating God? Such a conception is erroneous and is far from the general logic of life and evolution, which the more it develops the more diversity it creates. Thus, there must be a guarantee for religious pluralism.

The sophism "if there is only one God, then there must be only one religion" is invalid for the nature of God and the nature of religion are distinct from one another. The nature of God is the Mystery. This Mystery can never be fully understood by a language, by a symbol, by a doctrine. Everything that is said about the Mystery is in analogy and in symbolism.

The nature of religion is limited, is historic, is finite, is that which is created by human culture. Consequently, God as Mystery is within but also beyond religion. God is *within* because God is indicated through the use of language and symbols. But God is also *beyond* because God transcends all expressions due to its nature of Mystery.

This issue allows us to say with reason: it is important that there should be various religions and churches so that each of them reveals dimensions that are not portrayed by others. All religions and churches together, however, point out in unison the Sacred Reality. And at the same time all of them stand dumbfound for they realize that no language can truly express God. At this point it is appropriate to rest in silence.

This last reflection forces me to introduce a fundamental distinction between religion and spirituality.

By spirituality I understand the encounter with the Mystery of the world, with the Ineffable, with the Tao, with the Numinous, with that which is conventionally called God (but note that Buddhism is not comfortable with this expression). This encounter is neither imagined nor imposed. This encounter simply occurs as an original experience. The human being is a being open to the other, to the world and to the Ineffable. The human being is simply an open and dialogical being. The human being asks radical questions about its origins and destiny, about the meaning of the universe, about the meaning of life, about suffering and death. The human being is a cry to the universe. And the experiencing of reality encompasses the experiencing of that which we call Spirit. It is a way-of-being, of establishing relationships, of feeling part of a greater whole.

This phenomenon of spirituality is an ordinary anthropological given. It is not the monopoly of religion or of some spiritual pathway. Spirituality is something that precedes all. It has the same standing as libido, as will, as intelligence and as sensitivity. Just as there is *intellectual intelligence* through which we ordain rational and scientific knowledge and *emotional intelligence* through which we demonstrate feelings, care, and compassion, there is also *spiritual intelligence* through which we attain, beyond rationality and emotions, the global context of our lives, meaningful wholes, values, and the insertion into a major Whole.

It is appropriate for spirituality to be all encompassing and to be guided by a sense of the transcendental. Scientists have detected through the biological study of neurons the empirical basis for spiritual intelligence. Some neuron-scientists even spoke of a 'God Spot' in the brain. Within an evolutionary context this means: the universe has evolved up to the point in which intelligence emerged, an intelligence that is capable of perceiving the Mystery of the universe, the Mystery that penetrates and that weaves through everything. This 'God Spot' represents an evolutionary advantage for the species *homo* that is present in each and every human person. Logically, God is not only present in a particular point in the brain, but in the whole brain, in the whole being, and in each and every dimension of a being. But it is from this cluster of neurons that God lets itself be empirically perceived.[8]

This spiritual intelligence, also called spirituality, is at the basis of all religions and spiritual pathways. The way it has been historically expressed changes according to culture. Religions are cultural creations, are highly diverse, are attempts to express this foundational experience through the use of a doctrine, of celebration, of a sacred text and of an ethical code.

Religions are important to the extent in which they preserve, encourage, restate, and update spirituality for each and every person and generation. Religions vary, are numerous, are born, develop, and can disappear; but spirituality never disappears for it is part of the essence of the human being.

Mystics intuited this distinction between spirituality and religion when they made reference to the sacred fire that burns in the heart of every person and of every community and that must be continuously fed with resources from society and religion. If this fire starts to go out then religion faces a crisis or fossilizes. If this fire is continuously looked after, then it becomes the greatest reference. It opens the space for a fecund dialogue between religions that share this spirituality. Religions are varied and numerous, but spirituality is common to all of them. Spirituality enables understanding between religions. Spirituality is like a deep fountain feeding many rivers on the surface. All rivers are sourced from this fountain. This fountain is the place where human beings go to drink and quench their thirst.

Christians, however, hold onto an issue that can present difficulties to interreligious dialogue. Christians affirm the uniqueness of Jesus of Nazareth, in whom God would have said its last and definitive word to the whole of humanity. Christians feel they must bear witness to this affirmation due to their faith in the foundational texts and tradition. No matter how much dialogue is carried on, the bottom line is that all human beings are invited to join the Christian faith. This is the Christian position. This is a clear problem. How can we resolve it? I will try to provide an answer for I myself profess the Christian faith.

I believe that the global phase of humanity forces Christians to reevaluate their position. Christian statements are done within an enclosed system, which turn truths self-referential and absolute. A mental-

8. Cf. Zohar and Marshall, *SQ: Spiritual Intelligence.*

ity based on absolute formulations is characteristic of enclosed systems. The situation changes, however, when we realize that, just as it is the case with nature, systems are always open, never enclosed. Systems are moments of an ongoing process that is immeasurably vast.

We must think of the singularity of Jesus within the great process of evolution, of cosmos-genesis, of biogenesis and of anthropogenesis. Jesus represents an appearance in this incommensurable process.

At a certain moment in the evolution of the universe, of the Earth, of life and of consciousness emerged in the human being an awareness of the Mystery of the world and of its inner connection with this Mystery. Consciousness grasped God, God who was always present in every moment and phase of evolution. Moreover, consciousness achieved its apex when the human being felt itself to be a child of God. It calls God "Abah," dear Father full of goodness. Whoever calls God as Father feels itself to be God's son or daughter. This consciousness broke through in Jesus of Nazareth, our universal brother. But this consciousness is part of the process of evolution and of humanity, and as such it is not something exclusive to Jesus. It is the entirety of humanity that leaps forward towards the Mystery of the world through Jesus. Therefore, all human being are sons and daughters of God and this represents a new stage of anthropogenesis and of human consciousness.

The New Testament calls Jesus the Christ because of this awareness. *Christ* is not a name. It is a dimension, it is a conduct, it is a new state of consciousness of one who is connected and reconnected to God. To this person the Greek adjective *Christ* is applied, an adjective that means "anointed." This adjective was added on to the name *Jesus*.

But it is important to emphasize that the dimension *Christ* goes beyond Jesus. Jesus condensed the dimension Christ so much that the apostolic community end up calling him Jesus, the Christ, or simply Jesus Christ.

However, I repeat, it is important not to reduce Christ to Jesus. The dimension Christ is vast and it is always being realized in humanity. It gained body in the great mystics, sages, and scholars of all traditions when they intuited that the concept of spiritual journey is the immersion in the supreme Reality within a nondualistic experience. The follower of Tao enters in an ineffable union with Tao. The follower of Jesus, St John of the Cross stated: at the end of all we will be God through participation.

Is not this the profound truth that Christians want to express when they refer to divine incarnation and affiliation? Christians do not need thus to debase or depart from others so to affirm the singularity of the Christian pathway. Christians are in the same great pathway throd on by the rest of humanity, a great pathway in the direction of the Mystery that embraces all.

Some Christian sources point out this universal characteristic when they state that the Word was in the beginning, was God and that it illuminates every person that comes into this world (cf. John 1:1); or "For no other foundation can any one lay than that which is laid, which is Jesus Christ" (1 Corinthians 3:11); and "set forth in Christ, as a plan for the fullness of time, to unite all things in him, things in heaven and things on earth" (Ephesians 1:9–10). That is to say, the Christ is connected to the mystery of creation and as such it impinges on all beings and on every person that appears in the evolutionary process, including Jesus, the Nazarene.

If this is the importance of religions in the concrete reality of humanity, then I agree with the core thesis of the German theologian Hans Küng, a commentator of religions within the global phase of humanity, in his *Tracing the Way*. I quote:

> No peace among the nations without peace among the religions. No peace among religions without dialogue between the religions. No dialogue between religions without global ethical standards. No survival of our globe without a global ethic.[9]

The dialogue between religions cannot start with a discussion about doctrine; rather it must start with the awareness of the spirituality that unites all. And this starts mainly with prayer. To pray is to be immersed in spirituality. Through prayer people start to know each other, to discover the goodness of one and another, to discover the piety, the reverence and the sincere search for 'God'. Doctrines are revitalized through the concrete life that is inspired by the religious search. Certainly, everything that is healthy can become ill. All religions, despite being healthy, can incur deviations, hardenings and the fundamentalist attitude of some. This presents a vast ground for reciprocal criticism and for processes of purification. Just as illness is connected to health, in a similar way deviations are connected to the true essence of religion.

9. Kung, *Tracing the Way*, 266.

Out of this praying dialogue emerge points in common that provide the foundation for a possible peace between religions, and for peace in global politics.

In fact, the points in common in favor of peace were enumerated during the 1st World Conference of Religions for Peace in Kyoto, Japan, in 1970.[10] These points are

1. There is a fundamental unity to the human family in the equality and dignity of all its members.

2. Every human being is sacred and untouchable, particularly in its consciousness.

3. Every human community is valuable.

4. Power cannot be equated with right. Power can never be valued in itself, can never be absolute, and it must be limited by the right and by the control of the community.

5. Faith, love, compassion, altruism, the power of the spirit and the interior truth are ultimately much superior to hate, enmity, and egoism.

6. One must be, by duty, on the side of the poor and of the oppressed and against oppressors.

7. We strongly believe that at the end goodness will prevail.

It is clear that interreligious dialogue is not an end in itself. This dialogue is governed by something larger: peace between peoples, peace with the Earth, peace with ecosystems, peace of every human being with itself, and peace with the original Fountainhead, the source of all and to where all return.

Active tolerance between religions stands, therefore, for peaceful and happy co-living between the most diverse religions that are able to perceive this diversity as the richness of a sole and same Mystery fountain of Mystery.

---

10. Translator's note: check the following website for more information: www.wcro .org/.

Conclusion

By reaching the end of my reflections in this book it must have become clear how crucial the virtues of co-living, respect and tolerance are for a peaceful coexistence between the various tribes of the Earth, tribes which after so many years of isolation meet together for good in our Common Home.

To exist is always to coexist; to live is always to co-live. To coexist and to co-live requires as the initial attitude respect for the other, for the other as someone who is different from me. It is this initial gap between oneself and the other that enables an enriching approach, an exchange of complementarities, and a revitalization of one's own position.

In the encounter with the other we also verify the emergence of differences. These differences are not always immediately understood. Sometimes these differences cause estrangement and a feeling of rejection. It is at this point that tolerance enters as the effort to co-live in spite of differences, as the effort to place limitations on oneself because of the right of the other to exist as it is.

A great part of the conflicts in the world is due to a lack of respect for and tolerance of differences. Co-living is the outcome of hard learning. The final result of this is growth, is a convergence in diversity. This time, in this new global phase of civilization: we either learn to co-live, to respect each other, and to tolerate that which appears to us to be unacceptable; or we will face destruction and conflict as never seen before. We will all be victims given the interdependence of every one with everyone. The Earth, as Gaia, as a living supraorganism, whose vulnerability requires special care by all, will also be a victim.

The final effect of these virtues, if lived in articulation, is peace. Once more I refer to the Earth Charter definition of peace: "created by right relationships with oneself, other persons, other cultures, other life, Earth, and the larger whole of which all are a part."[1]

This shared peace is the major desire of humanity in our modern times, a humanity that is tired of conflicts, wars and decimations that blur the line of the horizon of hope that it need not always be like this, that history can be different, that history can be more humane, happy, and worth celebrating.

1. Translator's note: www.earthcharteraction.org.

Bibliography and Further Reading

Abdalla, Mauricio. *O princípio da cooperação: em busca de uma nova racionalidade.* São Paulo: Paulus, 2002.

Ali, Tariq. *The Clash of Fundamentalisms: Crusades, Jihads, and Modernity.* London: Verso, 2002.

Armstrong, Karen. *The Battle for God.* New York: Ballantine, 2001.

Augustine. *Confessions.* Translated by J. G. Pilkington. Nicene and Post-Nicene Fathers, 1st ser., vol. 1. Edited by Philip Schaff. Buffalo: Christian Literature, 1887. Revised and edited for New Advent by Kevin Knight. Online: http://www.newadvent.org/fathers/110101.htm

Bartholo Roberto dos Santos Jr. *Você e eu: Martin Buber, presence e palavra.* Rio de Janeiro: Garamond, 2001.

Bartoly, Emília. *Feng-shui e o desvelamento da morada humana: um estudo sobre os conceitos de espaço e de natureza na filosofia chinesa.* Rio de Janeiro: UERJ, 1998.

Basset, Jean-Claude. *Le dialogue interreligieux: histoire et avenir.* Paris: Cerf, 1996.

Bitterli, Urs. *Die "Wilden" und die "Zivilisierten": Die europäisch-überseelische Begegnung.* Beck'sche Sonderausgaben. Munich: Beck, 1976.

Bobbio, Norbert. *The Age of Rights.* Cambridge: Polity, 1996.

Boff, Leonardo. *Eclesiogênese: As comunidades eclesiais de base reinventam a Igreja.* Petrópolis: Vozes, 1977.

———. *Essential Care: An Ethics of Human Nature.* London: SPCK, 2007.

———. *Espiritualidade, caminho de realização,* Rio de Janeiro: Sextante, 2002.

———. *Ética e eco-espiritualidade.* Campinas: Verus, 2003.

———. *Experimentar Deus: A transparência de todas as coisas,* Campinas: Verus, 2003

———. *Novas fronteiras da Igreja.* Campinas: Verus, 2004.

———. *Princípio de compaixão e cuidado.* Petrópolis: Vozes, 2001.

———. *São Francisco de Assis: ternura e vigor: Uma leitura a partir dos pobres* Petrópolis: Vozes, 1981.

Borne, Étienne. "Tolleranza religiosa." In *Grande Dizionario delle Religioni.* edited by Paul Poupard, 2148–50. Assisi: Cittadella Editrice/Piemme, 1985.

Colorni, Felice M. "Laicità: Un concetto in cerca di senso." *Confronti,* Gennaio (2005). Online: http://www.confronti.net/

Corcoran, Peter Blaze, editor in chief. *The Earth Charter in Action: Toward a Sustainable World.* Amsterdam: KIT, 2005. Online: http://www.earthcharterinaction.org/.

Congar, F. Yves M.- J. *Je crois en l'Esprit Saint.* 3 vols. Paris: Cerf, 1979–1980.

Dupuis, Jacques. *Rumo a uma teologia cristã do pluralismo religioso.* São Paulo: Paulinas, 1990.

Eulenstein, Rolf. "Und wer ist mein Nächster (Lk 10,25–37)." *Theologie und Glaube* 67 (1977) 127–45.

Firpo, Massimo. *Il problema della tolleranza religiosa nell'età moderna*, Turin: Loerscher, 1978.

Francis of Assisi. *Writings and Early Biographies*. Chicago: Franciscan, 1996.

Freire, Paulo. *Educação como prática de liberdade*. Rio de Janeiro: Paz e Terra, 2004.

————. *Pedagogia da tolerância*. São Paulo: UNESP, 2005.

————. *Pedagogy of Hope*. London: Continuum, 2004.

————. *Pedagogy of the Oppressed*. New York: Herder & Herder, 1970.

Fuchs, Ottmar. *Die Fremden*, Düsseldorf: Patmos, 1988.

Fürst, Alfons. "Identität und Toleranz im frühen Christentum." *Orientierung* 66 (2002) 26–31.

Gandhi, Mahatma. *An Autobiography or the Story of My Experiments with Truth*. Penguin Classics. London: Penguin, 2001.

Gonzáles Faus, J. I. "La difícil laicidad." *Cuadernos Cristianismo e Justicia* 131 (2005) 29–30.

Habbermas, Jürgen. *The Theory of Communicative Action*. 2 vols. Cambridge: Polity, 1984–1987.

————. *The Inclusion of the Other: Studies in Political Theory*. Studies in Contemporary German Social Thought. Cambridge: MIT Press, 1998.

Hick, John, editor. *The Myth of God Incarnate*. Philadelphia: Westminster, 1977.

————, and Paul F. Knitter. *The Myth of Christian Uniqueness: Toward a Pluralistic Theology of Religion*. Faith Meets Faith. Maryknoll, NY: Orbis, 1987.

Huntington, Samuel P. "If Not Civilizations, What? Samuel Huntington Responds to His Critics." *Foreign Affairs* 173 (November–December 1993) 186–94.

Illich, Ivan. *Tools for Conviviality*. World Perspectives 47. New York: Harper & Row, 1973.

Jonas, Hans. *The Phenomenon of Life: Toward a Philosophical Biology*. New York: Dell, 1966.

Knitter, Paul F. *No Other Name? A Critical Survey of Christian Attitudes toward the World Religions*. American Society of Missiology series 7. Maryknoll, NY: Orbis, 1985.

————. "Toward a Liberation Theology of the Religions." In *The Myth of Christian Uniqueness: Toward a Pluralistic Theology of Religion*, 178–200. Faith Meets Faith. Maryknoll, NY: Orbis, 1987

Küng, Hans. *Tracing the Way: Spiritual Dimensions of the World Religions*. Translated by John Bowden. London: Continuum, 2002.

————. *World Religions*. Princeton: Films for the Humanities and Sciences, 2004.

Künsch, Dimas Antônio, Little Sisters of Jesus. *O renascer do povo Tapirapé: diário das Irmãzinhas de Jesus de 1952–1954*. São Paulo: Salesianas, 2002.

Leclerq, Joseph. *Histoire de la tolérance au siècle de la Reforme*. 2 vols. Théologie 31. Paris: Aubier, 1995.

Llull, Ramón. *Selected Works of Ramón Llull*. Edited and translated by Anthony Bonner. 2 vols. Princeton: Princeton University Press, 1985

Locke, John. *A Letter concerning Toleration; Concerning Civil Government, Second Essay; An Essay concerning Human Understanding*. Great Books of the Western World 35. Chicago: Encyclopaedia Britannica, 1952.

Marshall, I. Howard. *The Gospel of Luke: A Commentary on the Greek Text*. New International Greek Testament Commentary. Exeter, UK: Paternoster, 1978.

Melucci, Alberto. *L'invenzione del presente*. Bologna: Il Mulino, 1991.

Meyer-Abich, Klaus Michael. *Wege zum Frieden mit der Natur: Praktische Naturphilosophie für Umweltpolitik*. Munich: Hanser, 1984.

Monseleweski, Werner. *Der barmherzige Samariter: Eine auslegungsgeschichtliche Untersuchung zu Lukas 10, 25–37*. Beiträge zur Geschichte der biblischen Exegese 5. Tübingen: Mohr/Siebeck, 1967.

Moura, P. C. *Construindo o futuro: o impacto global do novo paradigma*. Rio de Janeiro: Mauad, 1994.

Müller, Robert. *O nascimento de uma civilização global*. São Paulo: Aquariana, 1993.

O'Leary, Joseph Stephen. *La vérité chrétienne à l'âge du pluralisme religieux*. Cogitatio fidei 181. Paris: Cerf, 1994.

———. *Religious Pluralism and Christian Truth*. Rev. ed. Edinburgh: T. & T. Clark, 1996.

Oliveira, Manfredo Araújo de. *Ética e sociabilidade*. São Paulo: Loyola, 1993.

———. *Desafios éticos da globalização*. Ética e sociedade. São Paulo: Paulinas, 2001.

O'Murchu, Diarmuid. *Evolutionary Faith: Rediscovering God in Our Great Story*. Maryknoll, NY: Orbis, 2002.

Panikkar, Raimundo. *The Intrareligious Dialogue*. Rev. ed. New York: Paulist, 1999.

Passet, René, and Jean Liberman. *Mondialisation financière et terrorisme*. Enjeux Planète. Paris: Atelier, 2002.

Pieres, Aloysius. *Liberación, inculturación, diálogo religioso: Un nuevo paradigma desde Ásia*. Estella: Verbo Divino, 2001.

Robinson, H. Wheeler. *The Christian Experience of the Holy Spirit*. Library of Constructive Theology. London: Nisbet 1952.

Scaccaglia, Luciano. "Siamo tutti laici." *Adista* 86 (2004).

Sellin, Gerhard. "Lukas als Gleichniserzähler: Die Erzählung vom Barmherzigen Samariter (Lk 10:25–37)." *Zeitschrift für die Neutestamentliche Wissenschaft* 66 (1975) 19–60.

———. "Lukas as Gleichniserzähler: Die Erzählung von Barmherziger Samariter (Lk 10:25–37)." *Zeitschrift für die neutestamentliche Wissenschaft* 65 (1974) 166–89.

Seoane, José, and Emilio Taddei. "From Seattle to Porto Alegre: The Anti-Neoliberal Globalization Movement." *Current Sociology* 50 (2002) 99–122.

Serres, Michel. *The Natural Contract*. Translated by Elizabeth MacArthur and William Paulson. Studies in Literature and Science. Ann Arbor: University of Michigan Press, 1995.

Simmel, Georg. *The Sociology of Georg Simmel*. Translated, edited, and with an introduction by Kurt H. Wolff. New York: Free Press, 1964.

Schoenborn, Ulrich. *"Gekreuzigt im Leiden der Armen": Beiträge zur kontextuellen Theologie in Brasilien*. Brasilien Taschenbuch 7. Mettingen: Brazilienkunde, 1986.

Schweitzer, Albert. *Ehrfurcht vor dem Leben: Grundtexte aus fünf Jahrhunderten*. Munich: Beck, 1966.

———. *Kultur und Ethik*. Munich: Beck, 1960.

———. *Reverence for Life*. New York: Harper & Row, 1969.

———. *Wie Wir Überleben Können: Eine Ethik für die Zukunft*. Spektrum 4264. Freiburg: Herder, 1994.

———, et al. *Was sollen wir tun?* Heidelberg: Lambert Schneider, 1986.

Suess, Paolo. "Über die Unfähigkeit der Einen, sich der Anderen zu erinnern." In *Anerkennung der Anderen: eine theologische Grunddimension interkultureller*

Kommunikation, edited by Edward Arens, Helmut Peukert, et al., 64–94. Quaestiones disputatae 156. Freiburg: Herder, 1995.

Sundermeier, Theo, editor. *Den Frendem wahrnehmen: bausteine für eine Xenologie.* Studien zum Verstehen fremder Religionen 5. Gütersloh: Mohn, 1992.

————. *Konvivenz und Differenz.* Missionswissenschaftliche Forschungen 3 Erlangen: Verlag der Evangelisch-Lutherischen Mission, 1995.

————. *Dem Fremden verstehen: eine praktische Hermeneutik*, Göttingen: Vandenhoeck & Ruprecht, 1999.

Teixeira, Faustino. *Teologia das religiões: uma visão panorâmica.* São Paulo: Paulinas, 1995.

Tourraine, Alain. *¿Poderemos viver juntos? Iguais e diferentes.* Petrópolis: Vozes, 1999.

United Nations Educational and Cultural Organization.. *The Delcaration of Principles on Tolerance 1995.* New York: United Nations, 1995.

Vatican Council, Second. *Dignitatis Humanae.* Online: www.vatican.va/archive/hist_councils/ii_vatican_council/index.htm/.

————. *Gaudium et Spes: Pastoral Constitution on the Church in the Modern World.* Washington DC: United States Catholic Conference, 1965. Online: http://www.vatican.va/archive/hist_councils/ii_vatican_council/index.htm/.

Vieira, Liszt. *Cidadania e globalização.* Rio de Janeiro: Record, 2000.

Vigil, José María. "Macroecumenismo: teología de las religiones latinoamericanas." *Alternativas* 27 (June 2004) 109–26

————. *Teología del pluralismo religioso: Curso sistemático de teología popular.* Quito: Abya-Yala, 2005.

————. *Theology of Religious Pluralism.* Berlin: LIT, 2008.

Voltaire, François-Marie Arouet. *Treatise on Tolerance.* Translated by Brian Masters. Edited and translated by Simon Harvey. Cambridge Texts in the History of Philosophy. Cambridge: Cambridge University Press, 2000.

Wilson, Edward O. *The Future of Life.* London: Abacus, 2003.

Wittgenstein, Ludwig. *Schriften*, vol. 1. Frankfurt: Surhkamp, 1969.

————.*Tractatus Logico-Philosophicus*, with an introduction by Bertrand Russell. International Library of Psychology, Philosophy, and Scientific Method. London: Routledge & Kegan Paul, 1981.

Zohar, Danah, and Ian Marshall. *SQ: Spiritual Intelligence; The Ultimate Intelligence.* London: Bloomsbury, 2000.

book 3

Feasting Together
and Living in Peace

Preface

This third book is the last of my reflections on those necessary and required virtues for the global phase of humanity so that humanity can be united and live in peace.

It only makes sense to philosophize about virtues if this philosophizing encourages virtuous living. More important than to know the virtues and about the virtues is to live these virtues and to become a virtuous person.

It is for this reason that the three books on virtues seek to combine theoretical reflections (which clarifies matters) with practical applications (which encourages acting virtuously).

To eat and drink together (i.e., communality) are primordial human activities. We do not only nurture our bodies, we also feed our souls. To eat and drink together represent rites loaded with meaning. It is through rites that we reveal our humanity and the degree of civilization that we have achieved.

Currently, more than half of humanity has no proper access to food and drink. This is a scandalous situation that constitutes a serious ethical and political problem. This situation points the finger at the other half of humanity, the well-nourished half of humanity, and charges it with being hardhearted, uncharitable, and barbarous. What strategies must be implemented if we are to place all at the table as brothers and sisters?

The final outcome of the virtues of hospitality, co-living, tolerance, and communality is peace. It is not peace as a ceasefire of a continuous war, but peace as the result of a development that starts to take root in human hearts, that spreads through communities, that is being implemented in societies, and that is anchored in God. What is being sought is a culture of peace. Peace is the aim, but it is also the means. Only peaceful means will produce peace.

The culture of peace creates an atmosphere of welcome, of care, of friendship, of love that transforms conflicts into dynamic tensions, it transforms competition into something healthy, and it transforms disagreements into opportunities for finding points in common within diversity.

The best definition for peace I have ever come across is stated in the Earth Charter, that is, peace is "created by right relationships with oneself, other persons, other cultures, other life, Earth, and the larger whole of which all are a part."[1]

Petrópolis, 24th June 2006

---

1. Translator's note: www.earthcharteraction.org.

twelve

Eating and Drinking Together: Communality

The apex of the process of hospitality, of co-living, of respect, and of tolerance is achieved in communality. Communality means to eat and drink together. All together at the table, as communal partners, eating, drinking, sharing communion, and celebrating being together in our Common Home. All together as a great human family meeting up in our Common Home, all together as brothers and sisters in humanity and as brothers and sisters of the other beings of creation. This is a dream. This is a dream that has been dreamt by humanity and by the great spiritual sages, such as Jesus of Nazareth and others. The dream is a virtual anticipation of something that can become a reality one day.

The table around which communality is realized is one of the most fundamental references of human families. It is at the table that family relations are continuously formed and reformed.

The table is not a mere piece of furniture; rather, it is connected to an existential experience and to a rite. The table stands for the privileged place occupied by the family, by communion and by fellowship. When we share a meal, we communicate the joy in being together; we communicate a feeling of well-being without faking it; we communicate a communion that is translated by an easiness of conversation about daily occurrences, by an easiness of expressing opinions about local, national, and international historical events without the fear of censure. At the table we can receive family members, friends and guests. It is at the table that we feel, in a way, members of the human family.

Food is much more than something material. Food is a symbol of encounter and of communion. Food is something that is appreciated and that becomes the object of discussions. The greatest happiness of a mother or of a chef is to perceive the happiness of communal partners at the eating of the food they have prepared. An important gesture at the table is to serve someone or to pass the food to someone. Civilized behavior encourages all to serve each other so that the food is passed around, reaching all.

But we must not be excessively romantic about this. The table is also a place where family tensions and conflicts take place, where issues can be discussed in the open, and where disagreements can be considered and resolutions established. It is at the table that disturbing silences reveal bad feelings between people. Thus, the table is the *human* table; it is a table that encompasses all contradictions of the human condition.

Modern culture has shaped time so much around work and productivity that it ended up weakening the symbolism of the table. The table is now reserved for Sundays or for special occasions, celebrations and birthday parties, which is when family members meet up. However, by and large, the table has ceased to be a point of permanent convergence for the family.

The family table has been replaced by other tables that are greatly secular: table of negotiations, games table, debating table, foreign exchange desk and client services desk, to mention a few. Even in their secular nature, all these tables still bear an irremovable reference; that is, tables are a place of encounter between people and it does not matter the reasons leading people to sit at the table, to be at the table to exchange, to negotiate, or work out resolutions that please all concerned. To abandon the table can stand for the failure of negotiations and the recognition of a conflict of interests. The table embodies all these contradictory features.

Despite this difficult dialectic, we must rescue the human sense of the table as a symbol of the family and of co-living. It is important to reserve time for the table as a place where communality and free and open conversation can happen in plenitude. The table is a permanent source of the reimplementation of humanity in its highest sense.

Narratives of Communality

Let me refer to some narratives about communality that are present in all cultures.

Let me start with the Judaeo-Christian culture for it is more familiar to me. In this culture there is a universal category, that is, the

Kingdom of God, which is the primal content of Jesus's message. This category is represented by the banquet to which we all are invited. We all sit at the table and become communal partners independent of moral standing. The Nazarene says:

> The Kingdom of Heaven may be compared to a king who gave a marriage feast for his son, and sent his servants to call those who were invited to the marriage feast; but they would not come . . . Then he said to his servants . . . Go therefore to the thoroughfares, and invite to the marriage feast as many as you find. And those servants went out into the streets and gathered all whom they found, both good and bad; so the wedding hall was filled with guests. (Matthew 22:2–3, 8–10)

Another narrative comes from east Asia. Perhaps, very few other stories are able to shed more light on the issue of communality than this one I shall refer to. Eating together in solidarity with each other represents the foremost human realization, which is something we call "heaven." And the opposite, the desire to eat in an egoistical manner, i.e., to eat alone, represents the ultimate human frustration, which is something we call "hell." The legend goes as follow:

> A disciple asked a Seer: "Master, what is the difference between the heavens, between the communality between the children of God, and the opposite?"
>
> The Seer answered: "The difference is very small, but it is of serious consequence. I have seen communal partners sit at the table where there was a great amount of rice. Everybody was hungry, almost starving. Everybody tried with no success to reach the rice. With the help of long chopsticks that were over one meter long each of them tried to take the rice to their own mouths. They tried hard but they did not succeed because the chopsticks were far too long. Hence, famished and alone they remained; they wasted away. This was hell, the negation of communality."
>
> The Seer continued: "I also saw a marvellous happening. I saw people sitting at a table, in the middle of which there was a great amount of steaming rice. They were all hungry. How marvellous! Each of them grabbed the rice with their own chopsticks and took it to the mouth of another. They served each other with extreme cordiality. They were together in solidarity. Each satiated the hunger of another. They felt as brothers and sisters in the

great table of Tao. This was heaven, the ultimate communality of
the children of the Earth."

This parable does not require explanation. Its content is obvious
and its argument is convincing. Unfortunately, nowadays, a great part of
humanity finds itself hungry and distressed because there are very few
people who are willing to help each other, to serve each other with the
abundance of food on Earth's table. The rich take hold of this food and
eat it with no regard for those who have been excluded. If only the rich
would let crumbs fall from the table so that the famished could dispute
these with dogs; but the rich do not even do this. There is a criminal
lack of communality between human beings and for this reason we are
wanting of humanity.

It is through eating and drinking together that human beings celebrate the joy of living and co-living. What is the point of being hospitable, of co-living humanely, of holding a mutual respect and a serene
tolerance if we cannot eat and drink together? When we eat and drink
together we collectively guarantee the continuation of life with all the
generosity, celebration and joy that accompany such an event. At the
end, as it is with the Kingdom of God, there is a table that has been
prepared so that communal partners can finally feast and celebrate the
re-encounter in our Common Home.

We are still far from achieving such a joyful happening. We have
a desperately raw and divided humanity, a humanity with 800 million
hungry people, with almost 2 billion undernourished people, 1 billion
people without enough drinking water, and 2 billion people with no access to proper drinking water.

On 11th of September 2001 when those terrorists threw their
planes against the Twin Towers in New York and against the Pentagon in
Washington, about three thousand people died. This was an atrocity that
stopped the world and humanity.

On that same day, exactly 16,400 children under five years old died
of hunger or of malnutrition; that is, five times more than the number of
people who died as a consequence of terrorism. Throughout that year,
12 million children died of hunger or of malnutrition, and nobody was
flabbergasted by this human tragedy.

Because of the existing and growing number of hungry people, we
must take notice of communality with urgency, we must remit to hu-

mane ideals and to a spiritual understanding of life and of the necessary bread that cannot be denied to any of the children of the Earth.

Communality: The Distinction between Man and Animal

Communality is so foundational that it is linked to the very essence of the human being. About seven million years ago the gradual and progressive separation between superior simians and human beings took place in a common ancestor. The particularization of the human being emerged in a mysterious way and it is very difficult to reconstitute it historically. However, ethnobiologists and archaeologists point to a particular event. Our anthropoid ancestors went out to collect fruits and seeds, and hunt game and fish, but they did not eat the results of their efforts alone; rather, they collected all those forms of nourishment and took them to the group, and once there they practiced communality. That is, they distributed food among themselves and ate it as a group and in a communitarian way.[1]

Therefore, communality, which presupposes solidarity and cooperation between individuals, allowed for the first leap from animality and towards humanity. This was just the very first step but it was a crucial step because it established the basic characteristic of the human species, which makes us different from other complex species (and between us and chimpanzees there is only 1.6 percent of genetic differential): that is, communality, solidarity and cooperation. This small difference makes all the difference.

Communality that in the past made us human is still at work today. If it is not present, then we become inhuman, cruel, and merciless. Is not this the unfortunate situation of humanity today?

But it was not only communality that made us into social and cooperative beings. Another factor emerged revealing the social and communitarian nature of the human being: speech in the form of a grammatical language. Certainly, the human being is the sole being with a language based on "double articulation" of words and of meanings. Both words and meaning are under grammatical rules. We speak; we do not merely emit sounds and grunts. As it was demonstrated by two well-known Chilean biologists, namely Maturana and Varela, language allows the human being to organize the world, allows the human being

1. Cf. Morin, *L'identité humaine.*

to name and classify things, allows the human being to develop imagination and ideas, and allows the human to develop concepts.[2]

Another element responsible for the rise of humanity is directly connected to communality, that is, gastronomy, i.e., the preparation of food. Claude Lévi-Strauss, an eminent anthropologist who worked for a long time in Brazil, noted well when he said that "engaging in cooking is a form of human activity that is truly universal. Just as there is no society without language, there is also no society that does not cook some of its food."[3]

About 500 million years ago the human being learned to make fire and to control it. And with fire the human being started to cook its food. The "culinary fire" is what differentiates the human being from other complex mammals. The transition from raw food to cooked food is considered to be one of the main factors in the transition from animal to civilized human being. With fire gastronomy emerged, a gastronomy that is particular to every people, to every culture, and to every region.

Every people has some food that is characteristic to it and that is part of its historical identity. For instance, the *feijoada* in Brazil,[4] the *taco* in Mexico, the burger in the United States, the pizza in Italy, the potato salad and the sauerkraut in Germany, the *kibbeh* in Arab countries,[5] the sushi and sashimi in Japan, to mention a few. This is not just about cooking the food but also enriching its taste. The seasoning used and the various flavours distinguish one cuisine from another, one culture from another. The various cuisines created different gastronomic habits, which are often connected to particular feasts, such as Christmas (when we eat turkey), Easter (when we eat chocolate Easter eggs), New Year's Eve (when we eat pork), and Feast of Saint John (when we eat corn on the cob), and so forth, all common to Brazilian culture.

2. Cf. Maturana and Varela, *The Tree of Knowledge.*

3. Lévi-Strauss, "El triángulo culinario," in *Lévi-Strauss: estruturalismo y dialetica*, 40. Translator's note: Passage translated directly from the Portuguese.

4. Translator's note: Feijoada is a typically Brazilian dish. It is a stew of black beans and various pieces of meat, offal, and sausages. Its origins are said to be connected to African slaves, who used all the pork meat and offal that the Portuguese masters did not care for and that were thrown out in rubbish tips.

5. Translator's note: *Kibbeh* is a Levantine Arab dish made of burghul and minced meat. The best-known variety is a torpedo-shaped fried croquette. It is a popular dish in Brazil.

Communality is connected to all these complex phenomena. These are all communitarian rites loaded with symbolism and meaning that reinforce the sense of belonging to a group and that consolidates the leap towards being a civilized human being.

In other words, to be nourished is not a biologically individual activity. When one eats in a communal manner, one takes communion with others. To do this is to enter into communion with those energies that are hidden in food, in its taste, in its smell, in its beauty, in its consistency. To do this is to enter into communion with those cosmic energies that underlie food, cosmic energies such as the fertility of the earth, solar warmth, forests, water, rain, and wind.

Due to this numinous character of eating/entering-into-communion, all communality is in a certain way sacramental. It is loaded with good energies that are symbolized in rites and artistic representations. It causes a joyful feeling in communal partners. The moment when we eat is one of the most awaited moments of day and night. We have an instinctive and rational awareness that without eating there is neither survival nor joy in existing nor fraternal coexistence.

For millions of years human beings, who first emerged in Africa, lived as nomads, wandering to places that offered them better chances of survival and expediency, such as the banks of a river, the banks of a lake, the banks of mangrove swamps, seaside areas, and green valleys. As tributaries of nature, they took from her what they needed to eat by collecting, hunting, fishing, and storing. By collecting fruits from nature they developed its production through agriculture, which presupposes the domestication and the cultivation of seeds and plants.

This domestication is a consequence of continuous habitation. Around ten to twelve thousand years ago, perhaps, the major revolution in human history took place: nomad human beings became sedentary. They founded the first settlements (12000 BCE), they invented agriculture (9000 BCE), and they started to domesticate and herd animals (8500 BCE). An extremely complex process of modern civilization started with successive revolutions, which were inaugurated by the first one, that is, the Industrial Revolution; then followed the nuclear revolution, the cybernetic revolution, the informational revolution, until we reached the current state of affairs.

In the first instance, wild vegetables and cereals were domesticated, probably by women, who were more observant of the rhythms of nature.

Everything seems to have started in the Middle East between the Tigris and Euphrates rivers and in the Indus Valley in India. There, wheat, barley, lentils, broad beans, and peas were domesticated. And in Latin America maize, avocado, tomatoes, manioc, and beans; in the Far East rice and millets; in Africa maize and sorghum were domesticated. This revolution took place between 9000 and 5000 BCE.[6]

Then around 8500 BCE animals were domesticated: first goats and sheep, then oxen and pigs. The chicken was the first fowl to be domesticated.

Hunting and collection of fruits and seeds continued to occur. But the domestication of vegetables, cereals, and animals guaranteed a better diet and overcame the stress of a daily search for food. This situation was further developed with the invention of the wheel, of the hoe, of the plough, and of other utensils made of metals around 4000 BCE. (Metal was already known around 7000 BCE.)

This sketchy data has been scientifically asserted in our modern times by archaeologists and by ethnobiologists through the use of modern technology such as carbon dating; electronic microscopes; and chemical analysis of sediments, ashes, pollens, bones, and charcoal. The results of these analyses allow us to reconstruct the local ecology and the economy of the time.[7]

However, it is important to bear in mind that this history is very short when it is compared with the history of life. If we start from the fact that human beings emerged only about 3 million years ago, then for 2,990,000 years the human being lived hunting and collecting. It is only about ten thousand or twelve thousand years ago that the human being emerged as a farmer and gatherer, and as someone who intervened with nature.[8]

By starting to plant and to harvest wheat or rice, it became possible for the human being to create reserves of food, to organize food provisions for the group, to expand the family, and in consequence of this, to expand human populations. At the same time that this happened, the human being started to lose the synergetic and cooperative relation it had with nature. This is so because the human being had to look after fields, to cut down forests, to till the soil, to plant, to harvest, and to take care

6. Cf. Pelt et al., *La plus belle histoire des plantes*.

7. Cf. Langaney, Bacharan et al., *La plus belle histoire de l'homme*.

8. Cf. Olson, *Mapping Human History*.

of animals, to provide food for herds, and to plan animal reproduction. In other words, the human being implemented working and production practices that provided surpluses. That which was at first liberating started to enslave the human being, for obligations and reliance on these activities started to take hold; these activities became the guarantee of sustenance. The human being had to start bringing home the bacon with the sweat of his face. And the human being did so with much effort. The expansion of agriculture and animal husbandry was responsible for the disappearance of around 10 percent of vegetable and animal life.[9] There was no awareness of responsible management of the environment. But it is also difficult to conceive of responsible management of the environment during that age given the richness of natural resources and the capacity of reproduction and regeneration of ecosystems at that time.

At any rate, the search for production and systematic storage of food happened relatively early. Thus, the Sumerians were the first to develop irrigation with the help of dykes and canals, and using the abundant waters of the Tigris and Euphrates rivers. Because of this development the Sumerians were able to considerably increase cereal output, which was used to feed their cities, and in doing so they were also able to feed armies and to wage wars.

As it happened, water started to infiltrate the ground causing a rise in the water table. Salt, which was encrusted on rocks, started to dissolve in the water, which then evaporated and caused the salt content of the soil to rise considerably. Consequently, fields became unproductive causing a scarcity of food, which is one of the reasons for the fall of this extraordinary civilization.

The Mayas, the most sophisticated civilization of Mesoamerica, disappeared due to a lack of concern for the environment, which made it impossible for the farming of maize and other cereals and vegetables. As a result of this, the Mayas found themselves forced to abandon their cities and pyramid complexes, which triggered the end of this civilization.[10]

The potato, a tuberous crop, which is original to lands of the Inca Empire (modern Peru), became the core food resource of the North of Europe, and in particular of those living in poverty in Ireland, from the seventeenth century. Between 1845 and 1847 CE there was an outbreak of a fungus-like disease that decimated potato plantations, which caused

9. Cf. Langaney et al., *La plus belle histoire de l'homme.*
10. Cf. Brahic et al., *La plus belle histoire de la Terre*, 176–78.

a terrible famine. Two million Irish either immigrated to the United States of America or simply died of hunger. Once again, this is an instance of a lack of ecological management that is associated with a lack of the minimum of solidarity possible, a lack of solidarity perpetrated by the English, which are at the heart of this terrible disaster.

At any rate, the Neolithic period set off a process that is unfolding to this day. The guarantee of food and the great banquet that the agricultural revolution promised to humanity, a banquet in which all sit as equal and communal partners, cannot be celebrated yet. Billions of human beings stand by the table awaiting falling crumbles in order to satiate their hunger. As far as food is concerned, these people possess neither sustainability nor guarantee.

The World Food Summit that took place in Rome in 1996 proposed to eradicate hunger by 2015 and it stated that: "food security exists when all people, at all times, have physical and economic access to sufficient, safe, and nutritious food to meet their dietary needs and food preferences for an active and healthy life."[11] Unfortunately, the Food and Agriculture Organization (FAO) reported in 1998 that these aims will not be reached unless the huge gap in social inequality is narrowed down considerably.[12]

In reality, the map of famine is daunting. According to the FAO, about 800 million people do not possess any form of food guarantee, and 283.9 million people are undernourished in South Asia; 241.6 million people are undernourished in Sub-Saharan Africa; 53.4 million people are undernourished in Latin America (of which 30 million in Brazil); 32.9 million people are undernourished in the Middle East and North Africa. Every day about 20 thousand people starve to death. This is a modern tragedy whose remote origins are found in the Neolithic period when human beings started to use aggressive practices in relation to nature and to natural resources, as well as the current unequal and unjust social order.

11. Translator's note: The Rome Declaration on World Food Security, available online: www.fao.org/docrep/003/w3613e/w3613e00.HTM.

12. Cf. Madeley. *Food for All*, 48–50.

Famine as an Ethical and Political Problem

The two basic innovations that were implemented during the revolution that took place in the Neolithic period are still part of our current economic practices: agriculture and animal husbandry. Certainly, practices are more sophisticated and the productive chain more complex now. But the aim is the same, that is, to produce surpluses so as to guarantee human life; though it is important to note that nowadays we are also concerned with guaranteeing the sustainability of the whole chain of life, of which the human being is a link among many others.

It has always been a great challenge to meet the requirements of providing food for all, whether due to weather conditions, the fertility of the soil, or social order. With the exception of the first phase of the Palaeolithic period, a period when human numbers were small and when there was an abundance of game, fish, fowl, fruits, and seeds, there has always been famines. The distribution of food has always been unequal despite the intrinsic communality present in human nature.

The scourge of hunger is not due to technical problems per se. Some production techniques are extremely efficient. Food production grows faster than the world's population growth. But there is bad distribution of food stuffs, that is, 20 percent of humanity has access to 80 percent of resources, whilst 80 percent of humanity has access to only 20 percent of vital resources. Thus, this distribution is unequal, unjust and sinful. Gandhi once said concerning famines caused by poverty: "Poverty is an insult, poverty stinks. It demeans, dehumanises, destroys the body and the mind, if not the soul. It is the deadliest form of violence."

The cause of this dreadful situation is a lack of ethical sensibility on the part of human beings towards other human beings. It is as if we had completely forgotten our ancient origins, it is as if we had completely forgotten that ancient communality and sense of cooperation that enabled us to become humans.

This deficit of humanity is the result of a kind of society based on a culture that privileges the individual over society, that values more private ownership of everything that is produced than an altruistic and fraternal co-participation, that reinforces mechanisms of competition over solidarity and cooperation, that gives centrality to values linked to masculinity (in men and women) such as rationality, power, use of force, will to dominate and instigation of competition over values connected to the feminine (also in men and women) such as sensitivity to the course of life, being caring and being willing to cooperate.

As one may gather, current ethics are utilitarian and elitist. It is not at the service of all and it is not concerned with taking care of every-body's life. Rather, it serves the interests of individuals and groups by excluding others, as it was well noted by Albert Schweitzer (1875–1965) in his *Cultural Philosophy*, volume 2: *Civilization and Ethics* (1923).

A basic injustice is at the heart of the current calamitous situation faced by part of humanity that faces famine and suffers. If an ethics based on solidarity, on care towards each other, on at least a minimum of communality is not implemented then there is no salvation. We do not want the terrible words Dante Alighieri saw at the gates of hell to become true: "Lasciate ogni speranza voi ch'entrate," that is, "Abandon every hope, who enter here" (*Divine Comedy*, Inferno, Canto III, 9).[13]

Another issue causing the human disaster of hunger is politics. Politics has to do with the organization of society, with the exercise of power and with the common good. For centuries in the West political power has been a hostage to economic power, which is articulated in a capitalist mode of production—and nowadays this situation is wide-spread across the globe due to the process of globalization. Capitalism aims at the maximization of gains in the shortest possible time and with the minimum investment. Gains are not democratized for the benefit of all but privatized by those who hold means, power, and knowledge; the benefit of others is something secondary for capitalism. Therefore, po-litical power does not serve the common good, but the privileged few. It creates inequalities that represent real social injustices, and today these inequalities are at a global level. As a consequence of this situation, mil-lions of people only have access to pitiful amounts of food and cannot meet their vital needs; or they simply have access to nothing and die of hunger and thirst, or die due to diseases caused by hunger and thirst, such as the millions of children under five years old, as I mentioned previously.

Until we change our values, until we put in place an economy that is subordinated to politics, and a politics that is guided by ethics, and an ethics that is inspired by at least a minimum of sensibility (which I would call the minimum of spirituality) towards others, there will be no

13. Translator's note: I have referred to Allen Mandelbaum's translation, which is available online: www.divinecomedy.org/divine_comedy.html/.

resolution to the problem of hunger and undernourishment at a global level. We will continue living this barbarous situation that blemishes the current process of globalization and that can no longer be ignored. Millions of people suffering in famine cry out to the heavens in search of help but no effective solution comes to them.[14]

Lastly, there is an issue that is worth mentioning when tackling the problem of global famines, that is, the importance of women in agriculture is generally unknown. According to the FAO, the UN organization that formulates policies concerning food and agriculture, women are responsible for a great part of the food produced in the world. Women produce between 80 percent to 98 percent of the food in Sub-Saharan Africa, 50 percent to 90 percent of food in Asia, and 30 percent in Central and Eastern Europe. There cannot be a guarantee of food supply without the participation of women in agriculture, and as such women must have a greater say over decisions concerning the destiny of life on Earth. Women constitute about 60 percent of humanity, and by their very nature they are more connected to life and to reproduction. It is absolutely unacceptable to deny the right to property and access to credit and to other cultural goods on the grounds that they are women. It is also absolutely unacceptable not to recognize a woman's right over her own body and her decision on reproduction, to schooling and to technical resources concerning the improvement of food production. All these rights are often denied them simply because they are women.

Trading Hunger: Food as a Business

By conducting research into the problem of famine we realize that it is the result of a philosophical view that underlies the whole of humanity's productive process. Food has become an opportunity for profit and the agricultural and food production process has become a profitable business.[15] The primary aim of agricultural and food production is to make a profit rather than to create accessible means to life for the greatest number of people.

Agriculture is no longer seen as the art and technique of producing the means for life; it is rather an enterprise aimed at achieving financial

14. Cf. Ramonet, *Géopolitique du chaos*.

15. Cf. Gonçalves, *Empresas transnacionais e internacionalização da produção*; Delpeuch, *Seed and Surplus*.

gain. Due to mechanization and the use of technology we can now produce much more food per acre than ever before. The "green revolution," which started in the 1970s and spread throughout the world, artificialized food production through the use of intensive irrigation, artificial fertilizers and pesticides, hybrid and genetically-modified seeds. The effects of this are now becoming very apparent: impoverishment of the soil, devastating erosion, deforestation, decreased river flows and the loss of thousands of kinds of natural seeds, which are important to have in reserve in the case of future crises.

Animal husbandry has changed a good deal due to battery farming, intensive practices, growth stimulants, vaccines, antibiotics, artificial insemination, and cloning.

In place of the traditional farmer we now find the agricultural entrepreneur who utilizes more machinery than human labor. Those who can no longer find work in the countryside migrate to cities, and nowadays about 70 percent of the world's population lives in cities. And the city puts considerable pressure on food production, which the city does not produce, but which is produced in the countryside. In addition to this, the production of agricultural produce on a large scale is done to the detriment of its quality and with the use of excessive chemical assistance.

Between core countries and peripheral countries there is a true trade war over the issue of food production. Rich countries subsidize their farmers in order to place their agricultural production at an advantageous price on the international commodities market, and this harms poor countries whose main source of wealth is quite simply the production and exporting of agricultural and animal produce. Very often and in order to become economically viable, poor countries see themselves forced to export cereals that will be used as animal feed by rich countries, cereals which could have been used by those countries to feed their poor populations.[16]

In the eagerness to make a profit, within a scenario founded on capitalist means of production and neoliberal politics, there is clearly a global tendency to privatize and trade everything, such as public assets, health, education, water, genes (i.e., genetic patents), and particularly seeds. Less than ten transnational companies control the totality of the

---

16. Cf. Houtard, *Délégitimer le capitalisme, reconstruire l'esperance*, 13–66.

market of seeds worldwide.[17] We have seen the introduction of transgenic seeds that do not reproduce themselves during harvests, and that therefore must be replaced each time, and this generates very high profits for the companies. The buying of seeds is just part of a "larger package" that includes technology, pesticides, machinery, and finance. These create a web of dependence that binds producers to the agricultural and food production interests of transnational companies.

This situation turns policies aiming at the eradication of hunger unviable and makes it impossible for human communality.[18] At the end of the day what is important within this scenario is to maximize an enterprise's gains and not to feed people. Thus, for instance, milk is seen less as a source of nourishment and more as a commodity and the source of profit through turning it into butter, cheese, yogurt, and so on.

Organic Farming: A Possible Solution

Despite the pressures and the standardization of agricultural industrialism for many years the power of organic farming has become increasingly evident. The more the production of food becomes increasingly mechanized and reliant on chemicals, the more we see resistance to them and the more we see a willingness for "clear" produce, for artisanal produce that is linked to traditional practices that avoid the use of chemicals and privileges organic enhancers and controls.

In order to make my argument brief I quote below the aims and principles established by the International Federation of Organic Agriculture Movements in 1981:

> To work as much as possible within a closed system and to draw upon local resources; to maintain the long term fertility of soils; to avoid all forms of pollution that may result from agricultural techniques; to produce food stuffs of high nutritional quality and sufficient quantity; to reduce the use of fossil energy in agricultural practice to a minimum; to give livestock conditions of life that conform to their physiological needs and to humanitarian principles; to make it possible for agricultural producers to earn a living through their work and develop their potential as human beings; to use and develop appropriate technology based

17. Cf. Shiva, *Protect or Plunder?*
18. Cf. Wilkinson, *O futuro do sistema alimentar.*

on an understanding of biological systems; to use decentralized systems for processing, distributing and marketing of products; to create a system which is aesthetically pleasing to both those within and outside the system; to maintain and preserve wildlife and their habitats.[19]

Such understanding gives a human face back to the production of food and discards the perspective that understands food production as a link in an industrial assembly line aiming at making a profit.

An increasing number of farmers, who are supported by a significant number of scientists and agricultural-ecologists and by organizations that postulate another kind of societal paradigm that is an alternative to the one we currently experience, practice *permaculture*.[20] This concept is formed by the abbreviation of the expression *permanent agriculture*, and it was introduced by the Australian Bill Mollison in the 1970s; and this idea served as the inspiration for the book *One Straw Revolution* by the Japanese Masanobu Fukuoka, who proves empirically in this book that it is possible to achieve high productivity without the use of chemical agents and without the eradication of weeds, and by favouring a partnership between species and by allowing plants and animals to fertilize the soil. Mollison defined *permaculture* as "the conscious design and maintenance of agriculturally productive ecosystems, which have the diversity, stability and resilience of natural ecosystems."[21]

The basic thesis of *permaculture* is to reaffirm the synergy between the human being and earth. Both must collaborate in the production of food for life: earth provides its fertility, its energies, its capacity to replace and to regenerate, and the human being enters with its work guided by knowledge, by techniques, by a caring and respectful attitude. In this way, food production is done *with* nature and not *against* nature. This effort assimilates modern knowledge and articulates it with traditional and local expertise to produce permanently sufficient food in a sustainable way for the current generation, but also for future generations, without sacrificing nature.

19. Quoted in Schwarz and Schwarz, *Breaking Through*, 156–57.

20. Cf. Altieri, *Agroecologia: As bases científicas da agricultura alternativa*; Gomes de Almeida et al., *Crise socioambiental*.

21. Madeley, *Food for All*, 43: this definition was personally given in a conversation with John Madeley in October 1991.

This mode of production is strengthened by those values proposed by the new ecological paradigm of civilization. This paradigm presents the Earth as Gaia, the name of an entity in Greek mythology that is used to designate the Earth as a living supra-organism, of which we are sons and daughters, of which we are its most advanced and complex expression. Our mission is to be the carers and guardians of the Earth, of its ecosystems, of its integrity, its beauty, and its fecundity. This understanding reaches its highest point when it is combined with *permaculture* and with organic agriculture, for such understanding is the philosophical, ethical, and mystical basis of these. To reinforce this understanding means to create the concrete foundations for a real communality that is viable to all the sons and daughter of the *Magna Mater*.

My reflections thus far lead me to tackle the issue of genetically modified (GM) food, and I shall deal with this briefly in the next section.

Genetically Modified (GM) Food: Market, Ethics, and Understanding of the World

Genetic modification is the result of the transference and alteration of the genes from a living being (e.g, plant, animal, human being, and microorganism) to another being with the conscious purpose of turning it healthier, more productive, or more resilient to pestilences and bacteria. Many producers, however, also have an additional hidden agenda to the above, that is, they aim at increasing business and financial gain.

This issue is highly polemical and causes concern at various levels: production, market, consumption, scientific research, government, ethics, and underlying all these, an understanding of the world.

Producers are keen on GM crops because they diminish costs and increase productivity, which is currently at about 20 percent of worldwide production, and with the added advantage of being resistant to plagues. The growing global demand for food reinforces their argument.

The market seeks gains. Some multinational companies (five in total) produce GM seeds that are slowly replacing natural seeds (due to the genetic erosion of the latter). And thus these companies now monopolize the seeds market (and one of these companies controls about 90 percent of the market), which makes producers economically and technologically dependent on these companies. And the supply of GM seeds involves a package of commitments, such as the payment of *roy-*

alties, buying pesticides, technical support, and bank loans. Crucially, such practices make it impossible for the kind of agriculture exercised on a small scale, at a family level, which employs natural seeds and that produces about 60 percent of all that we eat.

Consumers are reluctant to consume GM food because they fear for their health in the present and future. Science cannot tell us with absolute certainty that GM food is safe for consumption because it can only hypothesize about the future. And this, insofar as human health is concerned, is inappropriate. People require absolute assurance on such issues because people want a healthy life for themselves and for their children; that is, people want to live longer and do not want to risk death.

Opinion polls assert that about 60 percent of Europeans are against the consumption of GM food despite the untiring efforts by market forces to continue offering GM food. However, consumers, so as to safeguard their health, demand that any produce containing any form of genetically modified ingredient must be labelled accordingly. This rule is not always observed, and according to international conventions (especially according to the Cartagena Protocol on Biosafety) the obligatory labelling of genetically modified ingredients in food labels only started to be implemented in 2006.[22]

Scientific Research, aware of its freedom, continually penetrates into the mystery of life and unveils new pathways for a healthy and long life, especially through the development of biotechnology. However, more and more there is a demand for conducting scientific research consciously. That is to say: to conduct scientific research in a responsible and ethical way that is part of the social global process and that is attentive to what is happening to the wider web of life, which is currently under great pressure due to the voracious means of production and habits of consumption.

It is fitting of the sciences to call our attention to the implications of genetic manipulation for the environment, such as for instance, the risk of contamination of other plant species due to pollination, and consequently of the reduction of the biodiversity poll. And it may have a more serious implication (that is, for human health) as we do not know the long-term effects of ingesting GM food on our genetic code and on the good bacteria that inhabit our gut, bacteria that are responsible for our vital equilibrium.

22. Cf. *Convenção sobre a diversidade biológica [Convention on Biological Diversity]*.

Governments become bewildered. They are under pressure by consumers who demand the absolute quality of produce; they are under pressure from great conglomerates and market forces who demand the approval of GM food; they are under pressure because scientific research is contradictory, for some scientists assert that GM produce is safe both for human ingestion and for the environment whilst other scientists affirm that there is no conclusive research into the medium and long-term implications of GM produce for human health and the environment.

The Earth Charter postulates that to "prevent harm as the best method of environmental protection and, when knowledge is limited, apply a precautionary approach . . . place the burden of proof on those who argue that a proposed activity will not cause significant harm, and make the responsible parties liable for environmental harm."[23]

What decision should be taken? The mission of governments is to safeguard the common good and to resist the pressure of market forces. And due to its responsibility to the common good, it is also the mission of the state to go against immediate interests that do not take proper account of international treaties, such as the Convention on Biological Diversity and the Cartagena Protocol on Biosafety.

Ethics is imperative here. Public power, a delegated instance of popular power, must be guided by public *ethics*. Two principles are evoked here: responsibility and precaution.

The introduction of GM produce into the market must be guided by the principle of *responsibility*. This principle makes us take stock of the implications of scientific, technical and commercial practices for human health and the environment. The enforcement of this principle aims at guaranteeing that no direct or indirect global and cumulative ill can come to affect us and the community of life. Science cannot provide us yet with a conclusive answer to this matter due to its current stage of development.

What we do know is that GM organisms represent a challenge to sustainable agriculture, which is founded on respect and encouraging biodiversity. We also know that nature worked for billions of years to organize the genetic code of life through inter-retro-relations that encompass the physics and chemistry of the universe. A skin cell from our hands contains all the necessary information for the constitution of life, and this represents a fantastic instance of nanotechnology.

23. See the Earth Charter online: http://www.earthcharteraction.org/.

Another principle that must be respected is the principle of precaution. The scientist should dare to interfere with the complex game of life by assuming an attitude of great reverence and precaution. The scientist must be conscious that every gene is linked to other genes. No gene can be analysed without taking into account the web of relations that it bears with other genes.

The scientific community is increasingly aware that the Newtonian paradigm is inadequate when conducting research into biological phenomena, which are extremely complex, for this paradigm reduces and compartmentalizes everything. It is thus necessary to refer to a holistic and systemic paradigm, which is more adequate in trying to understand the implications of the manipulation of a genetic code.

Who can guarantee that the Roundup Ready crops will not disturb the environmental equilibrium? By referring to the principles of *precaution*, *responsibility*, and *respect* for life, we realize that we must impose a moratorium on GM produce. Research must continue so that we can achieve greater security and offer greater guarantees for life.[24]

A particular way of understanding the world underlies the issue of GM produce. And therefore the following questions need addressing: What is ultimately important? Is it market forces, is it profit, or is it being advantageous to producers? Or is it the health and well-being of humans, of the environment, of the chain of life, and the integrity of ecosystems and the preservation of the Earth as a Common Home?

If we choose—and it is imperative that we make such a choice—life and Earth, this does not imply that we are setting aside GM produce. These can be produced within certain boundaries and with care and by paying continuous attention to the implications of such production on the environment.

What must prevail is respect for all the works of the Earth and the universe, works that took billions of years to complete, and which are the outcome of a subtle equilibrium and that demonstrate extreme rationality that is present in all biological processes.

What is ultimately important is the maintenance of life and of the Earth with its capacity for evolving with a vast universe that is still expanding. A universe that is replete with beauty and greatness, which are grasped by our spiritual intelligence, the very expression of super-

24. Cf. Boff, *Essential Care*.

abundance of being and of life that comes from the Original Fountain, the source of every thing and to where every thing returns.

The Water Issue: Something Vital for Life or Mere Commodity?

I cannot leave the issue of water unanswered whilst dealing with the problems of hunger and food security. Water is directly connected to the issue of food for all food supplies require water.

Independent of all the debate, one can say of water that: it is a natural good that is connected to life, that it cannot be replaced by something else, and that is required by all beings. No living being, human or non-human, can live without water.

The future of life depends on the way in which we deal with the issue of water. Let me refer to some basic data about water and to some great problems connected to the issue of water.

There are about 1.3 billion km³ of water on Earth. This means that if we distributed all this water present in the oceans, lakes, rivers, underground water reservoirs, and polar caps over the Earth's surface in equal measures then continents would be submersed by 3km.[25] Ninety-seven percent of this water is salt water and 3 percent is fresh water. This 3 percent of fresh water is the equivalent of 8.5 million km³, of which only 0.7 percent can be directly accessed by human beings.

Water is abundant on Earth. The natural water cycle involves about 43 thousand km³ a year while total consumption is about 6 thousand km³ a year.

Thus there is a good deal of water, but it is unequally distributed. Sixty percent of this water is found in only nine countries, whilst eighty countries face a scarcity of this resource. About 1 billion people consume 86 percent of this water, whilst 1.4 billion people do not have enough (and in 2020 it is estimated that this figure will reach 3 billion people). Two billion people do not have access to water that has been properly treated, which is the cause of about 85 percent of the diseases contracted by these peoples. It is estimated that by 2032 about 5 billion people with be affected by a scarcity in water supplies.

25. Cf. Rebouças et al., *Águas doces no Brasil*; Tundisi, *Água no século XXI: enfrentando a escassez*; Zebidi et al., *Water, A Looming Crisis?* Shiklomanov, *World Water Resources* (1999); Shiklomanov, *World Water Resources* (2003).

There is no problem with water resources, but there is a problem with the management of these resources to allow for human needs and the needs of other living beings.

Brazil is the natural superpower of water, as it possesses about 13 percent of all fresh water on the planet (which is about 5.4 trillion m³). All this water is unequally distributed over the Brazilian territory: 70 percent in the Amazon Region, 15 percent in the Center-West Region, 6 percent in the South and Southeast Regions, and 3 percent in the Northeast Region. Despite the abundance of water supplies Brazil does not use its water resources well for 46 percent of all this water is wasted, which is something that could supply France, Belgium, Switzerland, and the north of Italy. Thus, it is imperative that a new cultural paradigm be constructed.

Because of the scarcity of fresh water resources, it is seen as a hydro resource and as an economic asset. Fresh water has become a commodity and a source of profit. And due to this understanding, there is a global drive for the privatization of water. Large multinational companies have emerged in this sector, such as the French Vivendi and Suez, the German RWE, the British Thames Water, and the American Bechtel Corporation, to name a few. This sector generates 100 billion dollars a year. Other companies, such as Nestle and Coca-Cola/Coke are strong in this sector, seeking to buy sources of mineral water all over the world.

From around 2000 onwards the renegotiation of foreign debt and of the granting of new loans to forty countries was conditioned by international financial institutions, such as the IMF and the World Bank— the condition being privatization of these countries' water supplies and services. This is what happened to Mozambique in 1999 in order that it could secure a new loan of 117 million dollars. The same happened in Bolivia in 2000 when it was forced to privatize the water supply and services in the city of Cochabamba. The Bechtel Corporation bought these and hiked up the prices by 35 percent. The organized reaction of the local population was so severe and efficient that it forced this company to abandon this enterprise and leave the country.

Water has become a factor of instability in certain regions of the planet. Some countries may resort to war in order to guarantee water supplies.

Understanding water as a mere commodity causes distortions in the relation of water-population:

- generates stiff competition between large companies in the sector, and this makes it impossible for cooperation between these companies, which harms local populations;

- places profit over and above any humanitarian and ecological interests;

- is socially insensible for it lacks in solidarity and it disrespects water systems, which transcend national limits;

- generates permanent disputes over transnational rivers. For instance, Turkey on the one side and Syria and Iraq on the other side; or Israel on the one side and Jordan and Palestine on the other; or the dispute between the USA and Mexico over the Rio Grande and the Colorado River.[26]

The spirit of privatization that took the globalized world by storm turns water into a commodity; it takes away from water its life-giving aspect, and in doing so, it crushes the idea that water must be shared to meet the needs of millions of people and vast areas of the planet.

In the face of these serious ethical and political deviations, the international community through the UN in meetings in Mar del Plata (1997), Dublin (1992), Paris (1998), and Rio de Janeiro (1992) consecrated "the right of all to have access to drinking water in sufficient quantity and quality to meet their essential needs." Therefore, the debate over water will necessarily fall within the following framework: Is water the source of life or the source of profit? Is water a natural good that is vital, communal, and irreplaceable or a hydro resource and a commodity to be traded?

One view does not exclude the other, and therefore we must link them properly. Fundamentally, water belongs to life and is connected with the right to life.

Within this understanding, drinking water, water that is used in the preparation of food, water that is used for personal hygiene, must be free. It is for this reason, and with reason, that the first clause of the Brazilian Law n. 9433 of 8 January 1997 over the National Policy on Hydro Resources states: "water is a good within the public domain; water is a limited natural resource with economic value; in situations when

26. Cf. Bouguerra, *As batalhas da água.*

it becomes scarce, the use of hydro resources must prioritize human consumption and the provision of drinking water for animals."

However, since water is limited and requires a complex structure of sourcing, storage, treatment, and distribution, it implies an undeniable economic dimension. But this dimension must not prevail over the other; on the contrary, the economic dimension must turn it into something accessible to all. Water is something so vital that its costs for human consumption and the provision of drinking water for animals should be covered by the government.

It is important to emphasize here: water is not a common economic resource. Water is connected to life and as such it must be understood as life. Life must not be turned into a mere commodity. Water is also linked to other dimensions that are cultural, symbolic, and spiritual, which turn it into something even more precious and loaded with value, which are priceless per se.

In order to understand the importance of water beyond its economic dimension, we must break away from the constraints of rational-analytic and utilitarian ways of thinking that are so prevalent in our societies. This way of thinking understands water as a commodity.

But beyond instrumental-analytic rationality there are other forms of reason. There is sensitive reason; there is emotional reason, symbolic reason and spiritual reason. These are forms of reason connected to the meaning of life. They do not provide us with the reasons for profit but with the reasons to live and to ascribe excellence to existence. These are reasons that allow us to understand water as life, as a common natural good, as the source and niche where life emerged in its immense diversity billions of years ago.

As a reaction to the *privatization* of water we must seek the *democratization* of water because it is a *common public and global good*, an asset of the biosphere and vital to all forms of life. By *democratization* here it is meant that the public sphere, from local to international, must formally recognize access to water as a right of the individual.

It is important to proclaim the formal recognition of access to water as an absolute right of the human being. It is fitting for the public sphere to create an adequate form of finance which covers the necessary costs to provide drinking water to all.

Due to these requirements, the People's World Water Forum was created in Florence, Italy, in 2003. This forum proposes the creation of a

World Water Authority, an instance of public government that is cooperative and based on solidarity with the special task of looking after international water basins so that the distribution of water meets regional needs.

We must put pressure on governments and companies so that water is neither traded nor considered a commodity. However, the water used in industry and agriculture must be paid for (and 90 percent of fresh water is used in this way).

We must encourage all kinds of cooperation that will help stop deaths due to lack of drinking water or untreated water. Six thousand children die every day of thirst. The media does not mention this. It is the same as ten Boeings crashing every day killing all passengers. Undoubtedly, such disasters would occupy the front pages of all newspapers. By providing drinking water to all we would also avoid the situation, where about eighteen million children do not attend school because they must fetch water, which can be some 5 to 10 km from their own homes.

The issue of providing drinking water for all is a serious one and as such it is imperative to establish a *World Water Contract*. This would be a social world contract around that which is of interest to all.

Water is life; it generates life and is one of the most powerful symbols of Eternal Life.

The Preconditions to Communality

The current socioeconomic structures of our globalized society and culture based on individualism that has taken root at all levels does not favor the ideal of communality. The vast majority of human beings are alienated from the true state of affairs of the Earth. They do not even discuss topics that concern us collectively, such as: the future of humanity, the scarcity of natural resources, and the tragic situation of millions and millions of people. They live in the sweet illusion that the Earth will continue to generously provide for us, and that we can continue on our current path forever, seeking year after year greater rates of growth and greater supplies of goods and services.

Experts on global scenarios, however, fear dramatic situations. The Earth Charter states in its introduction: "We stand at a critical moment in Earth's history, a time when humanity must choose its future . . . The

foundations of global security are threatened. These trends are perilous—but not inevitable. The choice is ours: form a global partnership to
care for Earth and one another or risk the destruction of ourselves and
the diversity of life . . . Our environmental, economic, political, social,
and spiritual challenges are interconnected, and together we can forge
inclusive solutions."[27]

In order to establish this alliance of universal care it is imperative
that another kind of paradigm that better answers the current crises and
that is more fitting to the planetary phase of humanity and to the history
of Gaia itself is constructed.

The current problems we face are so serious and so global that I do
not believe that a solution based merely on technical, political, and social resources will do. What is required is a coalition of peoples, groups,
and societies around certain values and principles for action so to forge
a new world order. Let me explain some of these values and principles.

The first of these is *care* for it is directly connected to the inheri-
tance we have received from the process of the evolution of the universe,
of life and of the human species.

The second is *respect* and *reverence* towards all alterity (i.e., otherness), from the Earth to ecosystems to each and every being of nature.

The third is found on the unconditional *cooperation* of all with all,
because we are all interdependent to the point of possessing a common
destiny.

The fourth is social *justice* in order to equalize differences and diminish hierarchical gaps and avoid the appearance of inequalities.

The fifth is unlimited *solidarity* and *compassion* towards all suffering beings starting with those who are facing more threats or who are
weaker.

The sixth is the *universal responsibility* over the future of life, over
ecosystems that guarantee human survival, that is, of the planet Earth.

The seventh is the *right measure* of all initiatives that concern all
so to counterbalance our current culture based on excesses and the creation of inevitable inequalities.

Lastly, is the *self-control* of our voracity to conquer, to dominate,
and to accumulate so that all can have enough to feel themselves—sons
and daughters of the Earth and members of the human family.

27. See the Earth Charter online: http://www.earthcharterinaction.org/.

Economy cannot be completely dismembered from society and independent from the control of social and political institutions for such a situation has as a consequence the destruction of the idea of society and of a common good. The truth is that the economy has become polarized between one side that produces wealth for some and another side that produces the impoverishment and the exclusion of many. The ideal to be sought in the economy is an economy that produces enough and decent stuff for all human beings and for the other beings in the chain of life.

Politics cannot be restricted to national interests; rather, it must undertake the governance of the whole of humanity so to attend collectively to global matters. The ethics in place must be the ethics based on care, on responsibility, on compassion and on biophilia.

Spirituality must be cosmic in order that we may "live with reverence for the mystery of being, gratitude for the gift of life, and humility regarding the human place in nature."[28]

Therefore, the challenge we must face is the following: to move from a society based on industrial production to a society based on the promotion of all life.

The final outcome to aim for is peace, which was incisively defined in the Earth's Charter as "the wholeness created by right relationships with oneself, other persons, other cultures, other life, Earth, and the larger whole of which all are part."[29]

These are the preconditions of ethical order and practical nature that on the one hand aim at criticizing the current paradigm and on the other hand at encouraging the new one. Logically, there must be technical, political and cultural mediations to turn this new paradigm into something viable. But these mediations will hardly be benevolent if they are not forged in the light of these guiding preconditions.

A precondition that could be immediately enforced and established in practice is *a new way of consuming*. The dominating form of society is consumerist. It is centred on consumption, ideally in an unlimited way, as an objective of society itself and of a person's life. One consumes not only to meet one's needs, which is something justifiable, but one also consumes unnecessarily, which is something questionable. This consumerism is only possible because economic policies that produce superfluous goods are continuously supported, encouraged, and justified.

28. Ibid.
29. Ibid.

Since these goods are superfluous, they require mechanisms of *marketing* or persuasion to induce people to consume them and to make them believe that the superfluous is actually necessary.

The crucial point in this form of *marketing* is to encourage habits in consumers that generate in them a consumerist ethic and a commanding necessity to consume. Increasingly, false needs are fomented and from this we see the rise of an apparatus of production and distribution. And since needs are unlimited, production also tends to be unlimited. In this way we see the rise of a society, which was denounced by Marx, that is marked by fetishes, abounds with the superfluous, and is replete with *shopping malls*, which are true temples of consumerism with altars loaded with attractive idols, but nonetheless merely idols; this is a society that is unsatisfied because nothing can satiate its thirst. Due to this, consumerism grows in an uncontrollable way, and it is impossible to tell for how long the Earth can stand the current levels of exploitation.

This perverse logic is wearing out nature, whose limited resources become depleted. It is alienating people, who believe they can find happiness and the meaning of life in the constant consumption of material goods and not in those human dimensions that are linked to spirituality such as solidarity, friendship, uninterested love, fine arts, music, the capacity to live together, tolerance, forgiveness, contemplation of the universe and of the Mystery that inheres in all things—these are dimensions capable of overcoming obstacles and of providing a feeling of awe in life.

Consuming Responsibly and with Solidarity

What should consumerism be if it is to allow for communality?

First, it is important for it to be *humane*. That is to say, that it ought to be fitting of human nature. The human being must consume if it is to live. But the human being is not merely a producer and consumer of material goods. The human being presents itself as an infinite project and as such it has other needs, it hungers after beauty and other nonmaterial goods.

On the one hand, every human being finds itself rooted in this spatial-temporal and cultural realm, but on the other hand, every human being finds itself connected to the infinite and to the unfathomable. As Blaise Pascal (1623–1662) correctly noted in his *Pensées* (1670) the human being is "a nothing in comparison with the Infinite, an All in

comparison with the Nothing, a mean between nothing and everything
. . . he is equally incapable of seeing the Nothing from which he was
made, and the Infinite in which he is swallowed up" (§72). As an infinite
project, nothing can fundamentally satiate our hunger, even less so the
accumulation of material goods, which is something that our civilization
is too ready to offer. Only an openness to the other, to the Great Other
and to the cultivation of that which is connected to spirit, to beauty and
to the Infinite can bring us some rest. Human consumption therefore
encompasses not only goods necessary for material life but also the ac-
quisition of those things that are necessary for spiritual life. Spiritual life
must also be fed so that it does not become anaemic and incapable of
dealing with the virulence of material urges.

Second, consumption must be *just* and *equitable*. The 1948 UN
Declaration of Human Rights states explicitly that food is a vital necessity and for this reason it is a fundamental right of every human being.
Food guarantees life, which is the basis for all other rights. Food must be
accessible to every human being (justice) and in accordance to its needs
and particularities (equitable). This right is the most fundamental of all.
If it is not accorded then the individual finds itself faced with starvation
and death.

It is for this reason that the Projeto Fome Zero (Project Hunger
Zero), which was implemented by the Brazilian president Luiz Inácio
Lula da Silva, gained international attention. This project seeks to uni-
versalize the right to food, which is a right to life. The first function of
the state, and of any governmental policy, is to guarantee the life of the
people. Without this guarantee politics and economics become inhumane, giving way to the systematic violation of a person's fundamental
human rights.

Third, to consume must be based on *solidarity*. Consuming with
solidarity means overcoming individualism and embracing moderation
in the name of love and compassion for those who cannot consume what
is necessary. This solidarity is based on an ethics of human sensibility. It
is to feel the other as an equal, it is to think of and to perceive the world
from the perspective of the other, from the perspective that takes into
account the other's needs and anguishes; or it is to think of and to perceive the world from the perspective of the community of life by taking
into account its degradation or conservation. Solidarity is expressed by
sharing, by being generous, by participating in movements in support of

the poor and oppressed, by the disposition and courage to defend their cause, by suffering and taking risks to defend their cause, by striving alongside and sharing in the joys of those who are in need, and also by deciding for an ecological attitude that is coherent with the system of life and with Gaia.[30]

This solidarity, I must emphasize, rescues the ancestral memory of our passing from the animal kingdom into the human kingdom, which happened due to the solidarity in sharing food; in short, due to the original communality. Solidarity is fully realized when we are able to eat and drink together at the same table, by celebrating the generosity of our Mother Earth and the ingenuity of human labour, which produces food for all.

Fourth, to consume must be *responsible*. Consuming with responsibility means becoming aware of the consequences of one's lifestyle and of one's levels of consumption. One can have a lifestyle and a level of consumption that is not satisfied by the sufficient and decent, and as such these become increasingly sophisticated and sumptuous. Such people consume too much of some things and in doing so these things become scarce for others, or they waste food that could meet the needs of people who are starving. Responsibility is translated by a moderate style of consumption, by being able to renounce things—not by asceticism but by love and solidarity for those who are in need. It is about opting for a voluntary simplicity and for a style of consuming that is consciously constrained, that neither gives in to desires nor to the tantalizing calls of advertising. This kind of consuming is free and completely human, for it is not the outcome of instinct but of the freedom to exercise it by thinking of others, who are our equals, who are our close and communal companions.[31] Even if this attitude does not have immediate and visible consequences, it has a value in itself. It demonstrates a conviction that cannot be measured by any anticipated effects; rather it must be measured by the value that this attitude has in itself independent of anything else.

Last, to consume must be *fulfilling* to the whole of the human be-ing. Without a doubt, we require nourishment. But nourishment alone is not enough. We also require knowledge and as such we consume information and discern which is required by us and which edifies us,

30. Cf. Cortina, *Consumo . . . luego existo.*

31. Etymologically the word *companion* means "those with whom we share bread."

which broadens our interdisciplinary understanding and which narrows it down within the confines of great specializations. We need to communicate and to establish relationships. We satisfy this need by feeding personal and social relationships which allow us to give and receive. Through this exchanging we complement each other and we grow.

Sometimes this communication is realized by visiting a popular neighbourhood, by taking part in groups based in poor suburban areas, by attending meetings at base-communities (*Comunidade de Base*), by demonstrating support towards demonstrations in the name of peace, justice, land reform, access and proper use of drinking water, preservation of forests; but also by watching a film, by attending a concert, by going to the theatre, by visiting an fine-arts exhibition, by participating in a debate. We need to love and to be loved. We satisfy this need by truly and unconditionally loving, by encouraging reciprocity, which allow us to take part in the life and destiny of others. We feel a need for transcendence, for daring, for going beyond imposed limits, for plunging into the Other, with whom we can dialogue, enter into communion, merge together—this is the supreme realization of existence, which comes out of itself to be completely with the Other.

All these forms of consuming realize human existence in its multiple dimensions. It we pay close attention, these forms of consuming do not waste energy, do not require expensive and superfluous items; rather they only require human effort and commitment as well as an openness to solidarity, to compassion, to beauty, to the capacity to admire another person and natural sceneries. We must be open to feel a gesture of human solidarity, to be touched by the love between two people, to experience happiness when seeing a situation turning for the better, to bear witness to how the poor organize themselves and produce their own food and share it in a communal manner.

Living these attitudes produces the most beautiful and desired outcome, that is happiness, which cannot be sought in itself. Happiness has a normative quality for it is the consequence of a life that is righteous, transparent, just, open to others, caring towards nature, aware of alternatives, conscious of the limits of the human condition; it is the consequence of a life lived with humility, courage, and hope.

The Ultimate Reality:
Communality of Jesus and in the Kingdom of God

It has already been said that eating is the representation of the soul of a culture. To know what is eaten, when it is eaten, how and with whom it is eaten is to penetrate the heart of a culture. Eating is a form of communion with people, with the Earth and with the universe. For this reason eating comes surrounded by rites and symbols, such as communality, which expresses the sociability that is characteristic of human beings.

Communality is essentially connected to hospitality. One does not welcome a guest/visitor without inviting him or her to the table and turning him or her into a communal partner. It is known, for instance, that the ancient Celtic tribes were hospitable to outsiders; when doing so, they offered food and drink even before asking these outsiders where they came from and why they were in the region.[32] They realized the deep meaning of hospitality and communality, that is, that these are fundamentally characterized by being open and unconditional.

It is important to recognize here that the difficulties that are inherent in hospitality in the modern, complex society are also present with respect to the issue of open communality. Communality, just as with hospitality, has a utopian and inalienable character. To give up on communality because of difficulties would represent a regress to the kingdom of apes and to abdicate that which makes us essentially human. We must use our personal and social skills and wisdom to identify on a case-by-case basis what kind of communality is appropriate, so that we do not negate it.

To end this chapter, I wish to focus on a utopian and practical reference of communality, that is the exemplary life of Jesus of Nazareth.[33] Jesus liked feasts to the point of being accused of being "a glutton and a drunkard, a friend of tax collectors and sinners" (Luke 7:34). He accepted eating, indiscriminately, with whoever invited him, with sinners and even with women, which was something scandalous at the time, such as in the case Martha and Mary (Luke 11:38–42). He introduced a conterculture that broke with the rigid rules of the time which pre-

32. Cf. Baron Tacla, "Hospitalidade e política da comensalidade nas tribos de Vix e Hochdorf," 21–48.

33. Cf. Aguirre, *La mesa compartida*; Koester, "The Historical Jesus and the Cult of the Kyrios," 13–18; Crossan, *The Birth of Christianity*.

scribed ablutions before eating (Luke 11:37–39) and the exclusion of many people for various reasons. He did not even respect the etiquette of the time, by saying that the last will be the first (Luke 13:29–30), and by also saying that even if he was the Lord, he was also the servant of all (Luke 22:27; John 13:4–15).

Jesus said and did all these things so that his listeners had an idea of the meaning of the Kingdom of God. In the Kingdom of God things were meant to be just as Jesus was saying and doing, that is, the opposite of the established customs of the time. For this reason, when Jesus spoke about the Kingdom of God, he drew the analogy of a banquet for which all were invited: all those who lived in cities and towns, including the poor and the handicapped as well as those who lived in suburban areas and those who wandered about, and also pagans and the impure and those who did not belong to the people of God (Luke 14:12–14). Communality was totally open and all were encouraged to participate. An abundance of food, equality, and dignity is what constituted the essence of the banquet idealized by Christ.[34]

On commenting on this revolutionary aspect of Jesus's teachings, Saint Paul said with reason: "He made of two people (Jews and pagans) a single people by bringing down the wall of unfriendliness that separated them. He nullified with his own flesh the law with its precepts and rules. He created a new humanity" (cf. Ephesians 2:14–15; Colossians 3:9–11).

Palaeo-Christianity (i.e., the original Christianity of the years before 50 CE, which was not organized into local parishes) kept the sacred memory of the communality lived by Jesus. Recent academic research on the "missing years of Christianity" (particularly in the 30s and 40s of the first century CE), that is, those obscure decades immediately after the execution of Jesus, has demonstrated the importance of communality.

From the 50s CE onwards, and starting with the Letters of Saint Paul and the four Gospels, we posses vast documentation on Jesus and on the communities that emerged around him. But what happened in the early years of Christianity, those years between his death on the cross and the appearance of written narratives? We have very few primitive sources, such as the *Gospel of Thomas*; the *Didache*, which is also called the *Teaching of the Twelve Apostles*; and the Q source, a subtext common to the Gospels of Luke and Matthew: these are the only documents dated before 50 CE. There are many Catholic and Protestant scholars investi-

---

34. Cf. Garcia, "Comida e dignidade," 20–25; O'Murchu, *Evolutionary Faith*, 20–25.

gating this area, such as Helmut Koester, John Kloppenborg, Dimitris Kyrtatas, to mention a few. However, the most incisive and notable of all is the Irish American Catholic John Dominic Crossan, member of the Society of Biblical Literature and cofounder of the Jesus Seminar, a group of academics studying the "historical Jesus." Of his many works notable are *The Historical Jesus: The Life of a Mediterranean Jewish Peasant*, and *The Birth of Christianity: Discovering What Happened in the Years Immediately after the Execution of Jesus*. This last work is an interdisciplinary work combining anthropology, history, literature, and archaeology, in an attempt to reconstruct the circumstances that permitted the rise of Christianity as an interaction between Jesus with his followers and with the historical context of the time.

We now know that many artisans and farmers in lower Galilee in the 20s CE, such as Jesus and his followers, lived a radical but nonviolent form of resistance against the urban development of Herod Antipas and against the mercantilism of Rome. A common feature within the wider context was the fierce opposition of Jews towards the internationalism of Greek culture and the military imperialism of Rome.[35]

According to Crossan, historical Christianity is the outcome of the merging of three traditions.

The first is the *Tradition of Life*, which emphasizes the sayings of Jesus and that puts forward a way of life inspired by his liberal behaviour. This tradition is rural in nature for it flourished in the rural parts of Galilee.

The second is the *Tradition of Death*, which sought to understand the reasons why Jesus had to die on the cross, for later he resurrected and appeared to many people. The issue of resurrection was interpreted within an apocalyptic framework, which affirmed the cosmic character of the phenomenon and the beginning of the renewal of the world and of the transfiguration of the human being. This tradition is more urban in character for it was elaborated in Jerusalem.

The third is the *Tradition of Communality*, that is, of "nourishing in community." This tradition refers to those common meals, which were abundant in nourishment and real in character, where food was shared in community. Its meaning was to symbolize the egalitarian character of the justice of God. The belief was that the God of the Kingdom, the God of Life, guarantees to all the means of life in a communitarian way. What

35. Cf. Kyrtatas, *The Social Structure of the Early Christian Communities*.

was important was not the bread placed on the table but the *sharing* of the bread and the passing of the bread to others. In the same way, the wine was not important, rather what was important was the cup that was *passed* from one person to another, it was the cup, which was *shared* between people that was important. Within this context, one can clearly identify the celebration of the Eucharist, which is something openly stated by Saint Paul (cf. 1 Corinthians 10; 11), and this was something done to fulfil a precept set by Jesus: "Do this in remembrance of me."

The common meal, as the *Didache* states, symbolizes the unity of the community of faith: "As this broken bread was once scattered on the mountains, and after it had been brought together became one, so may thy Church be gathered together from the ends of the earth unto thy kingdom" (*Didache* 9:4).[36]

What all this means is that it is in the food and drink that is shared by all—i.e. communality—that the presence of God takes place and that the renewal of the meaning of life and of Jesus's acts happen. As Crossan states: "Food and drink are the material bases of life, so the Lord's Supper is political criticism and economic challenge as well as sacred rite and liturgical worship. It may be all right to reduce it from a full eat-and-drink meal to a token nibble-and-sip meal as long as it still symbolizes that same reality—namely: Christians claim that God and Jesus are peculiarly and especially present when food and drink are shared equally among all."[37]

The tradition of communality united two traditions, the *Tradition of Life* and the *Tradition of Death*. For the primitive Church it was not sufficient to have the sayings, the life, the death, and the resurrection of Jesus, as important as these are. Everything had to end up at the common table, in communality, for it is communality that allows for the opening of one's eyes and the acceptance of Jesus and the divine presence in the world—just as it happened with the young ones, possibly a young couple, of Emmaus (cf. Luke 24:31). This data is very relevant for understanding Christianity in its more practical, than dogmatic, origins; this was a Christianity more centred on the community than on individuals.

The communality of Jesus and of the primordial Church was meant to anticipate the eternal communality with God in his Kingdom of

36. Translator's note: I have referred to Charles H Hoole's English translation of the *Didache*, which is available online: www.earlychristianwritings.com/didache.html/.

37. Crossan, *The Birth of Christianity*, 444.

Peace, of justice, of love, and of the super-abundance of everything that means life.

Historically, therefore, in the moment that utopia turns into reality, aspirations become concrete, the apex of the universal process will be realized; when this happens the complete communality between all beings of creation, all human beings, and God will take place. The table will be set, and all will be satisfied. There will be neither hunger nor thirst nor any other form of wanting because God itself will serve all with the produce of the universe and, this will mean a joyful plenitude for all.

thirteen

A Culture of Peace in a World in Conflict

Having implemented an unlimited form of hospitality, accomplished living together fraternally, established respect for all peoples and cultures, exercised active tolerance towards all differences, and lived in universal communality, it is understandable that we would expect, as the final outcome of this process, peace—the much desired peace.

It is perhaps appropriate to refer here to the beautiful definition of peace from the *Earth Charter*: "peace is the wholeness created by right relationships with oneself, other persons, other cultures, other life, Earth, and the larger whole of which all are a part."[1] A more encompassing and political definition of peace was expressed by the General Secretary of the United Nations, Kofi Annan at the time of the launching of the International Year for the Culture of Peace (2000): "True peace is far more than the absence of war. It is a phenomenon that encompasses economic development and social justice. It means safeguarding the global environment and curbing the global arms trade. It means democracy, diversity and dignity; respect for human rights and the rule of law; and more, much more."[2]

As one can gather, peace does not come into existence by itself. Peace is the outcome of values, behaviors, and relations predating it. Peace is the happy outcome of these; peace, which is perhaps the most desired and necessary outcome for humanity today.

1. Translator's note: See the Earth Charter online: http://www.earthcharterinaction .org/.

2. Annan, "Message on the Occasion of the Launch of the International Year of the Culture of Peace."

Why is peace something so much desired? Because the dominating culture, which is now globalized, is structured around choices that are contrary to peace. These choices focus on the will to exercise power and are expressed through the domination of one group by another, by social conflicts, and by violence against nature, which is turned into merchandise at the mercy of commercial interests.

Einstein and Freud: Can We Curb Aggression?

Within this scenario, can we achieve peace? History tells us that this is not easy. According to the historian Alfred Weber, bother of Max Weber, of the last 3,400 years of recorded human history, 3,166 were war years. The remaining 234 years were not exactly years of peace, rather they were years of truce and of preparation for war.

Most national days, national heroes, and the monuments on main squares are connected with deeds of war and violence in practically every country. The means of communication take the magnification of violence to its maximum, a fact epitomized by the *Terminator* films of Arnold Schwarzenegger.

Within this kind of culture, the soldier, the banker, and the speculator are worth more than the poet, the philosopher, and the saint. The formal and informal social processes do not create conditions for a culture of peace.

This situation brings to mind the question that Albert Einstein, who was a pacifist, put dramatically to Freud in 1932 in a letter dated 30th June: "Is there a way of delivering mankind from the menace of war? . . . Is it possible to control man's mental evolution so as to make him proof against the psychoses of hate and destructiveness?"[3]

Freud answered these questions in a frank manner: "In any case, as you have observed, complete suppression of man's aggressive tendencies is not an issue; what we may try is to divert it into a channel other than that of warfare . . . If the propensity for war be due to the destructive instinct, we have always its counteragent, Eros, to our hand. All that produces ties of sentiment between man and man must serve us as war's antidote . . . All that brings out the significant resemblances between

---

3. Quoted in Nathan and Norden, *Einstein on Peace*, 190.

men calls into play this feeling of community, identification, whereon is founded, in large measure, the whole edifice of human society."[4]

And later in his letter, Freud states in a realistic and resigned manner: "They conjure up an ugly picture of mills that grind so slowly that, before the flour is ready, men are dead of hunger."[5]

Despite this harsh truth, we continue to search for peace and we will never give up; we are not able to find an everlasting peace because this is something denied to mortals, but we can at least find peace as the will to dialogue and to find points in common.

In books 1 and 2 I introduced a referential narrative as a way of illustrating the topic I intended to discuss, and I shall do so below.

Symbols of a Humanity of Peace

Let me refer here to the symbolic-history by the journalist Ferran Sales that appeared in the Spanish newspaper *El País* on the 7th June 2001, page 8:

> Mazen Julani was a Palestinian pharmacist, 32 years old, father of three, who lived in the Arabic part of Jerusalem. On the 5th June 2001, when drinking some coffee with some friends in a bar, he became the victim of a fatal shooting by a Jewish colonist. This was done in revenge against the Palestinian group Hamas; forty-five minutes earlier, a suicide-bomber, had killed a number of people in a club in Tel Aviv. The bullet entered Julani's neck and exploded his brains. He was taken immediately to the Israeli hospital Hadassa, where he arrived already dead.
>
> The Julani family decided there and then to donate all his organs (heart, liver, kidneys, and pancreas) for organ transplants in Jewish patients. The head of the family spoke in the name of the whole family and said that this gesture did not have any political connotation. It was a strictly humane deed.
>
> According to Islam, he said, we are all part of a single human family, and we are all equal, whether Israelis or Palestinians. It does not matter who is going to receive the organs. The important thing is that they will help to save lives. For this reason, he continued, the organs will serve well our fellow Israelis.
>
> In fact, Julani's heart now beats inside Yigal Cohen. Julani's wife found it difficult to explain to their four-year-old daughter

4. Ibid., 199.
5. Ibid., 201.

the death of the father. She only said to the girl that her father had gone on a journey to a faraway place and that on his return he would bring her a beautiful present. To those who were close to her at the time, she whispered with eyes full of tears: given some time my children and I will visit Yigal Cohen in the Israeli part of Jerusalem. He lives with my husband's heart, he lives with the father-of-my-children's heart. It will be a great consolation to hear the heart of that who so much loved us; a heart which, in a way, still beats for us.[6]

This generous gesture is loaded with symbolism. Amid an extremely tense environment filled with hatred, a sign of hope and peace emerges. The conviction that we are all members of the same family, the human family, encourages attitudes of forgiveness, reconciliation, and unconditional solidarity. And set in the background, is that love brings everything together. Such virtues allow us to believe that a culture of peace is possible. According to Gilberto Freyre, one of the foremost theorists of Brazilian culture, the Brazilian civilizational experiment, despite its many contradictions, consisted in creating a people capable of joining the potentials of each and every culture and so with a great capacity to deal with conflict.[7]

Overcoming Obstacles to Peace

The pathway to peace is uneven and full of obstacles. Sometimes we are over optimistic, which leads us to utopian solutions, and at other times we are very pessimistic, which leads us to solutions that make peace itself impossible. In practical terms, I am thinking here of a limitless form of pacifism and of an extremist form of conflict. On closer inspection, these two pathways do not make justice to the complexities of reality, a reality in which one must bring about peace.

Limitless Pacifism

Historically, we can always find an attitude, usually with a religious background, of radical pacifism. Despite the real conditions of life,

---

6. Translator's note: This passage, originally published in Spanish, is directly translated from Boff's Portuguese.

7. Cf. Freyre, *The Masters and the Slaves*.

where violence, aggression, and war occurs, there have been people and groups who opted for a radical and limitless pacifism.[8] They prefer to die rather than fight back to defend themselves. Saint Francis of Assisi, the medical doctor and humanist Albert Schweitzer, the Russian writer Leo Tolstoy, and Marechal Rondon, who strongly supported the Brazilian native Indians (Rondon's motto was "better to die than to kill"), can be considered radical pacifists who renounced all kinds of aggression towards any being of creation. The Quakers are well-known for their practice of a 'quietist' radical (i.e., passive) pacifism.

This attitude of pacifism is born out of a deep religious feeling, of an unconditional respect towards every being and of a continuous search for "moral improvement." Whilst this behavior is very commendable, it is not very realistic on its own as it cannot bring about peace. There are moments in life when we must defend the innocents (e.g. children threatened by sexual abuse and death), we can justify intervention, for humanitarian reasons, when minorities are being exterminated, as happened in Bosnia and Kosovo in the late twentieth century—if we do not do so we may become accomplices to the crime.

Contradictory dimensions co-exist within reality, dimensions which are part of reality itself and that continuously undermine our efforts for absolute peace. How are we to deal with these? This is a question that radical (passive) pacifism cannot answer properly.

Active pacifism is injected with a larger dose of realism. It acknowledges the real conditions of a contradictory and conflicting reality but it refuses to make use of military power and war as a solution to problems. This is particularly relevant in our modern times as active pacifism is aware of the potential for great destruction in a war with "intelligent" weapons; such a war causes more victims among civilians than among military personnel. Active pacifism—also called active nonviolence, such as that practiced by Mahatma Gandhi and Martin Luther King Jr.—proposes affecting positively social and political reality without resorting to violence of any kind.

Nonviolent methods are used not for pragmatic or strategic reasons, but as a consequence of a strong conviction that the truth has a power in itself, so much so that it is capable of imposing itself.

8. Cf. Prat et al., *Pensamiento pacifista.*

Napoleon Bonaparte, not without reason, said: "There are two forces in the world, the sword and the spirit. In the long run the sword will always be conquered by the spirit."

Active pacifists believe in the invincible force of the spirit. Out of this conviction they make use only of peaceful means such as putting pressure on social and political authorities, great rallies, religious services in large public meetings, fasting, and hunger strikes. The use of such methods turn peace into the means to achieve peace, not simply peace as a goal itself; Gandhi achieved the liberation of India from Britain, and Martin Luther King Jr. gained civil rights for Black Americans by making use of such methods.

Last, there is also a *revolutionary pacifism*. It accepts the basic thesis of pacifism, which is the rejection of resorting to military force and war. But it further advocates that it is necessary to search for the causes behind militarism and the determination to go to war; these causes are the will to dominate others, conflicts rooted in geopolitical, ethnic, religious, and economic interests, and the existence of deep inequalities within societies and between peoples. Revolutionary pacifism seeks to deal with these hidden connections as a condition to a true and everlasting peace. It calls itself revolutionary not because it intends to make use of violent means but because it seeks to solve the causes of violence. It employs political means, it articulates with social movements, it mobilizes religions and churches, and it gets involved with groups involved in alternative practices. Chico Mendes subscribed to this revolutionary pacifism. He mobilized those living in the Brazilian jungle—native Indians and rubber tappers—to challenge those pockets of deforestation in the Amazon region; he organized the famous "matches," those public gatherings in which children, women, the elderly, and workers placed themselves in front of the machinery cutting down the forest.

Pacifism is more than a policy with a strategy and tactics; it is a fundamental attitude, it is an anti-militarist spirit that excludes war as a means of creating order between nations and human beings. There is neither just war nor holy war. All war is perverse because it decimates lives, especially innocent ones. War is in direct opposition to the transcultural commandment: "thou shall not kill." War is futile.

Extreme Conflicts

Reality is also an arena where conflict, struggles, and wars constantly take place. The human being is a lamb but it is also a wolf to another human being. It is possible for people, communities and nations to live together, but this is always challenged by threats and constant ruptures. The advent of the nation-state, and powerful countries, dominate the development of history and transform everything into a power struggle. The important thing is to be powerful and to have the capacity to be victorious over the other.

The jurist and political theorist Carl Schmitt (1888–1986) maintained in his *The Concept of the Political* the thesis that the identity of a people is defined and reaffirmed to the measure in which it is capable to identify and fight its enemy. This struggle gains the form of prejudice, smear and vilification of the other, the enemy. Carl von Clausewitz (1780–1831), in his *On War*, gives central stage to war in the development of history and understands politics as a war conducted by different means.

It was such perspectives, founded on violence, that produced the cold-hearted killings practiced by European colonialism in Africa, Latin America, and Asia, and which decimated millions of natives in a few years; what happened in Mexico and Peru in the sixteenth century is a good example of this.

After that there was the advent of total war (something initiated by Adolf Hitler with the Second World War) and of the *systematic production of cadavers in the Nazi death camps,* as put by the Jewish-German philosopher Hannah Arendt. These "death factories" did not have any military relevance. In these "factories" reigned the banal execution of people, reigned clinical and bureaucratic death carried out without any scruples or moral fibre. This was a sheer expression of racism and hatred.[9] In the twentieth century only, some 200 million people died in the many wars that occurred. This represents a high level of barbarism and the negation of any civilizational principle.

After 9/11 2001, after the terrorist attacks in the USA, a new kind of war emerged: the preventive war against world terrorism. This war is globalized. It divided humanity into "rogue" and "evil" countries, and "civilized" and "good" countries. The former are dealt with all the rigor

9. Cf. Stolcke, "Lo espantosamente nuevo," 101–19.

of the modern intelligence war, and the remaining countries are forced to take sides with the dominant super power, the USA. Human rights are no longer unconditional; rather, they are conditioned to an understanding of security for the global system. Fear, terror, insecurity are experienced by those core countries, which are constantly threatened by terrorism, which in turn keep these countries hostage of this logic.

Lastly, there is the issue of WMDs (weapons of mass destruction), which are capable of wiping out the whole human race and a great part of the biosphere. This mode of war altered deeply the understanding that the human being has of itself. The human being can put an end to itself. This end would neither be the result of a natural cataclysm, nor of divine will; rather, it would be the result of its own will. After taking hold of its own life, the human being now takes hold of its own death. This fact has metaphysical dimensions. It makes us think about our capacity for aggression, about our place in the evolutionary process, and who we really are. This fact has shaped an understanding of history as an uninterrupted process of wars and as an alternate succession of victory and defeat. Over and above this, there is another issue that aggravates deliberations on war and peace. This issue is the brutal situation of the poor and the excluded. The increasing number of these on a global scale may lead us to a conflict with dire consequences. These masses of those who are abandoned to their own devices can no longer be dismissed by the global system. Part of these masses constitute a reserve in the Mafia and terrorist economy, which mobilizes hundreds of thousands of people worldwide, which involves billions of dollars laundered by banks, that corrupts politicians and that even penetrates the highest levels of state security organizations. This complex phenomenon is seen by some commentators as equivalent to the third world war.[10]

The matter of rich and poor gains a geopolitical dimension and the eventual struggle between the opulent North and the impoverished South. This may cause us to experience organized acts of terrorism, public assets being vandalized, violence in public gatherings and eventually movements advocating urban warfare. Acts of great destruction should not be ruled out; acts such as the poisoning of the water system, the bombing of electricity stations, or even nuclear, power stations, or even of acts of incredible violence such as the ones that took place in New

---

10. Cf. Engelhard, *La troisième Guerre Mondiale est commencé*; I. Ramonet *Wars of the 21st Century*.

York, Madrid, and London. Along with these, we may also experience racism, xenophobia, religious fundamentalism and fascism, which are well-known causes of violence and death in civil society.

How are we to postulate peace in a world so troubled and violent? In real terms, the peace of the status quo is an armed peace, in a permanent state of siege. It is a truce and an armistice within a scenario of war, it is a pause for those involved to rebuild and re-arm themselves and restart the endless war.

In order for us to build a culture of peace we must overcome these radical perspectives and better our understanding of reality. Reality has more shades than the oversimplification of black/white, friend/foe, and war/peace.

Responsible Realism

Reality is by its very nature ambiguous. On the one hand it is marked by the conflicts I referred to earlier, and these are undeniable. On the other hand, it is woven through with the dynamics of order, harmony, and peace. These two sides do not change. They live together. They inter-combine. At one time the darker side reigns but bringing with it the lighter side, and other times the lighter side rules but carrying with it the darker side. One is not able to eradicate the other. They limit themselves, they complement each other, they challenge each other and they maintain the dynamic balance between each other, a balance which is never guaranteed but always in the making. Thus, the dramatic nature of reality.

The art is not to give primacy to a limitless pacifism at one time and primacy to extreme conflict at other times. The art consists in seeking a balance through establishing a convergence of forces that allows for things to organize in an orderly fashion, allow for the creation of institutions that are at least minimally just and inclusive, and for a way of organizing society that is minimally destructive. And this must be achieved by bearing in mind that the potential for conflict is like a shadow, always accompanying everything.

If this search for the "half way," for equilibrium, and for the right measure did not occur then sociability would be something impossible for the human being because human beings would have exterminated themselves.

Peace within this complex context cannot be understood as a secure state of affairs. It is a process through which conflicts are managed in such a way that it turns them into something non-destructive as well as the source of dynamism in human sociability. That is to say peace does not exist by itself. Peace must be continuously built, day after day, year after year, and in each person, group, community and society in the world.[11]

Peace is a way of managing conflicts through the use of non-conflicting means. Hence, for instance, in the establishment of social relations: allowing for dialogue, seeking to understand the position of the other, being open to the identification of common issues, being willing to establish harmony and even to forgive; these are attitudes that help generate peace. When searching for peace collective interests should gain priority over the interests of the individual or of particular groups, multiculturalism must prevail over ethnocentrism, a global perspective must provide guidance for local perspectives, and national citizenship must be open to a global citizenship.

If we do not take on this peaceful strategy collectively it will be difficult for peace to emerge.

Impossible Peace

If we want to achieve peace, it is important to realistically understand the potential for conflict that is present in the community of life and in the human being. Only by doing so can we achieve a sustainable peace and establish a culture of peace. I want to tackle this question from various points.

Violence at a Personal Level Is within Myself

It is important to be realistic and sincere. There is violence in the world because we carry violence within ourselves. I feel anger when driving if I am overtaken by another car in a reckless and dangerous way. I become irritated when the streets are full of people and I cannot walk in a hurry as I am already late for a medical appointment. I do not get on well with someone I meet who is arrogant and thinks that he or she is always right. I feel infuriated when I see a bully cowardly beat up someone smaller

11. Cf. Pureza, *Para uma cultura da paz.*

who tried to assert himself. Sometimes, I even surprise myself with what I feel as I struggle with someone who is arguing with me and who undoubtedly is distorting the facts and lying. How many times have we heard someone saying: "I am going to kill him or her"?

These feelings of violence and aggression are within us. They are manifested collectively in schools, in the workplace and in the community by the so-called phenomenon of *bullying* (and we do not have a direct or proper translation to this in Portuguese). It stands for attitudes that are intentional or non-intentional, concealed or explicit, for reasons of characteristics such as excess of weight, being skinny, not being very clever, parents' profession, health problems, way of dressing, etc., this turns someone into the object of fun, offence, humiliation, intimidation, and exclusion by part of the group through the use of kicks, slaps, etc. The victims usually are ascribed with jocular and even offensive nicknames, and become true escape-goats. The implications for the victims can be disastrous, as many become depressed, seek isolation, face panic attacks and eating problems. *Bullying* is nowadays a worry for schools and for the work place and it represents an obstacle for a culture of peace for students and workers are neither encouraged nor educated about respecting differences and tolerance.[12]

Explaining aggression has been a challenge to commentators. Sigmund Freud dealt with this issue throughout his life. Freud started with the fact that there exists two basic impulses in human life. The first is that which reaffirms and exalts life (called Eros in the same sense as ascribed by the ancient Greeks). The other is that which pushes towards death (Thanatos) and its psychological derivatives, such as hatred, revenge and exclusion. These two impulses co-exist and are constitutive of human reality.

Freud maintains that aggression emerges when the instinct of death is activated by a threat that comes from the outside. One can pose a threat to another by wanting to take the other's life. Thus, the threatened individual anticipates this and becomes violent towards, and eventually may even try to eliminate, the aggressor. The root of aggression is the fear that we can lose our lives.

However, if mutual trust prevails and if every one cares for everyone, then there is no reason for someone to feel threatened. Only then will an atmosphere of peace be established.

12. Cf. Fante, *Fenômeno Bullying.*

René Girard, a French scholar, asserts that aggression is rooted in the permanent rivalry that exists between human beings (which is something he calls "mimetic desire"). This rivalry creates permanent tensions and gives rise to sinister complicities. When society identifies someone as the source of evil and of threats, society turns this individual into a scapegoat. All unite against this individual so to cast him/her out. When this is done a momentary peace is established between those involved. When peace is no longer in place, new scapegoats are devised (e.g., terrorists, Muslims, globalization protesters, traffickers) and once again a union of all against him/her/them is established, and a new momentary peace achieved. This is an endless cycle.

But desire does not need to be mimetic and competitive. Desire can be guided by cooperation, by sharing, and by a collective ownership of that which is desired. In this way the conditions for a long-lasting peace are established, a peace which is no longer that momentary one established through the elimination of scapegoats.

Society, family, schooling and the cilivizational process teach us to dominate these hateful and violent dimensions that live within us and to put a stop to violent behavior and even to crimes. History, however, has shown that these are not sufficient in guaranteeing a long-lasting and sustainable peace.

There is another side to all this. There is a true source of goodness and affection, of good will and love within us, and which is never completely obscured.

Theorists of the human condition, and in particular those anthropologists who subscribe to the theory of cosmological, biological, and anthropological evolution, have made a strong case for understanding that these two dimensions are always in dialectical tension and dramatize our personal and social existence.

In every thing, inanimate or alive, these two forces are found in continuous tension. These are complementary forces. Each being must fight for and defend its space and affirm itself to live and survive. Otherwise it meets death. It was by reflecting on this particular aspect, and without considering the other, in respect to living beings that Darwin formulated his thesis about the survival of the fittest in the animal kingdom through natural selection.

However, there is the other force, that is there is the aspect of integration within a greater whole. No being survives by itself. Each being is a representative of a species, is a representative of a greater whole in which it is integrated, in which it feels itself secure, and in which its life and survival is guaranteed.

Self-affirmation and integration are part of every entity, even of subatomic elements. Certainly, it is possible that a being self-affirms itself with such force that it is no longer integrated with the greater whole. This is a deviation, which in the socio-political sphere caused the advent of capitalism. Within this deviation, what is important is the individual, the individual's achievements and the private accumulation of wealth. The individual forgets its part of a greater whole, which is society, nature and the universe. But the opposite can also occur: an individual integrates itself into the whole, develops the dynamics of cooperation and solidarity and of building the collective common good. Certainly, there may occur excesses: the individual may submerge itself so much within the greater whole that it loses its identity and its capacity for self-affirmation. This is what occurred with collective socialism: it was only able to envisage the "We" and it marginalized the "I," and this gave rise to a society without initiative, bureaucratic and destitute of creativity.

The art is combining permanently self-affirmation with integration, personal achievements with cooperation; the art is to give dynamism to personal and collective life processes.

Anthropologists have realized that we, human beings, are simultaneously *sapiens* and *demens*, and this condition is not due to degeneration but rather due to our evolutionary constitution. We are bearers of intelligence, wisdom, interior forces directed to generosity, collaboration, benevolence, love and forgiveness. And at the same time, we are bearers of madness, excesses, impulses of aggression and death. We are ambiguous, complex, bipolar; we are abysms of cruelty and pinnacles of affection. We are unfortunate beings for these two *Is* coexist and oppose each other inside each of us. Our hearts are divided. From our hearts springs the desire to do anything, and even to die, for the other. From our hearts springs the desire to reject, and even to kill, the other. We are a metaphysical enigma, a living contradiction, an angel and demon living together within the same vital space. In short, we are the meeting of two opposites.

How are we to bring about peace within this contradictory scenario? Peace will only be possible to the extent in which people, individually and collectively, predispose themselves to allow more space, and cultivate in a conscious and organized way the dimension of hospitality, cooperation, solidarity and love. A culture of peace depends on the predominance of these potentialities and on the care that every one takes with the other dimension, which is always present, the dimension of rivalry, egotism, and exclusion of others.

The Violence of Patriarchalism

Another cause of the reigning violence experienced by societies across the globe is due to a focus of patriarchalism. It has been demonstrated by scientific research, conducted under the auspices of feminism, that around 30,000 BCE societies were based on matriarchalism.[13] Women were at the head of society and organized relations with other groups. This was a culture marked by deep harmony with nature, for women felt connected with the rhythms of nature. Deities were feminine deities. Archaeological evidence of Mother-Goddesses are found practically everywhere in the world, particularly in the Mediterranean basin and in Southeast Asia. These were pacifist societies marked by a profound spiritual feeling for life.

Around 10,000 to 8,000 BCE patriarchalism started to slowly impose itself. For reasons not yet identified, men started to gain social and political power to the point at which they assumed control of society. Men imposed their interests, their vision for the world, and their understanding for the format of social relations. A slow and implacable process of re-structuring of social relations commenced, a process of subjugation and domination of women. The woman was banned from public life and confined to the family realm. Women continued to make a contribution in life for she carried on working and producing children, but she became invisible and marginalized. This process continuous to this very day despite struggles against this situation, the creation of organizations to tackle the issue, and vigorous feminist thought. The humiliations suffered by women due to discrimination in the labor market, due to the erotization of women for masculine use, due to the international trafficking of women, which forces women into being sexual slaves, denounce the continuation of patriarchalism. Patriarchalism reveals itself in even more radical forms in some African countries, who practice

13. Cf. Göttner-Abendroth, *Das Matriarchat*.

female circumcision and who condone unimaginable levels of violence against women.

The use of force is typical of male domination and the use of objective intelligence to implement its strategy to conquer and control the world is typical of males. For this reason men created the necessary instruments and apparatus for this task: the armed forces, war, the State which bears the legitimate right to make use violence, laws that legitimize these practices, a particular kind of science and technical expertise, as well as a reinterpretation of myths and traditions that legitimizes their new condition through divine authority.

Feminists argue that patriarchalism is more than an unequal and dominating relation of power of men over women. It is also a complex pyramidal political structure of domination and hierarchization that affects gender, race, class, politics, and religion.[14] Except for a few cases, practically all modern societies are patriarchal or patri-centered.

Faced by the strong opposition by a global feminist movement patriarchalism is undergoing a drastic process of dissolution. Patriarchalism lingers in the media and through the manipulation of female images for use in commercial marketing, but even in these cases it has started to feel the weight of resistance from society, society which seeks new forms of male-female relations, relations which are characterized by partnership, by the joint-responsibility of family tasks and by exchanging through differences, differences which are valued in equal terms.

Given this patriarchal culture centred on inequality and oppression, how do we achieve peace? Peace results from strategies of recovering the feminine aspect of society, of conveying dignity to women, of relations based on equality and sharing between the genders, of attitudes of continuous partnership between men and women, of attitudes that respect and value differences. The secular gender war can be replaced by a time of peace between men and women, of peace within families, and of peace in parental relationships.

Cultural Violence: The Will to Power-Domination

Patriarchalism gave rise to a kind of culture that organized practically all instances of society and projected and imposed its utopia and values upon all. The structural matrix of patriarchal culture is the will to

14. Cf. Schüssler Fiorenza, *Discipulado de iguais*, 151–59.

power-domination. This power-domination comes under the sign of Alexander the Great, or of Hernán Cortés, or of the conquest. This is an ambitious and promethean project of global conquest, of subduing peoples, and of subjugating nature. This project was carried out with iron and fire, and with extreme violence wherever its representatives found technical and political opportunity. Behind them they left a trail of blood, destroyed cities, crushed peoples, and devastated nature. This project knows no limits: it penetrated the heart of matter, it invaded the space of the sacred in life and it proposes conquering sidereal space. This will to power-domination was not stopped and does not stop in the face of any taboo, obstacle or limit. This will is essentially blasphemous for it is radically anthropocentric. The human being, through its will to conquer, becomes the benchmark for everything. Beyond the human being there is nothing.

It should not be surprising to find that, in its will to conquer, the human being developed the principle for self-destruction; the human being has built a "death machinery" so destructive that the human being is capable of bringing death to itself in various ways—which demonstrates its suicidal character—and to bring about the demise of a great part of the biosphere.

It was the will to power-domination that created the mercantile, colonial, neo-colonial, and now global-colonial modernity. Where will it take us if it is not constrained? Certainly, it will not take us to a kingdom of freedom, rights, respect, veneration, and peace. What peace can peoples long for when they see themselves simultaneously chained and forced to sing anthems of freedom?

Peace is only possible when it is the result of justice. A society has no future when it is built on structural and historical injustice. The basic idea of justice is encapsulated by the following statement, a true declaration of love for humanity: for each one according to its needs (physical, psychological, cultural, and spiritual) and of each one according to its capabilities (physical, intellectual, and moral). Within this framework, justice presupposes the equality of all and the search for a common good as defined by Pope John XXIII in his famous encyclical *Pacem in Terris*: "The common good 'must take account of all those social conditions which favour the full development of human personality.'"[15]

15. Pope John XXIII, *Pacem in Terris*, n. 58.

If relationships are not restructured so to become more just, egalitarian, and inclusive, then it will not be possible to live together in peace. Peace demands historical and political amends to compensate for the damages caused by domination over its victims, particularly those who for centuries were enslaved and transformed into "goods" to be sold for a price in the market. Those colonial, and once enslaving, powers still have not woken up to this reality, and do not even show themselves willing to apologize for the crimes against humanity they committed for centuries.

This peace is founded in that other dimension that is also present in the human being. The human being is not fatally condemned to power-domination. Alongside the paradigm of Alexander the Great and Hernán Cortés, those archetypes of conquerors, we find the paradigm of St. Francis of Assisi and Mahatma Gandhi, those who developed a spirit of universal fraternity and cherished "caring for" as a way of relating to all beings. The human being is able to live together and cooperate with others, become its allies, its brothers and sisters. History demonstrates that it is possible for human beings to relate to each other in a humane and fraternal way, and this is particularly the case with native populations—which still exist. Tensions and conflicts are resolved through dialogue, through negotiation, and through assuming commitments towards, and that are relevant to, all involved.

To give primacy to this dimension of the human being and to maintain the other under permanent scrutiny allows for at least a minimum of peace and of concord between people and societies.

The Violence of the Capitalist, Free-Market Economy

The will to power-domination gained its most palpable and perverse form in the capitalist, free-market economy. Historically, economy is about creating the material and technical conditions for life. Economy was an important aspect of society, but it was always in submission to politics, which is the way in which human beings distribute power among themselves, organize themselves, and construct a collective project. There is, however, a new historical development, in which economy has divorced itself from society, which created a perverse process of deterioration.

This was first hinted at by Karl Marx and it was brought to light by the American economist Karl Polanyi. Disassociated and divorced from any form of social, state, and human control, the economy has run wild. It functions by obeying its own logic, that is, the maximization of profit, the minimization of investments, and all this in the shortest term possible. And this is taking place on a global scale and without any form of ecological concern. Everything has become a *Big Mac*, everything can be put for sale in the market: health, culture, organs, religion. This is a sign "of general corruption, of universal venality," as Marx put it in his *The Poverty of Philosophy* (1847).[16] This is *the great transformation* as it was characterized by Polanyi, a transformation as has never before occurred.[17]

The most disastrous effect of this transformation is the lessening of the human being to a mere producer and simple consumer. There is nothing more unfortunate than this materialist and dignity-less human project.

As a member of a poor Base-Community (*Comunidade de Base*) in the Northeast of Brazil, who was very aware of the contradictions of life, said: "this person is so poor, really so poor, that the only thing he/she possesses is money." Goodness, generosity, spirit of cooperation and of care were totally lacking in this person.

In 1847, Karl Marx prophetically wrote in his *The Poverty of Philosophy*: "Finally, there came a time when everything that men has considered as inalienable became an object of exchange, of traffic and could be alienated. This is the time when the very things which till then had been communicated, but never exchanged; given, but never sold; acquired, but never bought—virtue, love, conviction, knowledge, conscience, etc.—when everything, in short, passed into commerce. It is the time of general corruption, of universal venality, or, to speak in terms of political economy, the time when everything, moral or physical, having become a marketable value, is brought to the market to be assessed at its truest value."[18]

Dead labor (machinery, apparatuses, robots) surpasses living labor (the workers). What is important is to conquer markets and to accumulate limitlessly. The driving force behind this logic is fierce competition. Only the strong survives; the weak does not endure, it gives up and ceases to exist.

16. cf. Marx, *The Poverty of Philosophy*.

17. Cf. Polanyi, *The Great Transformation*; Lowy, "Eco-socialism and Democratic Planning," 294–309.

18. cf. www.marxists.org/archive/marx/works/1847/poverty-philosophy/cho1.htm.

As it happens, this ferocity faces a restriction: nature with its limited resources and its limited capacity to sustain itself. However, nature is not respected. If it was, then this kind of economy would destroy itself. For this reason this kind of economy must continuously open new frontiers for production and for the development of agricultural businesses, which inevitably implies sacrificing, for instance, vast parts of the Brazilian Amazon jungle and of the Brazilian Pantanal, regions holding the largest hydric resources in the world, a luxurious biodiversity, as well as the largest reserves of biomass and of alternative energy resources.

The Earth has shown its revulsion recently: global warming, the thinning of the ozone layer, barrier reefs dying (which are largely responsible for the ocean's vitality), tornadoes, droughts, powerful floods, and at the human level, the growth of violence in social relationships. Research on weather patterns carried out by the Pentagon in 2004 warns: in the next three decades humanity can fall into a form of generalized anarchy due to severe changes in the Earth's ecosystems.

Humanity has reached an unsurpassable obstacle. It is no longer about building peace; rather, it is about collective survival. This situation characterizes the high degree of madness and barbarism humanity has reached. We risk destroying, or seriously damaging, the future of Gaia and of human life.

Some thinkers have started to speak out and even to make desperate appeals concerning these dark prospects. One of the first to do this is the Italian philosopher and social scientist Norberto Bobbio. Throughout his life and in his vast number of works he has always defended a belief in those two great contributions made by the West: human rights and democracy. He advocates that both are the foundations for a judicial and political pacifism that is capable of solving the problem of violence in disputes between states. But the advent of a globalized terrorism and the ecological time-bomb has shaken his convictions on this thesis.

In one of his last interviews he declared: "I would not know what to say about the third millennium. I am not sure of anything anymore and only one question troubles me: will this be the millennium of a ravaging war or the millennium of concord between human beings? I have no answer to this question."

The great historian Arnold Toynbee (1889–1975), after having written twelve tomes on the great civilizations, held a similar opinion at the end of his life. In his autobiography titled *Experiences* he says sombrely: "I . . . have lived on to see the ending of human history become a mundane possibility that would be translated into fact by an act, not of God, but of Man."[19]

And just to re-enforce my concerns here, I refer to the impartial Samuel P. Huntington, former advisor to the Pentagon and a prominent commentator on the process of globalization. At the end of his book *The Clash of Civilizations* he says: "Law and order is the first prerequisite of Civilization and in much of the world—it appears to be evaporating . . . On a worldwide basis Civilization seems in many respect to be yielding to barbarism, generating the image of an unprecedented phenomenon, a global Dark Ages, possibly descending on humanity."[20] And I could refer to other commentators here.

Given this threatening scenario for humanity and life on Earth, how do we achieve peace? Peace will only happen with radical changes to the paradigm of production and distribution of those items that are necessary for life. Peace implies overcoming the system of death, the *society of industrial production*, and the establishment of its alternative, which is a *society of sustainability of all life*. Within this new paradigm the focus is no longer the unlimited accumulation of goods and services, but the production of an adequate and decent amount for all, including the other members of the community of non-human life. The Earth will no longer be regarded as a chest of illusory and unlimited resources; rather, the Earth will be regarded as the Great Mother, as the supra-organism Gaia, of whom we are all sons and daughters.

The Original Violence of the Cosmos

My analysis would not be complete if I did not include a fundamental issue connected to the very structure of the universe. Every single being, galaxy, star, planet, form of life, human being, and consciousness comes from the original Fountainhead, the Abyss of plenitude, also called the quantum Vacuum, which is not vacuous at all. It is that unapproachable background energy that is always in the present, in the past and in the future. In it are present infinite possibilities of being, of energy, of matter and of knowledge. From it, our universe came to be; and possibly and according to string theory many other different and parallel universes. Out of this unapproachable Source without end an immeasurable explo-

19. Toynbee, *Experiences*, 371.
20. Huntington, *The Clash of Civilizations*, 321.

sion was produced, the *Big Bang*, and we do not know the reasons for this. Nanoseconds after, another mysterious violent event took place, which has yet to be explained by science. All existing matter, with the exception of an infinitesimal part of it, was annihilated by antimatter. The existing matter is what was left from that inexplicable obliteration.[21]

This remaining matter, under the influence of the *Big Bang*, was thrown in all directions. Energies with billions of degrees of heat were thrown everywhere. When they cooled down immense clouds started forming, slowly increasing in density. These clouds gave birth to red stars, which are furnaces, which forge inside themselves the main phys-ical-chemical elements that enter into the composition of every entity in the universe: oxygen, iron, nitrogen, phosphorus, and others. When they exploded, billions of years ago, they launched these elements in all directions giving origin to galaxies, stars, planets like the earth, and supplied the physical-chemical structure that made it possible for life to emerge in all its forms, including an extremely complex and conscious form, human life.

In the origin of everything is thus present an unimaginable original violence. This is the primal chaos. But to the measure in which these primordial elements started to expand, order was being simultane-ously established, and entities increasingly more complex and systems increasingly more interlinked and coherent appeared. Chaos is never merely chaotic. Chaos is rather generative and inventive.

The universe, to the extent in which it expands itself, shows itself to be creative, self-organizing and self-regulating. Chaos does not van-ish; it lingers and is present in each phase of the evolutionary process. Galaxies devour other galaxies in an inferno of explosions and de-struction. Meteors continuo to fall on and bring unbalance to planets, just as it happened 67 million years ago in the Yucatan Peninsula and Caribbean—this event killed the dinosaurs who had triumphed all over the Earth for over 100 million years. Tectonic plates are continuously shifting, encroaching on each other and producing devastating earth-quakes and tidal waves, such as the *Tsunami* that happened on Christmas 2004 and which decimated part of Southeast Asia.

But this systemic chaos has its destructive power contained to the measure in which new balances are established, balances which main-

21. Cf. Hawking, *A Brief History of Time*; Swimme and Berry, *The Universe Story*.

tain the evolutionary process unfolding as an open system capable of innovations and of extraordinary new orders never seen before.

The organizing and regulating systems articulate with their medium, exchanging energies, matter, and information so that they continue to enrich themselves and develop a subtle dynamic equilibrium, which is never enclosed on itself but rather open to adaptations, flexibilities, and incorporations; these systems are part of a global system and co-evolve with this same global system. Even when a system faces a crisis and can no longer react, its composition shows itself to be creative by giving origin to new orders and forms of life that adapt to the mediums in which they are inserted.

The important point of this very brief reflexion on this issue is to bear in mind: there is an original chaos, a structural violence and an instability proper to the constitution of the universe and to all realities contained in it.

This fact does not mean that there is no peace and that peace is from the start impossible. This means that peace is never a given, is never something established once and for all. Peace must be continuously built upon those orders, systems, and webs of relations that continuously emerge.

If violence is something structural, then the challenge is: how do we manage it? What strategies must be follow to curb its destructive powers? How do we transform the intrinsic dynamics of chaos into something positive for nature and human beings?

Peace is a way of imposing limits and of sublimating conflicts inherent in the whole of reality (cosmic, social, and personal). This will only be possible if we have at the heart of things the dimension of order, harmony, and establishment of interdependences and webs of cooperation.

The Possible Peace

My reflections up to this point demonstrate how complex and full of obstacles the path to peace is. Peace seems to be something almost impossible. But humanity has never completely given up on its search for peace. The heart does not rest if it does not find peace, something which is as important as love. I believe in peace and in the human capacity to build it.

But I believe in it, provided two conditions are met, conditions that are revealed by analyzing reality and its dimensions, which encompass the heart and the cosmos, the cosmos and the Big Bang.

The first condition is that we should seriously embrace the polarity *sapiens/demens*, love/hate, chaos/cosmos, symbolic/diabolic as belonging to the structure of the universe and the human being; we are the living unity of oppositions.

The second condition is that we should reinforce the luminous side of these opposing forces in such a way that it is able to keep under control, put a limit on, and integrate the dark side, and once this is done then we can achieve the desired peace.

This was and is the pathway trod by humanity and exemplified by its greatest spiritual leaders, such as Mahatma Gandhi, Pope John XXIII, Dom Helder Camara, Martin Luther King Jr., and others, to mention a few from our modern times.

An Efficient Strategy to Build Peace

This pathway was prepared centuries ago by *the first after the Unique*, and maybe *the last of the Christians*, St. Francis of Assisi (1181–1226). He developed a strategy capable of building peace.

This strategy gained its best expression in the "Peace Prayer of St. Francis of Assisi," which is the object of a book of mine on this topic, *The Prayer of Saint Francis*. This prayer is always said when religious leaders from around the world meet. It stands for a belief with which all identify. Curiously, this prayer was written anonymously during the First World War (1914–1918) by a devotee of St Francis of Assisi from Normandy, France. He captured extremely well the spirit and the core teachings of St. Francis of Assisi, who left us very few writings, that the prayer was attributed to St. Francis of Assisi himself.[22]

This prayer spread throughout the world when it was published in the *Osservatore Romano*, an official publication of the Vatican, on the 16th of January 1916. From this moment onwards it spread everywhere as a source of inspiration for peace and affection between human beings and peoples. The language of the prayer is religious but its content is universal and can be taken on by followers of any religion or even by those who do not follow any religion.

22. Cf. Boff, *The Prayer of St. Francis*.

Despite its radical pacifism and its sensitivity, for it calls all creatures brothers and sisters, this prayer does not lose a sense of our contradictory reality. It understands that the world is a minefield; it understands that the world is intertwined with grace and sin. It does not even question the reasons for this. It understands, following the wisdom of simple people, that we should not try to understand evil but to overcome it with good. It ascertains that the sane part of us will heal the sick part and that light is more righteous than the darkness that accompanies it.

It is not without reason that Dante Alighieri (c. 1265–1321) in his *Divine Comedy* calls St. Francis of Assisi "un sole . . . Però chi d'esso loco fa parole, non dica Ascesi (Assisi—translation insertion), ché direbbe corto, ma Oriente, se proprio dir vuole" or "a sun . . . therefore let him who names this site not say *Ascesi* (Assisi—translation insertion), which would be to say too little, but *Orient*, if he would name it rightly" (*Paradiso*, Canto XI, 50–54).[23]

It is within this integrating understanding that evil ceases to be completely absurd, despite being part of the composition of all things. Hence, St. Francis of Assisi states with certainty and open heart:

> Lord, make an instrument of your peace;
> Where there is hatred, let me sow love;
> Where there is injury, pardon;
> Where there is doubt, faith;
> Where there is despair, hope;
> Where there is darkness, light;
> And where there is sadness, joy;
>
> O Divine Master, grant that I may not so much seek to be
>   consoled as to console;
> To be understood, as to understand;
> To be loved, as to love;

23. Translator's note: I have referred to Allen Mandelbaum's translation, which is available online: http://www.divinecomedy.org/divine_comedy.html; interestingly, all English translations seem to maintain 'Ascesi' instead of 'Assisi' as is the case in Portuguese. Ciardi notes: "It is such passages that certify the failure of all translation. *Ascesi*, which can mean 'I have risen,' was a common name for Assisi in Dante's day. *Oriente*, of course, is the point at which the sun rises. Let no man, therefore, call Assisi 'I have risen' (i.e., a man has risen), but let him call it, rather, the dawning east of the world (a sun has risen)" (134).

For it is in giving that we receive;

It is in pardoning that we are pardoned;

And it is in dying that we are born to Eternal Life.

Amen.[24]

As one may gather from this prayer, the pathway to peace opens up when we reinforce love wherever there is hatred, forgiveness wherever there is insult, union wherever there is discord, faith wherever there is doubt, truth wherever there is error, hope wherever there is despair, happiness wherever there is sadness, light wherever there is darkness.

The negative side is neither negated nor shunned. It is assumed but it is also submitted to the logic of the positive side.

The outcome of this wise strategy is the peace that is possible in contradictory entities, such as we are, in this turbulent Earth. The peace that springs from this, to paraphrase and remind ourselves of the previously stated conception of peace in the *Earth Charter*, is the plenitude resulting from good relations that people and societies maintain with each other, with life, with other cultures, with nature, and with the *whole* behind which God is hidden.

This is the path of Saint Francis, a path which can be lived at every moment by turning peace not into a desirable goal but into a righteous and short pathway towards it. Only peaceful means lived by peaceful minds can produce peace.

The Ethics of Care and of Universal Justice

The predominance of the masculine principle, which is historically expressed through the domination of men over women, and over everything else around it, has impoverished the human condition. As I have already pointed out, the predominance of the masculine principle has exacerbated power, reason, and violent means and it has weakened the feminine principle, sensitivity, emotional intelligence, being caring and caring for, the symbolic perception of reality and spirituality.

The presence of this bias in foundational human experiences has greatly impinged on ethics. The focus of the classical understanding of morality, which has its roots in ancient Greek philosophy and which culminated in Kant or in Habermas, has an unconscious basis on the

24. Online: http://www.prayerguide.org.uk/stfrancis.htm/.

masculine principle. For this reason it is based on two pillars: 1) the autonomy of the individual, that is, on the premise that only a free being is capable of being an ethical being; and 2) in the justice that is expressed by the rights and duties of men (this did not apply to women according to ancient Greek philosophy).

Hence, this understanding, however correct it is, is only a partial one. It leaves out fundamental dimensions such as affective relationships, such as family relationships, relationships with friends, with others and with all those with whom we feel emotionally involved. Without these relationships society does not function. It is here that we must refer to an essential category, that is, to care.[25] To care is that relation in which one is concerned and feels responsible for the other, in which one is involved and allows oneself to be involved with the life of the other, in which one shows solidarity and compassion. To care is that relation in which one perceives the contextual reality of problems and in which one is not merely being faithful to principles and duties.

The empirical basis for this is the knowledge that we all need to be cared for, welcomed, valued, and loved and that we all desire to care for, to welcome, to value, and to love—and this is something which was so finely analysed by Winnicott in his *Human Nature*. The privileged bearers, but not exclusive bearers, of these experiences are women. Women are directly connected to a life of care such as when bringing up children, preparing food, showing devotion during sickness, and educating. These characteristics are not exclusive to women, but proper to the feminine principle, which is also present in men, who are able to realize it.

Underlying this ethics of care there is an anthropology that is more fecund than the traditional one, which serves as the basis for prevailing ethical approaches; that is, the ethics of care starts with the relational character of the human being. The human being is fundamentally an entity of affection, bearer of *pathos*, of the capacity to feel, to affect and to be affected. It possesses intellectual reasoning, *logos*, but it is also gifted with emotional reasoning, with sensibility reasoning and spiritual reasoning. The human being is a being-with-the-others and for-the-others in the world. The human being does not exist isolated in its magnificent autonomy; it rather lives within a web of concrete relations and always finds itself connected to this web. The human being does not require a

25. Cf. Boff, *Essential Care*; Noddings, *Caring*; Noddings et al., "Justice, Caring, and Universality," 21–36.

social contract to live with others; rather, the human being already lives in community.

In order for us to have a culture of long lasting peace we must articulate these two ethical traditions: care with justice.[26] These two traditions are not in opposition to each other; rather, they compose and complement each other.

It is important to have institutions that are just. But the functioning of these institutions must not be formal and bureaucratic; they must be humane, caring and sensitive to the contextual situation of people. Above all, we must implement an universal culture of care towards the Earth, ecosystems, peoples, and especially toward those in need.

As I have maintained elsewhere, care is so central that it belongs to the essence of the human being and of all life.[27] To care is a precondition for all actions if these actions are to be righteous and directed towards a peaceful living together between human beings.

It is proper, due to "to care" and "to the least minimum of justice," to pay attention to the instinctive side of the human being, which is connected to its self-affirmation and to its physical and psychological survival. Within this context the law of the stronger prevails. This is the *natural-instinctive* side of the human being. But the human being is never only *natural-instinctive*. Ever since the emergence of language and of the spirit of cooperation, the human being became a *cultural* being. Objects are not merely objects to be used. Objects are also symbols through which the human being communicates meaning. If the natural being functioned instinctively through the logic of stimulus-response (e.g., only went after the first source of food it found or the first sexual partner that appeared, or beat up the individual who was being annoying), now as a cultural being the human being is ruled by the logic stimulus-reflection-response. The human being feels the influence of instincts but submits it to reflection, to self-control and to the right measure, which allow the human being to gain satisfaction without being prejudicial to others. In this way, the human being shows itself to be civilized.

Instead of the gaining-and-losing, the gaining-and-gaining takes over. Every side gains something, which diminishes the potential for tension and conflict. This is particularly true of political conflict. Instead

26. Cf. Mesa, "La ética del cuidado y sus implicaciones en la formación moral de la escuela," 21–33.

27. Cf. Boff, *Essential Care*.

of brutal force, repression, and war being used, dialogue and negotiation, the use of forums of arbitration, and reconciliation are employed. These forums take into account the various interests of the involved parties and seek a solution that satisfies all involved, which avoids the parties resorting to violence.

The challenge consists in creating a culture of gaining-gaining, that is to say, of implementing this strategy in groups, schools, communities, neighborhood meetings, unions, and family affairs so that it becomes something natural, and not something which we need to think about. In this way all would learn to dialogue, to listen to other's arguments, to consider one side and the other, to seek points in common between all that can then be practically implemented. The culture of peace emerges from a similar strategy.

However, we can never forget the personal efforts of each and every individual in turning itself into an instrument of peace. The individual only effectively collaborates with the communitarian strategy of peace if it turns itself into a subject of peace who emanates peace through words and deeds. The relevance of virtues becomes apparent within this scenario: humility, the search for perfection, being open to dialogue and listening, and being welcoming towards others. And the relevance of religious dimensions also become apparent within this scenario: prayer, meditation, and the capacity to forgive received injuries. It is perhaps one of the highest manifestations of spirit that it has the capacity to remain silent when it has every right to speak up, not to complain about an injustice when it had all the right to do so, to forgive when suffering an injury. This triumph can only be claimed by such an individual. Only the human being can savor the interior happiness of spirit and enjoy a peace that is already fitting of the kingdom of those who are free from these worldly limitations, from this world in which the sons and daughters of Adam and Eve suffer and grieve.

The Ethical-Political Paradigm for a Global Peace

I want to conclude my reflections on peace by referring to an ethical-political project suggested by Immanuel Kant (1724–1804) in his well-known text *Perpetual Peace* (*Zum ewigen Frieden*) of 1795.[28] This

---

28. Cf. Kant, *Zum ewigen Frieden*; Kant, *Perpetual Peace*; Guinsburg, *A paz perpétua*.

philosopher was one of the first to envisage a globalized world, though not through the economy but by law and democracy.

Ahead of his time, Kant proposes a "world republic" (*Weltrepublik*) or a "state of peoples" (*Völkerstaat*) founded on "global citizenship" (*Weltbürgerrecht*). This global citizenship, Kant says, is first characterized by a "universal hospitality" (*algemeine hospitalität*) (cf. §357).

Why is hospitality so fundamental? Kant's answer is: because all human beings are on this Earth and all, without exception, have the right to be in it and to visit its various corners and peoples. The Earth belongs to all (cf. §358).

This citizenship expressed through "universal hospitality" is governed by law and not by violence. Kant proposes disassembling the war machinery and disbanding all armies—just as it is proposed in the Earth Charter—for if the potential for resorting to such violent instruments remains in place, then there is a continuation of the powerful threatening the weaker and of tensions between states; it is only by destroying these violent instruments that we can achieve a long-lasting peace.

The rule of law and the spreading of universal hospitality will create an awareness of the rights in the minds and hearts of all global citizens and in doing so, will generate a "community of peoples" (*Gemeinschaft der Völker*). This community of peoples, Kant asserts, can become something so conscious that the violation of a right in one place will be felt everywhere else (§360). Ernesto Che Guevara expressed this same conviction many years later. Solidarity and the spirit of hospitality will be something so strong between human beings that the suffering of one person will be the felt by all, and the improvement of one person the improvement of all.

As a response to those who question the political practicalities of this (practicalities which generally lose sight of the ethical content of social relations) Kant asserts that global citizenship is not utopia; it is rather a necessary outcome of long-lasting peace (§360). If we want an enduring peace and not merely a truce or a momentous reconciliation, then we must live universal hospitality and respect the universal rights of each and every citizen.

Kant's ethical-political views established the foundations for a paradigm of globalization that is pertinent even nowadays.

Peace is the result of the rule of law, of institutional and coordinated judicial cooperation between all states and peoples. The respect of rights—rights which Kant considers "the apple of God's eye" or "the most sacred thing God has put on Earth"—creates a community of peace and security that puts a definite end to the "infamous warmonger."

Modern international law, seeking the rule of peace, is guided by these Kantian principles. This is in contrast with the views of another political theorist on globalization, Thomas Hobbes (1588–1679), who also established a paradigm for globalization and peace. For Hobbes, the concept of peace can only be characterized negatively, that is, peace stands for the absence of wars and represents equilibrium in the tensions between states and peoples. This understanding dominated for centuries, and in particular during the Cold War years. It made a strong comeback recently in the politics of those core countries that are led by the USA when, after the terrorist attacks of 9/11, 2001, they decided to combat terrorism by taking terror to those countries which, allegedly, supported terrorist acts, such as Afghanistan and Iraq.

They abandoned a perspective of peace by implementing a regime of national and international security based on a logic of generalized suspicion: it sees in any stranger, such as an Arab or Muslim, a potential terrorist. In the name of security, citizens find themselves under surveillance and constitutional rights are cancelled, rights which were a customary and rightful perquisite of American democracy. Those who are suspected of links with terrorism are arrested and submitted to measures that are equivalent to torture, and are kept in secret places, sometimes outside the country, cut off from the rest of the world, without access to their families, lawyers, and even to the International Red Cross, which totally disrespects the Human Rights Charter and other international agreements. Moreover, these core countries propose preventive military measures, support international cooperation only to the extent that their own positions are strengthened and to the extent that they can still manipulate international organizations for their own ends. This is the triumphant and threatening comeback of the Leviathan-State, the unforgiving enemy of any kind of hospitality.

Godly Peace

All factors and practices at a personal and social level should be directed towards contributing to the building of peace. My reflections would be incomplete and would hinder our search for peace if I did not include the issue of spirituality.

Spirituality is that dimension of the human being that deals with those great and ultimate questions that always accompany our thoughts: Where do we come from? Where do we go to? What is the meaning of the universe? What can we expect of the afterlife?[29]

It is usually the case that religions deal with these questions. But religions do not hold a monopoly on spirituality. Spirituality has an anthropolitical foundation and it is present in each of us and in all stages of our lives in this world. Spirituality is not so much about knowledge; it is rather more to do with feeling. It is the heart that awakens great dreams and seeks ultimate questions.

Human consciousness arose out of the evolutionary process. There was a moment in the history of this consciousness in which we became aware that we are part of a limitless Whole. Moreover, we became aware that things were not just thrown together at random or aimlessly. On the contrary, they form a great whole. We intuite that a thread interweaves everything and turns the many into one and in the one finds all kinds of diversity. The stars that so much fascinate us at night in the tropics, the majesty and imensity of the Amazon forest, the great rivers such as the Amazon River (which is rightly called the sea-river), the abundance of life in the prairies, the synphonic sound of birds and animals in the woods, the multiplicity of human cultures and faces, the mystery of birth of a fragile infant filled with emotions, the miracle of love between two people, and so on and so forth; these and other experiences reveal to us the diversity and the oneness of our planet and universe.

Human beings call these unifying thread by a thousand names, such as Tao, Shiva, Allah, Yahweh, Olorun, and many other names. All these stand for the word God. When a human being says this word something happens in its mind and heart. Neurologists, neurolinguists and other neuroscientists identified the "God module" in the brain (cf. Zohar 2000). This module increases the hertz frequency of neurons. This means that the evolutionary process provided the human being with a way of capturing the presence of God in creation. Evidently, God is not only in the "God module: but in the whole brain, in all life, and in the whole universe. But it is from this module that we are able to capture God's presence. Furthermore, we are capable of dialoguing with God, of

29. Cf. L. Boff, *Experimentar Deus*.

taking our pledges to God, paying tribute to God, and thanking God for the privilege of existing. But at other times we say nothing to God; we only feel God's presence in silence and in contemplation. It is in these moments that our hearts open to universal dimensions, and that we feel as absolute as God or perceive that God comes down to our own level. This is a unique experience of immersion in the nameless mystery, of union between the lover with the Beloved.[30]

Spirituality is not only about knowing; it is mostly about feeling radical human dimensions. The effect is a profound and sweet peace. Peace that, as Jesus said, is "not as the world gives" (John 17:24). This is the peace of God.

Humanity is in great need of this peace of God. This peace is the secret fountain feeding human peace in all its forms. This peace breaks through from the inside, radiates in all directions, sets standards for relations, and touches the "inner heart" of people with goodwill. This peace is composed of reverence, respect, tolerance, benevolent understanding of the limitations of others and the embracing of the Mystery of the world. This peace feeds love; care; the will to be welcoming and to be welcomed, to understand and to be understood, to forgive and to be forgiven.

The culture of peace finds in this spiritual peace its most solid foundation, its limitless source and the certainty that it is one of the most reliable foundations for guaranteeing the future. Only then will peace flourish in the Mother Earth, in nature, in the immense community of life, in the relations between cultures and peoples and thus appease the human heart, which is tired of so much searching.

30. Cf. L. Boff, *Espiritualidade, caminho de realização.*

conclusion

The Blessedness of Virtues

After this extensive and complex argumentation in which I tackled the main *virtues for another possible world*, it is important to look back and emphasize some salient points. I want to do this in the style of the blessings we find in the gospels. The utopian character will be emphasised from the very beginning and may awaken in us energies that can encourage practices that bring about concrete transformations.

Blessed are hospitable people, for without knowing they could be welcoming God itself and its messengers.

Blessed are those who live together with those who are similar and those who are different, for they are enriched in their humanity.

Blessed are those who respect every and each creature: the ant in the pathway, plants, animals, and every human being, independent of gender, origins, ethnic background, and religion; and especially those who respect the poor and needy, for they will gain the honorable title of universal brothers and sisters.

Blessed are those who demonstrate tolerance with those who are different, who for love renounce trying to convince the other, who do not even attempt to change the other for the better, and who warmly embrace that which they do not understand of the other's culture. They will be called sons and daughters of God; for, just like God, they have an attitude of tolerance toward all, good and bad, just and unjust.

Blessed are those who sit at the table as brothers and sisters to eat, drink, and celebrate together the generosity of the Earth, its various foods, fresh vegetables, and colorful fruits. They will be considered the truest sons and daughters of the Mother Earth.

Blessed are those who promote peace, who encourage feelings of mutual affection, who defuse possible conflict, who cultivate a caring attitude between peoples, and who cause the rise of love in the heart. These are the first citizens of the new Heaven and new Earth.

Blessed are those who engage in the study of those *virtues* that can guarantee *another possible world*, not simply to gain more education, but that they may improve their lives and become virtuous people. They will inaugurate the new era of global ethics based on a culture of care, responsibility, compassion, and love, which are the foundations of a long-lasting peace

Bibliography and Further Reading

Aguirre, Rafael. *La mesa compartida: estudios del NT desde las ciencias sociales.* Colección Presencia teológica. Santander: Sal Terrae, 1994.

Ali Brac de la Perrière, R. *Plantas transgênicas, uma ameaça aos agricultores.* Petrópolis: Vozes/Trilce, 2001.

Alighieri, Dante. *The Divine Comedy.* Translated by Allen Mandelbaum. Everyman's Library 183. London: Campbell, 1995. Online: www.divinecomedy.org/divine _comedy.html/.

Altieri, Miguel A. *Agroecologia: As bases científicas da agricultura alternativa.* Rio de Janeiro: Fase, 1989.

Annan, Kofi A. "Message on the occasion of the launch of the International Year of the Culture of Peace." Address delivered in Paris on September 14, 1999. Online: http://www.unesco.org/bpi/paix2000/kofi.htm/.

Araújo de Oliveira, Manfredo. *Desafios éticos da globalização.* São Paulo: Paulinas, 2001.

Arendt, Hannah. *The Origin of Totalitarianism.* London: A & U, 1967.

Arribas Jimeno, Alejandro. *El laberinto del comensal: los oscuros simbolos de comensalidade.* Madrid: Alianza, 2003.

Baier, Annette C. "The Need for More Than Justice." In *Justice and Care: Essential Readings in Feminist Ethics.* edited by Virginia Held, 47–58. Boulder: Westview, 1995.

Baron Tacla, A. "Hospitalidade e política da comensalidade nas tribos de Vix e Hochdorf." In *Laboratório de História Antiga,* 21–48. Rio de Janeiro: UFRJ/Phôinix, 2001.

Barrau, Jacques. *Les hommes et leurs aliments—Esquise d'une histoire écologique de l'alimentation humaine.* Paris: Tèmes Actuels, 2003.

Boff, Leonardo. *Essential Care: An Ethics of Human Nature.* London: SPCK, 2007.

Bouguerra, Mohamed Larbi. *As batalhas da água: por um bem comum da humanidade* Petrópolis: Vozes, 2004.

———. *Experimentar Deus: a Transparência de todas as coisas.* Campinas: Verus, 2003.

———. *The Prayer of St Francis: A Message of Peace for the World.* Maryknoll, NY: Orbis, 2001.

———. *Espiritualidade, caminho de realização.* Rio de Janeiro: Sextante

Brahic, André, et al. *La plus belle histoire de la Terre.* Paris: Seuil, 2001.

Buey, F. F. "Sobre el pacifismo de Albert Einstein." In *Pensamiento pacifista,* edited by Enric Prat et al., 65–86, Barcelona: Icaria/Antrazyt, 2004.

Ciardi, John, translator. *The Paradiso,* by Dante Alighieri. New York: Signet Classics, 2001.

Clausewitz, C. V. *On War.* London: Trübner, 1873.

Convenção sobre a diversidade biológica. Instituto de Estudos Avançados da Universidade das Nações Unidas, November 2005. *[Convention on Biological Diversity.* Online: www.cbd.int/convention/convention.shtml/.]

Convention on Biological Diversity. *Handbook of the Convention on Biological Diversity.* 3rd ed. Montreal: Secretariat of the Convention on Biological Diversity, c2005

Corcoran, Peter Blaze, editor in chief. *The Earth Charter in Action: Toward a Sustainable World.* Amsterdam: KIT, 2005. Online: http://www.earthcharterinaction .org/.

Cortina, Adela. *Consumo . . . luego existo.* Cuadernos Cristianismo i Justicia 123. Barcelona: Cristianismo i Justicia.

————."La paz en Kant: ética y politica." In *Kant: la paz perpetua, doscientos años después,* edited by Vincent Martínez Gusmán, 67–81. València: Nau Libres, 1997.

Crossan, John Dominic. *The Historical Jesus: The Life of a Mediterranean Jewish Peasant.* San Francisco: HarperSanFrancisco, 1991.

————. *The Birth of Christianity: Discovering What Happened in the Years Immediately after the Execution of Jesus,* San Francisco: HarperSanFrancisco, 1998.

Delpuech, Bertrand. *O desafio alimentar Norte—Sul.* Translated by Márcia Poncioni et al. Rio de Janeiro: *Vozes/FASE, 1990.*

————. *Seed and Surplus: Illustrated Guide to the World Food System,* London: Catholic Institute for International Relations, 1994.

Duarte, Joao-Francisco Junior. *O sentido dos sentidos.* Curitiba: Criar, 2004.

Engelhard, Philippe. *La troisième Guerre Mondiale est comencé.* Paris: Arléa, 1999.

Falk, Richard. *Predatory Globalization: A Critique.* Cambridge: Polity, 1999.

Fante, Cleo. Fenômeno Bullying: como prevenir a violência nas escolas e educar para a paz. Campinas: Verus, 2005.

Fiddes, Nick. *Meat: A Natural Symbol.* London: Routledge, 1991.

Fisas, Vinçenç. *Cultura de la paz y gestión de conflictos.* Barcelona: Icaria/UNESCO, 1998.

Food and Agriculture Organization of the United Nations. *Rome Declaration on World Food Security and World Food Summit Plan of Action.* Rome: FAO, 1996. Online: www.fao.org/docrep/003/w3613e/w3613e00.HTM/.

Freyre, Gilberto. *The Masters and the Slaves: A Study in the Development of Brazilian Civilization.* New York: Knopf, 1964.

Galtung, Johan. *Peace by Peaceful Means: Peace and Conflict, Development and Civilization.* Oslo: International Peace Research Institute, 1996.

————. *Tras la violencia, 3R: reconstrucción, reconciliación, resolución—Afrontando los efectos visibles e invisibles de la guerra y la violencia.* Bilbao: Balkeaz/Guernica Gogoratuz, 1998.Garcia, Paulo Roberto. "Comida e dignidade, um banquete cristão." *Tempo e Presença* 343 (Set-Out) 20–25.

Gomes de Almeida, Silvio, et al. *Crise socioambiental e conversão ecológica da agricultura brasileira,* Rio de Janeiro: AS-PTA, 2001.

Gonçalves, Reinaldo. *Empresas transnacionais e internacionalização da produção.* Petrópolis: Vozes, 1992.

Göttner-Abendroth, Heide. *Das Matriarchat.* 3 vols. Stuttgart: Kohlhammer, 1988–2000.

Guinsburg, Jacò, translator. *A paz perpétua,* by Immanuel Kant. São Paulo: Perspectiva, 2004.

Gupta, Joyeeta. *Our Simmering Planet: What to Do about Global Warming.* A Global Issues Title. London: Zed, 2001.

Hassner, Pierre. *La violence et la paix: de la bombe atomique au nettoyage ethnique*, Paris: Seuil, 2000.

Hawking, Stephen W. *A Brief History of Time: From the Big Bang to Black Holes.* Toronto: Bantam, 1988.

Held, David. *La democracia y el ordern global: del Estado moderno al gobierno cosmopolita.* Madrid: Paidós, 1997.

Houtard, François. *Délégitimer le capitalisme, reconstruire l'esperance.* Essais. Brussels: Colophon, 2005.

Huntington, Samuel P. *The Clash of Civilizations and the Remaking of World Order*, New York: Simon & Schuster, 1996.

John XXIII, Pope. *Pacem in Terris.* Online: www.vatican.va/holy_father/john_xxiii/encyclicals/documents/hf_jxxiii_enc_11041963_pacem_en.html/.

Kant, Immanuel. *Zum ewigen Frieden.* Hamburg: Meiner, 1992.

———. *Perpetual Peace.* New York: Cosimo, 2005.

Koester, Helmut. "The Historical Jesus and the Cult of the Kyrios Christos." *Harvard Divinity Bulletin* 24 (1995) 13–18.

Kyrtatas, Dimitris. *The Social Structure of the Early Christian Communities.* New York: Verso, 1987.

Langaney, André, Nicole Bacharan et al. *La plus belle histoire de l'homme: Comme la Terre devint humaine.* Paris: Seuil, 2000.

Leme Machado, Paulo Affonso. *Recursos hídricos: direito brasileiro e internacional.* São Paulo: Malheiros, 2002.

Léonard, H. J., editor. *Meio ambiente e pobreza—Estratégias de desenvolvimento para uma agenda comum.* Rio de Janeiro: Zahar, 1992.

Lévi-Strauss, Claude. "El triangulo culinario." In *C. Lévi-Strauss: estructuralismo y dialetica.* Edited by B. Pingaud. Buenos Aires: Paidós, 1968.

Lowy, Michael. "Eco-socialism and Democratic Planning." *The Socialist Register* 43 (2007) 294–309.

Macy, Joanna, and Molly Young Brown. *Coming Back to Life: Practices to Reconnect Our Lives, Our World.* Gabriola Island, BC: New Society, 1999.

Madeley, John. *Food for All: The Need for a New Agriculture.* Global Issues in a Changing World. London: Zed, 2002.

———. *Hungry for Trade: How the Poor Pay for Free Trade*, London: Zed Books, 2000.

Magalhães, D., editor. *A paz como caminho.* Rio de Janeiro: Qualitymark.

Maturana, Humberto R., and Francisco J. Valera. *The Tree of Knowledge: The Biological Root of Human Understanding.* Translated by Robert Paolucci. Boston: Shambhala, 1992.

Marx, Karl. *The Poverty of Philosophy.* Online: http://www.marxists.org/archive/marx/works/1847/poverty-philosophy/ch01.htm

McKibben, Bill. *The End of Nature.* New York: Random House, 1992.

Mesa, José Alberto. "La ética del cuidado y sus implicaciones en la formación moral de la escuela." In *La educación desde las éticas des cuidado y la compasion*, 21–33. Bogotá: Pontificia Universidad Javeriana, 2005.

Moita, Luis. "Que é o pacifismo no nosso tempo?" In *Para uma Cultura de. Paz*, edited by José Manuel Pureza, 20–39. Coimbra: Quarteto.

Morin, Edgar. *L'identité humaine.* Méthode 5. Paris: Seuil, 2001.

Moltmann, Jürgen. editor. *Friedenstheologie, Befreiungstheologie*, Munich: Kaiser, 1988.

Nathan, Otto, and Heinz Norden, editors. *Einstein on Peace.* London: Methuen, 1963.

Noddings, Nel. *Caring: A Feminine Approach to Ethics & Moral Education.* Berkeley: University of California Press, 1984.

———, et al. "Justice, Caring and Universality: In Defence of Moral Pluralism." In *Justice and Caring: The Search for Common Ground in Education,* edited by Michael S. Katz, Nel Noddings, et al., 21–36. New York: Teachers College Press, 1999.

Olson, Steve. *Mapping Human History: Genes, Race, and Our Common Origins.* Boston: Houghton Mifflin, 2003.

O'Murchu, Diarmuid. *Evolutionary Faith: Rediscovering God in Our Great Story.* Maryknoll, NY: Orbis, 2002.

Ossami, Marlene C. M. "Cultura alimentar: alguns elementos para a formulação de um programa alimentar." In *Educação cidadã: novos atores, nova sociedade—Fome Zero,* Brasília: Cadernos de Estudo 2 (2004) 101–15.

Pascal, Blaise. *Pensées.* Translated by W. F. Trotter. Online: www.oregonstate.edu/instruct/phl302/texts/pensees-contents.html/.

Pelt, Jean-Marie, et al. *La plus belle histoire des plantes.* Points. Paris: Seuil, 1998.

Perles, Catherine. "Les origines de la cuisine—L'acte alimentaire dans l'histoire de l'homme." *Communications* 31 (1979) 4–14.

Petrella, Riccardo. *The Water Manifesto: Arguments for a World Water Contract.* London: Zed, 2001.

Pingaud, Bernard C., et al., editors. *Lévi-Struass: estructuralismo y dialéctica.* Letras mayúsuculas 1. Buenos Aires: Paidós, 1968.

Polanyi, Karl. *The Great Transformation: The Political and Economic Origins of Our Times,* Boston: Beacon, 2001.

Prat, Enric, editor. *Pensamiento pacifista.* Barcelona: Icaria/Antrazyt, 2004.

Pretto, Adão. *A soberania alimentar da produção e o comércio de sementes,* Brasília: Centro de Documentação e Informação, 2002.

Pureza, José Manuel. editor. *Para uma cultura da paz,* Coimbra: Quarteto, 2001.

Ramonet, Ignacio. *Géopolitique du chaos.* Collection L'espace critique. Paris: Galilée, 1997.

———. *Wars of the 21st Century: New Threats, New Fears.* Melbourne: Ocean, 2004.

Rebouças, Aldo da Cunha et al. *Aguas doces no Brasil.* 2nd, rev. ed. São Paulo: Escrituras, 2002.

Rosnay, J. *O homem simbiótico: perspectivas para o terceiro milênio.* Petrópolis: Vozes, 1997.

Schmitt, Carl. *The Concept of the Political.* Translated by George Schwab. Chicago: University of Chicago Press, 1996.

Schüssler Fiorenza, Elisabeth. *Discipulado de iguais,* Petrópolis: Vozes, 199

Schwarz, Walter, and Dorothy Schwarz. *Breaking Through: Theory and Practice of Wholistic Living.* Bideford, UK: Green Books, 1987

Schweitzer, Albert. *Cultural Philosophy.* Vol. 2, *Civilization and Ethics.* Translated by John Nash. London: A. & C. Black, 1923.

Serres, Michel. *The Natural Contract.* Translated by Elizabeth MacArthur and William Paulson. Ann Arbor: University of Michigan Press, 1995.

Shiklomanov, Igor A. *World Water Resources at the Beginning of the 21st Century.* St. Petersburg: UNESCO, 1999 (conference publication).

———. *Water Resources at the Beginning of the Twenty-first Century.* International Hydrology Series. Cambridge: Cambridge University Press, 2003.

Shiva, Vandana. *Protect or Plunder? Understanding Intellectual Property Rights*. Global Issues. London: Zed, 2001.

———. *Monocultures of the Mind: Biodiversity, Biotechnology and Scientific Agriculture*. London: Zed, 1998.

Stolcke, Verena. "Lo espantosamente nuevo: guerra y paz en la obra de Hannah Arendt." In *Pensamiento pacifista*, edited by Enric Plat et al., 101–19. Barcelona: Icaria/Antrazyt.

Swimme, Brian, and Thomas Berry. *The Universe Story*. San Francisco: HarperSanFrancisco, 1994.

Tourraine, Alain. *Um novo paradigma para compreender o mundo de hoje*. Petrópolis: Vozes, 2006.

Toynbee, Arnold. *Experiences*. London: Oxford University Press, 1969.

Tundisi, José Galizia. *Água no século XXI: enfrentando a escassez*. São Carlos: Rima/Instituto Internacional de Ecologia, 2003.

United Nations Scientific and Education Associaton. *Declaración y Plan de Acción Integrado sobre la Educación para la Paz, los Derechos Humanos y la DemocraciaI*. Paris: UNESCO, 1995.

———. *Educación para el desarollo y la paz: valorar la diversidad y aumentar las oportunidades de aprendizaje personalizado y grupal*. Paris: UNESCO, 1996.

Waldow, Vera Regina. *Cuidar, expressão humanizadora da enfermagem*. Série enfermagem. Petrópolis: Vozes, 2006.

———. *O cuidado humano: o resgate necessário*. Porto Alegre: Sagra-Luzatto, 1998.

Weil, Pierre Gilles. *Liderança, tensões, evolução*, Belo Horizonte: Itatiaia, 1972.

———. *A arte de viver em paz*, São Paulo: Gente, 2004.

Wilkinson, John. *O futuro do sistema alimentar*. Dossiê FAST/Comissão das Communidades Europèias; Estudos rurais. São Paulo: Hucitec, 1998.

Winnicott, D. W. *Human Nature*. London: Free Association, 1988.

Zebedi, H., et al. *Water, A Looming Crisis?* Paris: UNESCO, 1998.

Zohar, Danah, and Ian Marshall. *SQ: Spiritual Intelligence; The Ultimate Intelligence*, London: Bloomsbury, 2000.